Talleyrand's Last Duchess

◆

Talleyrand's

STEIN AND DAY/*Publishers*/New York

Last Duchess

FRANCOISE DE BERNARDY ❖

TRANSLATED FROM THE FRENCH BY DEREK COLTMAN

FOR MY FRIENDS

Juliet Munet

AND

Françoise de Vauxmoret

CONTENTS

ILLUSTRATIONS

Following page 192

"Il me reste vous, restez-moi bien."

TALLEYRAND

Part One

DOROTHEE

OF

COURLAND

(1793-1809)

❖

W

ARSAW, MAY 3, 1791. For the first time since the partition of 1722, there was a tide of gaiety rising in the city as it
came back to life after a long winter. The new constitution
had just been voted, and the King, Stanislas-Auguste Poniatow-
ski, was on his way to offer God his thanks in the cathedral of
St. John.

As he was walking through the narrow passage linking the
Zamek Palace to the royal box, a young, fresh, and lovely
woman, the Duchess of Courland, threw herself at the sovereign's feet and thanked him, quivering with emotion, for having accepted this new constitution, which was to regenerate,
which was to save the country.

Anne-Charlotte-Dorothée of Medem had married Pierre
Duke of Courland in 1779, when she was eighteen and he fifty-
five. Duke Pierre's father, Jean-Ernest Biren (gallicized into
Biron), was a former favorite of Empress Anne, who had raised
him from the position of a clerk in the Chancellery to that of a
royal Duke and a Regent of Russia. He incurred disfavor, however, and was banished to Siberia along with his son. Pierre,
the present Duke of Courland, had returned from that 20 years
of exile with a soured and irritable character. Two previous
wives, the Princess of Waldeck followed by the Princess Yous-
soupoff, had already fled from his fits of anger and his tyranny.
Lately, the Duke's temper had become somewhat sweeter, perhaps because of advancing age, perhaps because of his passion
for a wife so very much younger than himself. Moreover, it
seems beyond doubt that the latest Duchess was "patient and
resigned"—and still virtuous. Whatever the truth of the matter,
for ten years their household remained an harmonious one, and
numerous children were born into it. First, three daughters,
Wilhelmine, Pauline, and Jeanne, in 1781, 1782 and 1783; then
a son, Pierre, in 1787; another daughter, Charlotte, in 1789. The
last two both died in early childhood.

Pierre had been disagreeable not only as a husband but also as a ruler. Strong in the knowledge of her Courland origins and "seven centuries of illustrious ancestry," the young Duchess had been obliged to intervene more than once between the Duke and his subjects. Though as it happened, Pierre felt no particular desire to live at Mittau. He preferred his properties in Bohemia and Silesia, particularly the château of Sagan, the fief of Wallenstein, purchased in 1786.

Urged on by emissaries from the Empress Catherine, who wanted to annex this little country squeezed against the Baltic between Russian Livonia and Lithuania, which was still Polish, the aristocracy of Courland had risen against its ruler in 1790. The Duke decided to appeal for help to Poland, former suzerain of the country. He also decided that his wife would be his best ambassador. The Duchess had therefore arrived in Warsaw during the autumn of 1790.

Being both lecherous and ostentatious by nature, Stanislas-Auguste accorded this amiable and pretty woman a generous welcome and placed a palace at her disposal. The Duchess immediately flung her doors wide to everyone who was of any account in the kingdom, and particularly to members of the Diet whom it was her business to win over to her cause.

Many she did win over, but the most advanced among them, the "young Deputies," continued to elude her. Republican in spirit, active and bold in pursuit of their beliefs, ardent supporters of constitutional reform, they often swayed the Diet's decisions, and the duchess grew uneasy. It was absolutely essential that she gain the support of their leader, Alexander Batowski. Batowski, about thirty years old, with black, unpowdered hair, a handsome face and expressive eyes, did not belong to any of the country's leading families. Nevertheless, polished by a long stay in France, imbued with all the new ideas—enlightened, in short—he had gained an ascendancy over the younger deputies.

A friend of both parties, Count Zabiello, acted as intermediary and brought Batowski to visit the Duchess. After several visits, in the course of which he displayed an extreme coldness of manner, he finally accepted an invitation to dinner. The Duchess did not mean to let this opportunity slip through her fingers. Drawing Batowski into a side room, she sat down on a divan and explained the dangers of her situation. Vitrolles * tells us: "The Duke was holding her responsible for the outcome of the matter, and with a character as terrible as his there was no way of telling to what lengths his resentment might carry him. All this was extremely well expressed, with sufficient emotion to lend power to her eloquence, and a few tears rolling from her lovely eyes." Batowski was completely subjugated by so much charm and such powers of seduction.

"Very well, Madame la Duchesse," he said, "is that what you want? I will take the whole conduct and success of the affair upon my shoulders since it is so very important to you. But only upon one strict condition: that I alone am empowered to act in the matter, and that you will ask advice of no one but myself."

Though taken aback at first by this imperious demand, the Duchess nevertheless agreed to it, and daily consultations followed between them for the next few months.

At the beginning of 1792, the Courland affair came before the Diet. Thanks to a piece of clever juggling—a second vote taken when the chamber was half empty, after the first vote had proved unfavorable—Batowski succeeded in winning the Duke's case against his subjects.

Vitrolles reported the subsequent events: "The happy deputy immediately made his way up into the Duchess's box, where, to his surprise and alarm, he found her pale and senseless! It was to the sound of his voice, as he himself informed her of this unhoped for turn of fortune, that the Duchess regained consciousness in the very arms, as it were, of her friend. Her gratitude was as ardent as it was natural. She bestowed upon Count Batowski all the marks of an ardent friendship that was never to be effaced."

The Diet had not been unaware of the intrigue: when the

---

* Vitrolles was a young officer in Condé's army. He had emigrated to Germany where he married Mlle de Folleville, the adopted daughter of the Duchess of Bouillon. The Duchess lived at that time in Erfurt with her cousin the Prince of Salm. Both were thoroughly familiar with the notorious behavior of the Duchess of Courland, and it was from them that Vitrolles learned the story.

question of choosing a Polish Commissar for Mittau came up, they appointed Batowski.

Catherine decided to play the spoilsport. Once peace had been signed with Sweden and Turkey, the Tsarina turned her attentions to Poland. A kingdom bedeviled by anarchy she would have left alone, but she had no wish to see a regenerate monarchy there. On May 19, 1792, her armies invaded Lithuania and routed the Polish garrison: the second partition was imminent.

Courland was also occupied. It did not occur to the Duke to resist: with his Duchess, but without regret, he left for Sagan.* Batowski attempted to delay his departure, and Catherine had it intimated to him that, as a supporter of the constitution of 1791, he must choose between leaving the country, or Siberia. He chose the first, withdrawing by way of Warsaw to Berlin, where, on August 21, 1793, at No. 7, Unter den Linden, in the baroque palace built by Frederick II for his sister Amelia, the Duchess of Courland gave birth to a fifth daughter, Dorothée.

◇   ◇   ◇

The Duke of Courland had accepted his wife's liaison with Batowski calmly. Doubtless the Duchess's long stay in Warsaw had prepared him for such an event, while at the same time the effects of encroaching age—Varnhagen † states quite baldly that he was already practically dead ‡—led him to show understanding towards the errors of a wife who had displayed such generosity of temperament.§ Perhaps he thought to himself, when all was said and done, that ten years of fidelity, and the three charming daughters whose maturing beauty was by that time

---

* In 1795, the Duke ceded his principality to Russia officially in exchange for 8 million francs, a pension of 250,000 francs, and a settlement for his wife.

† Varnhagen von Ense (1785-1858), Gemran diplomat and writer, born in Dusseldorf, died in Berlin. At the age of 28 he married Rachel Levin. She presided over an important literary salon in Berlin and was one of the first to recognize Goethe's genius. Varnhagen's 15-volume journal was published from 1861 to 1870.

‡ *Dieser sogar schon todt war.*

§ Her daughters took after her.

illuminating his last years with a warm glow of pride were well worth a measure of indulgence. Even though he must surely have recognized that he was not her father, his only reaction to the birth of Dorothée was one of indifference.

He went even further: he gave his wife back her freedom, and authorized her to set up a separate establishment where she might spend six months of every year with Batowski, the other six being spent with himself and their three eldest daughters at Sagan. After considering the purchase of a villa in Switzerland, on the shore of Lake Geneva, the Duchess finally acquired the château of Löbikau near Altenburg a long house in the classic style with trophies, a colonnade, and a large park.

The Baron de Vitrolles, an *émigré*, was living at Altenburg waiting for his opportunity to return to France; he became acquainted with Batowski and soon afterwards with the Duchess. "She was still young; though not tall she was beautifully proportioned, her face had that fresh skin one sees in Northern girls, her features were full of grace, her eyes charming, her mouth delicate, her teeth superb. The only possible defect in her face was a nose that was perhaps a trifle too long. . . ."

Vitrolles became a constant visitor at Löbikau. One summer's day, the Duchess and Batowski were walking together in the gardens when he arrived. "The Duchess was leaning on Count Batowski, and carrying over her arm a heavy basket of fruit that she had just picked. On her head she was wearing a wide straw hat with its untied ribbons flowing down over her shoulders.

" 'Well, dear Monsieur de Vitrolles,' she said to me, 'don't you think we look just like a solid bourgeois couple?' "

Life could have been sweet in that beautiful place. But there were times when it was not. The Duchess herself was of a gay and even temperament, but Batowski was by nature unstable and melancholic. His ambitions had been thwarted, he was in exile, and he was embittered: even the kindness of those most sympathetic to him he found irksome. A Romantic before his time, neurasthenic without knowing it, he was constantly willing himself to be unhappy and abandoning himself to moods of despair that were without any real justification. One fine day, he suddenly decided that he must have a separate establishment to which he could retire when the fancy took him; so the

Duchess had a little lodge built for him in the woods two miles away from Löbikau itself. They named it Tannenfeld.

When Vitrolles came to visit them, the Duchess enacted the role of the tender and passionately adoring mother. "She was constantly bringing her daughter Dorothée to see us, a charming child, about four or five years old, with a precocious mind and imagination, lively and animated in all her movements. One might perhaps have said that her eyes were too large. Her hair was very black, her face dark-skinned and full of expression. In short, by no means an ordinary child."

In fact, however, this very likeable woman, in whose life the most important things were love and Society, scarcely paid any attention at all to her daughter. The child was more like a pet to her, something one stroked from time to time but never allowed to get in the way and left others to take care of. Dorothée was actually left entirely to the mercies of an old English governess whose rule was as harsh as her knowledge was limited. The education she imposed upon her delicate and nervous charge seems to have consisted mainly of beatings and cold baths.

Sullen and somber by nature, the little girl was also torn by the two modes of existence between which she alternated every six months. She ought to have preferred life at Löbikau, for despite Batowski's periods of gloom the atmosphere there was always animated and restrictions were few. But she was a precocious and very sensitive child so that this easy-going environment made her feel uncertain and insecure. She wondered why she was the only one who was always taken away from the haven of the family circle at Sagan—the château [of Sagan] "at once grave, imposing and magnificent," of which she constantly dreamed, never climbing into the carriage that was to take her back there without childish cries of joy.

"Our life at Sagan was more or less the same as that in any small German court," Dorothée wrote in 1822. "My father, with that lavishness of hospitality then customary in the North, was always ready to entertain not only his neighbors but also a great many foreigners, who came, some from Berlin, some from Prague, some from Dresden, to stay with us at Sagan. Since my father's household included a troupe of quite passable actors, some Italian singers, and several good musicians, the long winter evenings, already preceded by superb hunts and rather lengthy meals, could always be counted on to provide agreeable enough entertainment."

With those huge blue eyes set between their long, black lashes, Dorothée gazed round at Sagan and tried to penetrate its secrets. Although the château gave her a sense of security that she lacked at Löbikau, nevertheless, when surrounded by her sisters, who were so much older than she and whose life she hardly shared at all, the little girl experienced a vague uneasiness, an obscure impression of being different. This uneasiness also assailed her when in the presence of the old man who ruled over Sagan, that unknown and distant father whom she knew so little, who usually ignored her, who almost never spoke to her, and whom she loved nevertheless with the timid and anxious love of a child who is looking for human warmth and protection.

Later, her eyes opened by experience, Dorothée wrote down her memories of this time. Whereas Batowski's name is barely mentioned—and then with bitterness—for Duke Pierre she had nothing but words of gratitude and affection. "Even though I was no more than six at the time [of his death], I have nevertheless retained a very vivid memory of his appearance and behavior, and I have always kept very carefully a little pile of Courland ducats he gave me in exchange for the two crowns he asked me for one day, complaining jokingly that he was ruined. The willingness with which I handed him my little store earned me a very tender kiss, of which I can still feel the impression."

❖ ❖ ❖

While spending so much time complaining of imaginary misfortunes, Batowski had failed to observe a more immediate peril: the Duchess of Courland's growing indifference. In 1798, at Carlsbad, the young woman had made the acquaintance of the Baron d'Armfelt. A former favorite of Gustav III who had been banished after the latter's tragic death in 1792, Armfelt was in Germany waiting for some change in his fortunes that would enable him to return to Sweden. Tall, with a chest too heavy for his short legs and a face on whose fine features pleasure had left its marks, this high-class adventurer was attractive to women; and he attracted the Duchess of Courland.

She saw him again in 1799; he completed his conquest. Together, they returned to Löbikau. Since Batowski was there with them it would be possible to derive no little amusement from conjectures as to how this imbroglio, one not unworthy of the Italian Comedy, might have ended. Would the Duchess have departed as usual for Sagan, leaving her two lovers face to face? The problem was resolved by a dispatch from Prague informing them that the Duke of Courland was seriously ill: Armfelt accompanied the Duchess to her husband's bedside.

Pierre of Courland died on January 13, 1800, at Gellenau in Silesia. His widow, now free, found herself extremely embarrassed by that freedom. At a time when she was still in love with Batowski, she had promised to marry him a year after the Duke's death. Failing this, she was bound by their contract, a document drawn up with all the proper formalities, to pay a forfeit of fifteen hundred thousand francs.

Marry him? The Duchess no longer wished to. Pay the forfeit? The sum was rather large. She explained the alternatives before her to Armfelt, who immediately took her to task. He put it to the Duchess that she owed a duty to her daughters. Now that the Duke was dead, the three older girls would be living with her. Since they were as charming as they were pretty, princesses of Courland and the richest heiresses in Germany, they ought all to make the most brilliant matches. But what suitor would come near the stepdaughters of a Polish upstart? Furthermore, the King of Prussia still considered himself Dorothée's protector; would he continue to extend his patronage to Mme Batowski? It would be better to pay up. Armfelt spoke with the voice of reason: the Duchess decided to sacrifice herself for her daughters.

There remained only to inform Batowski of her decision. The Duchess wrote a letter summoning him to an interview with her at Meissen, just outside Dresden. Armfelt, who escorted the Duchess to the appointed rendezvous, remained in the background while his mistress talked things over with Batowski, but nevertheless encouraged her from the wings. The discussions were painful, passionate, and also interminable.* Batowski, finally realizing the depth of the abyss he himself had dug, was at first rebellious, then passed from anger to supplication.

The rivals met only at mealtimes. Nevertheless, Armfelt's constant presence at such a moment of crisis finally opened Batowski's eyes and forced him to a decision. In the course of the final interview, he snatched up the contract and flung it with a noble gesture into the fire. The Duchess then fell upon his neck and swore eternal friendship more everlasting than her love.

Whereupon, still faithful to the commedia dell'arte style in which they had begun, all three returned to Löbikau. Armfelt and the Duchess took up residence in the château, Batowski at Tannenfeld. He soon found the situation intolerable, however, and decided to leave. The Duchess was distressed at the idea of his going and would only consent to it on condition that he accept a pension of three thousand ducats.† His traveling expenses thus provided, Batowski left for Hamburg. He went out of the Duchess's life, and also, for many years, out of Dorothée's.‡

❖   ❖   ❖

Once Batowski was ousted and the Duchess of Courland was safely in Prague, where she was to spend the statutory year in

---

* "It is said that they spent more than twenty-four consecutive hours in these discussions," Vitrolles tells us, with visible admiration for such a verbal marathon.

† The Duchess thus created a precedent later followed by two of her daughters. Wilhelmine, when she was Duchess of Sagan, announced to the Congress of Vienna, "I am ruining myself with husbands," alluding to the pensions she was paying to Prince Louis de Rohan and Prince Wassili Troubetzkoi. For more than thirty years, Dorothée was also to provide an income for Edmond de Périgord, after he had fled to Florence to escape his creditors.

‡ In Hamburg, Batowski renewed an old friendship with the banker Walckiers. He shortly married the latter's daughter. Walckiers was a partner of Simons, with whom Talleyrand did a great deal of business. Returning to Poland in 1807 on the heels of the French Army, or rather on the heels of Talleyrand, Batowski threw in his lot with Russia in 1814, but returned to spend the last years of his life in France. He died in Lorraine about 1836.

mourning for her husband, Armfelt was free to occupy himself with the destinies of his mistress's daughters.

The three eldest were of marriageable age, and there were numerous suitors. The second eldest, Pauline, came to her decision very quickly, and there is no evidence to make us think that Armfelt was in any way responsible for her choice. "Pauline . . . very pretty, very sweet-natured, naturally high-spirited, but a little giddy and lacking in experience, still irked by my father's authoritarian discipline, put out by the indifference with which he had greeted the requests that had been made to him for her hand, frightened by my mother's extremely withdrawn attitude at that time, eagerly accepted the first husband she was offered. This turned out to be the Prince of Hohenzollern-Hechingen, head of the elder branch of the reigning house of Brandenburg, a very great lord certainly, and one of whom the worst I have to say is that I am totally unable to find any other quality to praise in him than the brilliance of his birth." Such is Dorothée's brief and somewhat melancholy account of the motives that influenced her sister when deciding "the only really important question in a woman's life."

Both in figure and in face, Wilhelmine, the eldest, was the most beautiful of the three elder sisters, the Three Graces of Courland. She was also the richest, since she inherited Sagan, which Frederick II had decreed should descend through the female line in order to attract the rich Duke of Courland into Prussia. Earlier, a prince of Wurtemburg had wanted to marry her, and Zoubof, Catherine the Great's last lover, to seduce her. Now, Princess Louise Radziwill, by birth a princess of Prussia, an intimate friend of the Duchess of Courland and Dorothée's godmother, was anxious to marry Wilhelmine to her brother, Prince Louis-Ferdinand. A meeting was arranged at Leipzig and everything appeared to have been settled. Then suddenly, on the advice of his ministers who were alarmed at the prospect of seeing the prince, a man of bold and adventurous spirit, becoming so wealthy when the court itself was in such financial straits,* the king of Prussia withheld his consent. Angered by

---

* Dorothée recalled later: "The court of Berlin was so deeply in debt at the time of 'Fat Wilhelm's' death [Frederick-Wilhelm II, who died on November 16, 1797] that the treasury was found to contain insufficient funds to cover even his funeral expenses, and a courier was despatched to Sagan with a request that my father advance the sum required for that ceremony."

what she termed "the wrongs done her by the Prussian Court," urged on by Armfelt whose own interest in her was stronger than it should have been and who wanted to see her with a husband at once dependent and malleable, Wilhelmine threw herself into the arms of Louis de Rohan and married him on June 23, 1800. "A great name, the misfortunes of exile, and a handsome face in which I have never been able to discern either nobility or intelligence were his only claims to a preference that wounded a great many rivals and distressed all our family's friends," Dorothée wrote later.

Jeanne, the third sister, had already been involved, while her father was still alive, in a most distressing escapade. One of the musicians attached to the little court at Sagan had persuaded the young girl—still a child, for she was scarcely sixteen, and almost completely abandoned by a mother so often absent and a father who was too old—to elope with him. He took her to Erfurt and left her there with one of his friends. Then he went on himself to Hamburg with the intention of getting a good price for the Princess's diamonds and arranging their passage to America.

The Duke her father swore that he would never set eyes upon the fugitive again. Nevertheless he sent the officers of the Sagan garrison in pursuit of her. One of them went to Erfurt and there discovered the princess, "a prey to indescribable alarm, as frightened as a dove caught in a net." The governor of Erfurt, Charles-Théodore de Dalberg, coadjutor of the Archbishop of Mainz, took the young girl under his protection and saw to it that she was taken back to Sagan with the Prussian officer as an escort and chaperoned by a respectable woman. True to his word, the Duke her father had left the château for Prague.*

This affair had created rather a stir in Germany, and it proved necessary to go to the farthest reaches of the kingdom

* The Duke of Courland placed his daughter Jeanne under the tutelage of the Count of Wratislaw, Bohemian Chief of Police. The Count read all the young girl's letters and intercepted those addressed to her by the musician, who refused to relinquish his prize and was trying to persuade Jeanne to attempt a second flight. Perceiving the man's obstinacy, Wratislaw set a trap for him. Using the princess's name, he lured him to a supposed rendezvous at Egra, on the Bohemian border, and had him arrested there. The musician was thrown into prison and then, it is said, beheaded.

of Naples to find Jeanne a husband. On March 18, 1801, she married the Duke of Acerenza, a prince of the Pignatelli family. "The letters written on his behalf by the Queen of Naples and the officious zeal of certain persons my sister believed at that time to be among our friends sufficed to sway her decision. I have never been able to discover any reason for this marriage other than my sister's inability, at the age of sixteen, to resist persuasion." Dorothée had obviously learned from Talleyrand the art of half-truths, and perhaps also, if one weighs her words carefully, that of subtle innuendo.

The seven year old Dorothée did not have to be found a husband of course, but it was time to give some thought to her education. "I was a small, very young child, excessively thin, constantly suffering from some illness or other, and with dark eyes so large that they were quite out of proportion to my emaciated face. I should have been frankly ugly if it had not been for the great expressiveness that my face was said to possess; since I never remained still for a moment, people overlooked my wan complexion and supposed, quite rightly, that I possessed some hidden fund of energy in my constitution. I was by nature taciturn, and aside from my fits of petulance displayed none of the normal characteristics of childhood. . . . I doubt whether it would have been possible to find a more disagreeable or a more unhappy child than I was at the age of seven."

Although possessed of a lively curiosity and a ready understanding, Dorothée did not even know her alphabet. On the other hand, she could speak three languages: French, "picked up in the drawing room, German, which came to me via the antechamber," and English, which she had learned from the old governess whom the Duchess of Courland, from weakness and lack of interest, had allowed to remain in charge of her youngest daughter.

Armfelt was amazed that this child, whose eyes brimmed with intelligence, could not read. "He determined to find out for himself whether my ignorance was a result of wilfulness on my part, stupidity, or defective methods of instruction. He himself taught me to read, and my progress was so rapid, I learned everything in so short a time, that he was able to assure my mother of his conviction that something might yet be made of me and that it was high time I was provided with a well-educated governess who would be capable of instructing me properly."

Having delivered himself of this advice, the only happy memory of a reign that was as brief as it was tyrannical, Armfelt yielded openly to his infatuation for Wilhelmine and became her lover,* to the combined fury of Rohan and the Duchess. The former quieted down again quickly enough.† As for the latter, Armfelt suggested that she accept the offer of marriage she had received from the Duke of Ostromania, Gustav III's second brother, whom she had met at Carlsbad in 1800.

The Duchess of Courland decided to give the matter her consideration. But the King of Prussia and the young Dorothée's guardians, somewhat dissatisfied with the foreign and Catholic marriages made by the other Princesses of Courland, made it clear to the Duchess that they would not permit her to take their young ward away with her to Sweden. The Duchess had become accustomed to her independence. She was rich and free, why should she encumber herself with a husband? She decided that it would be wiser, and more convenient, to console herself for Armfelt's treachery with a new lover, Baron d'Alopeus, whom she met in Berlin.

She also decided to leave Prague, to spend her summers in Saxony, and to take up residence during the winter in some large city that offered resources suitable for Dorothée's education. Almost the whole of the child's fortune was in Prussia, and it seemed certain that her future, too, would be spent there. Princess Radziwill was asking for her godchild, the King for his ward, and the latter "was insistent upon his wishes in the matter." The choice of city therefore fell upon Berlin. For seven years, from 1802 until 1809, except for a long break occasioned by her visit to Courland, that city, together with Löbikau, was to be the principal setting of Dorothée's young existence.

❖　❖　❖

---

* This liaison led to the birth of a daughter, whom Wilhelmine brought up in her own household in the guise of a foundling.

† In December of 1801, the Duchess of Sagan went to Paris escorted by the Prince and the Baron, her husband and her lover.

She settled in with her mother at No. 7, Unter den Linden, which was by now the little girl's own property. The immense palace, parts of it extremely dilapidated, was a sad and dismal place. At night, "one could hear the shouts of the guard at the Brandenburg gate and the footsteps padding past in the snow of the man who called the hours."

The Duchess had her own establishment and Dorothée another, made up of her own servants, her tutor, and her governess. Ashamed, no doubt, of her former neglect, the Duchess had now gone from one extreme to the other and was trying to turn her child into a little phoenix. As soon as she arrived in Berlin, Dorothée was obliged to submit to two separate powers which before long were at swordspoint. The Abbé Piattoli and Mlle Hoffman had begun by loving one another far too well, and they ended up loathing one another.

Regina Hoffman was of German origin. She was engaged to marry a Frenchman in her youth. She had apparently followed her betrothed to Paris, but he had died the day before the wedding. Regina, by then a Catholic, immediately withdrew into a convent and was about to take the veil when she discovered that she was a freethinker. She left the convent, Paris, France itself, and moved to Poland, where she had been Christine Potocka's governess before accepting the same position with Dorothée. Generous-hearted, high-principled, ardent and imperious by nature, but with more imagination than intelligence, Regina Hoffmann provided her pupil, who soon became extremely attached to the governess, with an education that was more brilliant than rational.

The Florentine Scipione Piattoli, once a Piarist Friar, had been given permission in 1774 to leave the order. Since then, an Abbé in name only, a friend of the philosophers, particularly Jean-Jacques Rousseau and Condillac, he had devoted himself to the teaching profession. In 1785, he had undertaken the education of two young Polish aristocrats, Prince Henri Lubormirski and his cousin Prince Adam Czartoryski. Before long, however, he found himself caught up in politics. Singled out by King Stanislas-Augustus, Piattoli became his librarian and confidential secretary, a post that guaranteed him the principal role in the drawing up of the 1791 constitution. It was for this that Catherine the Great had him imprisoned in 1792. Freed once more, thanks to the Duchess of Courland and Adam Czartoryski, who had been sent to Russia as a Polish hostage and subsequently became a close friend of the new Tsar, Alexander, Piattoli had arrived in Berlin during the spring of 1802. The Duchess took him into her household and charged him with the task of transforming her daughter into the hoped-for phoenix.

Taking the humanities and sciences upon himself, Piattoli hired assistant masters to instruct his pupil in the arts. In vain. The dancing master failed to teach Dorothée a single step, and the piano teacher proved no more successful. After the first quarter of an hour, the little girl was unable to conceal her boredom. She would have liked to draw and seemed to have some talent in that direction, but the lessons had to be interrupted, then discontinued altogether, because of her extremely poor eyesight.

Mlle Hoffmann, on the other hand, had a great deal more luck with the various female accomplishments. Dorotheé quickly showed herself to be very nimble-fingered; she enjoyed sewing and embroidering during the long winter evenings while listening to passages read aloud from history books. She was a lonely child, leading a very unchildlike life.

While developing in her charge those feminine talents that were to provide an occupation during her hours of conversation, Mlle Hoffmann was also keeping an eye on the child's health. Subjected to the theory of hygiene laid down in *Emile*, obliged, despite her distaste for walking, to take a daily outing in the Tiergarten, the Hyde Park of Berlin, Dorothée soon recovered her strength and color. Though it is reasonable to believe that if the little girl's sensitive and nervous constitution * now grew stronger, it was to a large extent because her heart was at last opening to the passionate warmth of affection with which she was surrounded by her governess and Abbé Piattoli.

Her intelligence was also coming into flower, with a rapidity that may perhaps be attributed to the length of time it had

* "I am convinced that at the age of seven, though the remark applies to all the rest of my life as well, I had never suffered from any illness that was not a form of protest."

been allowed to lie fallow. In no more than a few months, Dorothée learned to write correctly in German, French, and English. Arithmetic too came very easily to her, and at the age of ten she began to study algebra and other branches of mathematics.* But above all, Dorothée discovered the joys of reading, and she began to devour any and every book that fell into her hands with an avidity that was to remain with her all her life.

Satisfied that her daughter had now been entrusted to what she supposed were good and trustworthy hands, and which were so as far as devotion to duty and affection were concerned, the Duchess of Courland had by now returned to her former state of indifference toward Dorothée. Her summers were spent for the most part in travel, her winters in social engagements. Even when they were both in residence beneath the same roof, mother and daughter scarcely ever saw each other. Dorothée came in to kiss her mother's hand every morning, and the Duchess occasionally ate dinner with her daughter; but very occasionally, for she disliked having to tolerate the constant presence of Regina Hoffmann, who was determined not to let her authority be undermined and consequently never let her pupil out of her sight.

Keeping the child away from a mother so remiss in her duties was easy and almost justified; such exclusive tenderness was balm to Dorothée. Yet one is forced to express unqualified regret that Mlle Hoffmann should have taken advantage of her young charge's boredom with children of her own age in order to isolate her. Dorothée scarcely saw any other children at all except for Mlle de Goeckingk, her guardian's daughter, Princess Radziwill's children, and those of the Queen. For of course it was impossible for Mlle Hoffmann not to comply when she was asked to bring the little girl to Court or to the Radziwill palace.

❖   ❖   ❖

The Duchess of Courland and her daughter had been in residence in Berlin for about two years when, in 1804, a dispute

* In 1806, the astronomer Bode took a fancy to Dorothée and she spent many evenings with him in the Berlin Observatory.

arose between the late Duke of Courland's heirs and the children of his brother Charles, who were claiming a share in the sum previously allotted by Russia as an indemnity for the loss of Courland. Moreover this indemnity had in fact never been paid. It had therefore become necessary to vindicate the claims of the Duke's heirs and at the same time to collect from Russia the monies that were due.

M. de Goeckingk, the King of Prussia's confidential advisor and one of Dorothée's guardians, left for St. Petersburg with full authority to act on behalf of the Duchess and her daughters. Since he spoke French badly, and Russian not at all, he took Piattoli with him. Dorothée was consequently forced to say good-bye to a tutor who, though he had opened up for her the world of the intellect, had failed to provide her with any religious foundation for it, or with anything more than a few basic principles of morality.

Piattoli's interest in his pupil did not cease when he went to St. Petersburg, and during the two years that he spent in Russia he continued to write to her, frequently and with affection. He offered moral guidance of an entirely non-religious and worldly kind, in which pride of ancestry and self-respect played the leading roles. He taught Dorothée to be truthful and polite; * himself a devotee of order,† whether in the running of a household or in the sphere of the passions, he also advised her never to give way to any emotion that had not first been approved by her reason. These were all external virtues, and ones that provided no defense against the weaknesses tolerated by society, those weaknesses of which the child had only too many examples all around her. Above all, an Abbé but no preacher of the Gospels, Piattoli instructed her in neither meekness of heart nor humility of mind. It was to take many years, grief, and the sublime words of Bossuet to teach Dorothée's noble but overly proud soul to understand at last the meaning of the Beatitudes.

---

* "Always be scrupulous in fulfilling what are termed your duties to society and you will then be repaid by those solid and lasting pleasures that it is proper to expect from it; be equally scrupulous in fulfilling the duties of friendship and you will not want for friends . . ."

† "I am certain, dear child, that I should find your study as neat and orderly as it is possible to be. Orderliness is one of the prime virtues of a rational person . . ."

Still a pedagogue at heart, Piattoli criticized or approved the handwriting or the spelling of the letters he received in return, expressed an interest in the hated piano lessons, and kept a strict eye on the purity of his former student's French.

Finally, since he knew that his own education had afforded him a more delicate awareness of such matters than Dorothée's "kind friend" (Mlle Hoffmann) could have acquired in the course of her somewhat sketchy upbringing, Piattoli also initiated the little princess into the ways and the exigencies of society. He expressed pleasure upon hearing that she no longer showed annoyance when losing at games. When Dorothée complained that she had been bored at a reception, the Abbé immediately replied that such things were an excellent apprenticeship. It was essential to know how to accommodate oneself to the tastes of other people. Several days later, the Abbé added: "Always behave toward others as you would have them behave toward you. Thoughtfulness, compliance with the wishes of others, and the pleasure of giving pleasure should be your guiding principles, in games as well as in conversation."

Director of conscience, director of studies, head of protocol, Piattoli was also concerning himself with Dorothée's future. In St. Petersburg he had renewed acquaintance with his former pupil, Prince Adam Czartoryski, who had by now progressed from being Alexander's favorite to the post of Minister for Foreign Affairs. He was in a position to help the Courland family win their case. Piattoli saw him often, then moved into his house, and quite naturally told him a great deal about his beloved pupil. Despite the twenty-three year difference in their ages, the idea of a marriage between Czartoryski and Dorothée insinuated itself into the Abbé's overimaginative mind. Without displaying any great enthusiasm, the Prince * did not for all that reject the idea entirely, and the Abbé mentioned the matter in a letter to Berlin. Dorothée's imagination was immediately captured by the idea of this stranger whom she insisted on thinking of as persecuted and unhappy, while her heart conceived the hope that this man who was so very much older than herself would prove a source of protection and support.

The Duchess of Courland was one of the first ladies of

---

* Perhaps he was still in love with the Tzarina Elizabeth?

Berlin, but the guests in her salon came from every class of society. Jews and Christians, scientists and great lords, great ladies and actresses, all these mingled and accosted one another there without making any distinctions as to creed or birth. It was a humanist and cosmopolitan salon, though with the French influence predominating. Dorothée rarely appeared there, although the liveliness of her intelligence would certainly have enabled her to hold the interest of some of the guests. But these latter, enchanted by the mother, still so blond and fresh, failed to notice the haughty and taciturn child, her dark eyes too big for her thin face, always buried in the skirts of a stiff, self-conscious governess. As soon as she was able, Dorothée would disappear back to her own quarters, where, moreover, she could rejoin her own little court.

Despite all his letters, which were read with affection and preserved with great care,* Piattoli's departure had left Mlle Hoffmann with a great deal more room to maneuver. Once free from the constraints imposed upon her by the Abbé, the impetuous governess threw aside all moderation, both in the adulation she lavished upon her pupil and in her efforts to keep the girl away from her mother.

Since she was herself fond of society and also the mistress, for all practical purposes, of a lavishly provided household, Mlle Hoffmann created a salon of her own, though it was also Dorothée's, composed of several merchant families, some artists, such as the actress Unzelmann and the manager of the Iffland theater —with whom the governess had an "intimate relationship"— as well as some men of letters, Jean de Müller the historian, and the great Schiller when he was visiting Berlin. It was an entirely German salon, as opposed to that of the Duchess, and one of which Piattoli would not have approved, not only because of its social level and acceptance of actors, but also because of its exclusive preference for everything German.

A child in years, but already possessing the mind of a woman, Dorothée at the age of thirteen still had the same huge eyes as before, apparently black at a distance, but in fact deep blue

---

* When she returned to Silesia in 1840, after being away for twenty-five years, Dorothée discovered these letters at Günthersdorf, stowed away in an old desk.

when seen close up. The forehead was pure, the nose delicately traced, but rather too long, a family feature also observable in her mother and sisters. The upper lip was finely molded, the oval of the face impeccable. The hair, shining and black as a raven's wing, was drawn down on either side of the brow from a central parting. When she spoke, it was with a slight impediment in her speech that she retained for many years. This fortunately lent a certain charm to her way of talking which might otherwise have been slightly pedantic, an effect echoed by the way in which the usually serious expression on her face was sometimes irradiated by a great burst of childish laughter.

As for her inner life, Dorothée herself has left us a perspicacious moral portrait of what she was at that age. "So I was happy then! Yes, certainly, but not happy the way most children are happy, and that was the cause of innumerable mistakes later in my life. For it was with tastes not rightfully belonging to my years, with an inordinate pride, an awareness of my own independence, weakened family ties, and only the faintest notions of religion, it was with a determination to eschew evil, but a determination that sprang from pride, with a fear of censure, but a fear that sprang from my own arrogance, that I walked, presumptuous and blind, towards the flower-strewn reefs ahead . . ."

The lawsuit dragged on, and Piattoli became uneasy. In May of 1806, the Duchess of Courland decided to go to St. Petersburg and plead her cause herself. The day after her arrival, she was still in her peignoir, eating breakfast and talking with the Abbé, when a Russian officer walked in without waiting to be announced. It was the Tsar. When he kissed her hand, the Duchess offered him her cheek. "She was still pretty enough," her daughter wrote in 1822, "for a complete lack of adornment to do her no disfavor. The Emperor found her to be as beautiful, as amiable, and as great a lady as anyone in the world, all of which in fact she was." In two months, the lawsuit that had been postponed again and again for two long years was brought to a conclusion, and in the most satisfactory manner.

The Duchess was in the midst of preparations for her journey back to Prussia, where she was to rejoin Dorothée whom she had left in Berlin, when the kingdom of Frederick the Great was swept by a sudden wave of madness. On November 12 and 13, 1806, after signing an alliance with Russia, which was still at war with France, the King of Prussia invaded Saxony. Napoleon's reaction was swift. By October 4 the Grande Armée had been concentrated in Franconia, and ten days later the Prussian armies had been crushed at Jena and Auerstadt.

The wave of madness was succeeded by one of terror. While the remnants of the Prussian armies were still being scattered like leaves in an autumn gale, Queen Louise fled from Berlin with her children and the entire royal family. Terrified at the thought of remaining in a city about to be occupied by the French, Dorothée and Mlle Hoffmann imitated this royal exodus. The governess had a quantity of clothing thrown into trunks which were then hauled up onto the carriages, and they drove away as fast as they could. But once on the packed highways, the two fugitives could only make very slow headway, and did not dare even to lean out of the windows for fear they might see French scouts.

In Koenigsberg, everything was unobtainable. The Duchess of Courland sent for her daughter to join her at Mittau. Dorothée decided to risk the attempt. It was a painful journey, made through dismal and bitingly cold autumn weather along the melancholy Baltic coast. "From Koenigsberg to Memel the road runs for forty leagues across a stretch of quicksands, which would have dragged us to a halt at every step if we had neglected the precaution of always remaining close enough to the sea to be washed by every wave. But the Baltic is very stormy in November, and the waves sometimes broke so high over our carriage that there was good reason to fear that they might drag it back with them into the sea." On the evening of the second day, Dorothée arrived with her governess on the promontory that lay across the water from Memel. It was impossible to cross. It was impossible to spend the night in the carriage because of the intense cold. The two women were obliged to take shelter in a smoky bar full of drunken sailors waiting for the dawn.

Huddled behind a big stove, Dorothée was just attempting

to snatch a little sleep when the door flew open to admit an emissary from the Duchess of Courland. M. de Butler had brought her letters, but also food and furs.

The Duchess had taken up residence with her elder brother at the castle of Altautz. Dorothée did not enjoy the life there. She had become too accustomed to her quiet and studious life in Berlin; the autumn weather, her solitude and her sad thoughts began to weigh upon her. She was too much the princess to take any enjoyment in the rustic abundance of this country life; she was too much an intellectual for country pleasures, hunts, long meals, and evenings spent in drinking to have any attraction for her. Cut off from the other residents by her habits and her education, entirely lacking in "gregariousness," she was totally unable to feel at home in that family circle.

And to make matters worse, she was terrified by the Courland winter's extreme cold and refused to leave the house. "Deprived . . . of all form of exercise, unable to find anything to read except one solitary prayer-book, far from my friends and ignorant of what had befallen them, excessively bored by the conversation of my aunts and cousins, I longed impatiently for our exile to end. . . ."

There was no question of returning to Prussia while the war was still in progress. A house would have to be found for the winter. Another of the Duchess's brothers offered her a house in Mittau. It was a handsome building, but melancholy and lonely, facing the castle which had been half destroyed by a fire.

Dorothée liked Mittau no more than she had Altautz. Irked by the thought that she was now dependent on her mother,* she turned back once more into the sullen and rebellious child that she had been before. And Mlle Hoffmann was delighted to observe that relations between mother and daughter, which had steadily been rendered easier by the recent years of indifference and, above all, of independence, were now becoming sour again.

Just at that time, however, Piattoli returned, and this event fortunately produced a relaxation in the atmosphere and helped

* "There was no reason for my mother to decrease her expenditure because three-quarters of her income came from Russia; but all my lands were in Prussia, laid waste by the French army, and I now found myself forced to live at her expense. It was a thing that had never happened to me before, and one that galled my independent spirit. . . ."

Dorothée to reconcile herself to Courland a little. Less absorbed in her own regrets, the young girl was now able to take more interest in the curious spectacle presented by the palace of Mittau.

The only wing that still remained habitable was occupied by the Count of Provence and his phantom court. Dorothée looked upon these survivors of an age that seemed to belong wholly to the past with an eye devoid of indulgence. The Countess of Provence startled her out of her wits the first time she met her: "I have never seen an uglier or a dirtier woman. Her gray hair, cut so that it looked like a hedgehog, was topped with a terrible straw hat all frayed at the edges; her face was long, thin, and sallow; her tiny, stout figure was somehow or other draped in a dirty skirt over which there flapped the tattered remains of a little black taffeta cape. . . ."

And then, although the Duchess of Angoulême was noble, magnanimous, resigned, and touching in her adversity, the Duke of Angoulême was able to fill every moment of his day quite happily, what with Mass, and Vespers, and Benediction, and hunting, while the Duke of Gramont, the former Duke of Guiche, once married to Mlle de Polignac by Marie-Antoinette, spent all his time looking for a good dinner.

An extremely tender friendship sprang up between Mlle Hoffmann—who was by no means a novice in such matters—and the Duke of Avaray, future favorite of Louis XVIII. This intimate connection on the part of her governess was instrumental in winning Dorothée the good favors of the Duke of Provence.* "M. d'Avaray was constantly appearing on his master's behalf to tell us that we must go over to the château. The King used to take me on his knees, kiss me, call me his little Italian girl because of my black [sic] eyes, ask me questions about my lessons, and, in a word, was kind to me in a thousand ways."

Both born intriguers, Avaray and Regina Hoffmann hit upon

* "It is impossible for me to doubt the truth of this," Dorothée wrote in 1822, "since the King has never displayed even the slightest recollection of his former kindnesses to me, whereas he has several times spoken of her to M. de Talleyrand in 1814, the day when M. de Talleyrand went to meet him at Compiègne. One must agree that this is proof of an accurate, but extremely incomplete, faculty of recollection."

the idea of marrying Dorothée to the Duke of Berry, since it was known that a rich wife was wanted for the Duke and the young Princess of Courland had not only a considerable dowry but expectations that were even more magnificent still. The question of religion scarcely presented itself: Dorothée did not practice any form of worship. Mlle Hoffmann, certain of the influence she exercised over her pupil's mind, flattered herself that she would be able to win Dorothée's approval for the match and also to make her reject all other suitors. Everything had therefore been decided between the conspirators, both in general outline and in detail, even though the principal party concerned had not as yet been informed.

The castle in the air quickly faded. The fortunes of war having just brought Talleyrand and Batowski to Warsaw, they now drove the Count of Provence out of Courland and started Adam Czartoryski on the way to Mittau.

D

II ❖
THE FORCED MARRIAGE
(1807-1809)

URING THE two years he stayed in Russia, Piattoli had continued to pursue his idea of a marriage between Dorothée and Czartoryski. The prince himself remained reticent and had rejected the Abbé's suggestion that he take some positive action in the matter. Nevertheless, happening to see a miniature of Dorothée in Piattoli's rooms, Czartoryski had made off with it and not given it back. Nor had he forbidden the Abbé to send his own portrait to Berlin.*

Though Mlle Hoffmann had apparently subscribed to Piattoli's project—at least until his arrival at Mittau—, the Duchess on the other hand had viewed it with displeasure from the first. She admitted that it was a good match, that the suitor was distinguished and his fortune respectable; but the family had a reputation for being difficult and temperamental as well as for professing a rooted disdain for all things German. Rightly, the Duchess also took offense at the way in which Dorothée had been isolated in her own household and advantage taken of her childish imagination in order to make her fall in love with a stranger. But to exert any influence over her daughter she would first have been obliged to win the child's confidence, and Dorothée herself, cold and respectful, made this impossible.

Such was the situation at the time of the Abbé Piattoli's arrival in Mittau: a suitor more concerned with politics than with emotions, and subject to the imperious will of a mother determined to impose upon him a happiness of her choosing; and an excitable child, ambition already budding within her, enjoying the thought of the role she would be called upon to play at the Russian court, and beguiled by the picture that her

---

* Dorothée preserved this miniature religiously until the day when, already betrothed to Edmond de Périgord, she placed it in the Abbé Piattoli's coffin, which was then closed upon the first hopes, the first illusions of the future Duchess of Dino.

39

still untutored imagination painted of a tranquil and blissful life at the side of her perfect hero.

Piattoli answered Dorothée's eager questions with paeans for his friend and excuses for the latter's apparent indifference. Though extremely curious to make the young girl's acquaintance, the Prince was alarmed at the difference in their ages, and could not bring himself to believe that a child could accommodate herself to the tastes of a man matured by exile and misfortunes. Dorothée listened without a word. Still too young to perceive that the Prince was doubtless right, she congratulated herself on possessing tastes so far in advance of her childish years and undertook to become older still, to lose "the small traces of childishness that still remained in her conversation and her behavior."

The victory that had still hung in the balance after Eylau in February was decided finally in favor of the French at Friedland in June. Since Czartoryski was an enemy of the French government, he resigned from his post as Minister of Foreign Affairs; while the potentates were conferring at Tilsit he came to Mittau to await the results of their negotiations.

The Duchess had not changed her mind and was still hostile to the idea of his marrying Dorothée. Nevertheless, she seized this opportunity of demonstrating her gratitude to Czartoryski for the help he had given her in St. Petersburg. The Prince did not leave her house for three weeks.

Entering her mother's drawing room one evening before dinner, Dorothée found herself in the presence of a serious-looking man, still handsome, whom she recognized by his sad face and disdainful mouth. To her great confusion, Adam Czartoryski sat beside her at dinner. During the meal, although he observed her attentively, he maintained an almost absolute silence.

Such a coldness of manner, such deliberate taciturnity, and the excessive length of the scrutiny to which she had been subjected might have been thought sufficient to dishearten the young girl, but Dorothée was moved by the Prince's melancholy air and thought that she could "read in his face the marks left by great passions and touching misfortunes." As for the scrutiny, she saw nothing "in his observant gaze but a flattering curiosity."

On his way back to St. Petersburg after signing the peace treaty at Tilsit, Tsar Alexander paid a visit to Mittau. He was charming to the Duchess, cold to Czartoryski. Nevertheless, the Prince decided to accompany the Tsar back to Russia in order to settle all his affairs before returning to Germany, and these intentions were duly announced to the Duchess.

Czartoryski had been favorably impressed with Dorothée. She was rich and would also doubtless be pretty. But outside of politics the Prince was a weak and indecisive man; he dared not make any further advances until his mother had ratified his choice. The day before he left, dropping his reserve at last, he asked Dorothée to return to Berlin by way of Warsaw; that was where his mother lived, and he would like the young girl to visit her.

A visit to Warsaw? Dorothée was only too willing, but how was she to get there? Her wealth seemed her only hope in this fateful moment when all her future, perhaps her only chance for happiness, was at stake. But would even her wealth suffice?

Recognizing the impossibility of her scheme for marrying Dorothée to the Duke of Berry, disgruntled by the departure of the Count of Provence and d'Avaray's silence, Mlle Hoffmann was now once more in favor of the Czartoryski marriage. Unfortunately, however, she was unable from a material point of view to organize so difficult a journey, and insufficiently equipped from a worldly point of view to prepare the ground for so delicate an encounter. Piattoli could have managed both things successfully, but he had gone back to St. Petersburg.

Cut off, distressed at her plight, Dorothée resolved to confide in her mother. If the Duchess had agreed to help her daughter at that point their indifference to one another might well have changed into affection. But the Duchess affected a complete detachment in the matter and refused to commit herself.

Truly a strange attitude for a mother to take toward her daughter, this neutrality in the face of so serious a problem. The Duchess was within her rights in not approving of the Czartoryski match. The weak character and apparent reluctance of the

Prince, his mother's undisguised hostility, and the ever increasing divergence of their political opinions all entitled her to be critical in her attitude. She should have explained all these things to her daughter, frankly but firmly, and made the child understand how unwise it would be, at the age of fourteen, to commit herself for life without being certain that she was both in love and beloved. She should have pointed out to Dorothée, a Princess of Courland and proud of the fact, that she was entitled to expect even better offers, and that she ought not to humiliate herself before a family who bore her ill will, or impose herself upon people against their wishes.

But the frivolous and self-centered Duchess, who had already left the task of marrying her three eldest daughters to Armfelt, now displayed an equal lack of concern in the case of her youngest. It may well have been during the course of this year, 1807, that the young girl's indifference, as she realized the extent to which her mother had failed her, was finally replaced by animosity.

◇   ◇   ◇

Accompanied by Mlle Hoffmann, and preceding her mother by several weeks, Dorothée set off on the journey back to Berlin in September of 1807. The two women broke their journey for one day at Memel, where the royal family had taken refuge. Dorothée saw Princess Radziwill and went to pay her respects to Queen Louise. Then, with beating heart at the idea of her first encounter with the French outposts, she continued on her way. All the dismal sights of war assailed her. On every side were burned-down houses, abandoned villages, and the effects of famine and typhus. The two women did not dare to stop again and stayed the whole time inside the carriage; milk, butter, and meat were all infected; for three-quarters of the journey they lived on nothing but barley bread and a little rum mixed with water.

No. 7, Unter den Linden was occupied by the French. Dorothée had flattered herself that the French commander, M. de Saint-Hilaire, being an extremely courteous man, would allow her to move back into her own apartments. It was too much to expect of a conqueror, and when Dorothée and her governess finally stepped down from their carriage one fine evening they were escorted through to two wretched rooms off the second courtyard.

For a week, Dorothée isolated herself in these quarters, not wanting to meet any of the occupying forces and bitterly distressed at the idea of seeing Berlin populated by foreigners. When she did finally make up her mind to emerge from her miserable lair it was only to be filled with indignation at the filthy state of the house and the damage that she now realized it had suffered. Far from attempting to raise her spirits, her guardians filled her ears with even louder groans about the depredations inflicted on her lands, most of which were situated along the military routes. The Duchess returned just as this concert of lamentations was at its height and, without allowing such things to trouble her, immediately began to invite the officers of the occupying forces into her house. The rift between mother and daughter was growing wider day by day.

Neither Piattoli, who believed "metaphysical ideas to be more reliable as guides than the Gospels," nor Mlle Hoffmann, who had emerged from her affiliations to two different religions with none at all, had made any provision for Dorothée's religious education. She never said her prayers for the simple reason that she knew none. She had been to church only once. The sermon had been a bad one: Dorothée had fallen asleep and announced upon her return home that she had no desire to repeat the experiment.

Since she had by now passed her fourteenth birthday however, it was high time that she made her first communion. This ceremony, and the confirmation that preceded it, was the sign of a young girl's entry into Prussian society in those days. Since the unhappy state of the country was at that time making a withdrawn life obligatory, Mlle Hoffmann decided that the winter of 1808 could not be better employed than in providing her charge with some religious instruction.

It was arranged that a pastor named Riebeck should come and spend an hour with Dorothée twice a week. He made her read Old and New Testaments and gave her the benefit of a great many moral exhortations with no basis in any particular form of religion. After several weeks of this, Pastor Riebeck announced that Dorothée was sufficiently prepared for her confirmation. Good Friday (April 15 in 1808) and the church of St. Nicolas were selected as the time and the place for the ceremony.

In this dark edifice, lit only by a few scattered candles, her head draped with a black veil, dressed in a long frock of the same color, a gold cross at her neck, Dorothée answered the pastor's questions and was duly confirmed in her faith. She then proceeded to the altar, surrounded by a numerous crowd of interested, or merely curious, co-religionists. At the end of the long and exhausting ceremony, she fainted.

Dazzled by Napoleon's successes, the Duchess of Courland had for many years been anxious to go to France. There had been a rumor that she was about to do so during her stay in St. Petersburg in July of 1806; the rumor had reached the ears of Fouché, who then made sure that it reached the Emperor's also. Whereupon, for what reason we cannot be certain, though it may have been fear of possible intrigues on her part, Napoleon forbade the Duchess entry into France while at the same time extending this embargo to a number of other Russian nationals.

Now the wheel had come full circle. The Emperor and the Tsar had achieved their reconciliation on the banks of the Niemen, and the Duchess, entering joyfully into the spirit of Alexander's new political alignments, was once more assailed by a passionate desire to visit Paris, to become acquainted with Napoleon, and perhaps to snare him in her toils. Moreover there was nothing to keep her any longer in Berlin. Life was already uncomfortable enough there in a house three-quarters full of occupying troops, and when the court returned to the city she would be in a very difficult position because of her Francophile sentiments and her present friendly attitude towards the victors. She would do better to leave.

The day after Dorothée's confirmation, the Duchess announced that she was going to leave Berlin and take up residence in Saxony, where she would remain until such time as her daughter's marriage had set her free to travel where she pleased, and above all to take up residence in France, which was what she most desired.

Dorothée listened without a word. Her mother's departure would have left her completely unmoved had it not also entailed her own. She was too young to live alone and she was aware of it. The Duchess insisted that the young girl come to live with her at Löbikau, and Dorothée agreed to this without much difficulty. She made only two conditions: that she was to be allowed a completely independent establishment at Tannenfeld, the small house built earlier for Batowski, and that she was to return to Berlin during the winter in order to continue her studies.

Once the Duchess had left, Dorothée was in no hurry to set out upon so long and wearisome a journey. Saxony was infested with brigands. Apparently bearing her no grudge for the ill grace with which she had behaved towards him, and perhaps feeling a degree of pity for the helpless state in which she had been left, M. de Saint-Hilaire offered the services of two aides-de-camp as escorts for the young girl and her governess. Touched by this gesture, Dorothée accepted, and it was as well she did so. Half a day's journey from Löbikau the travelers were attacked, and one of the aides-de-camp, Lafontaine, was seriously wounded. With the greatest difficulty, they managed to transport him with them as far as Tannenfeld, where he remained for ten weeks. "While nursing him, we grew to feel a friendship toward him, and also toward his general, with whom this accident had brought us into correspondence."

❖ ❖ ❖

Released from his religious vows by the Pope, Charles-Maurice de Talleyrand-Périgord, the former Bishop of Autun who had become Minister for Foreign Affairs to the Directoire, then to the Consulat, had married Catherine Grand * on Sep-

---

* Née Catherine-Noël Worlée, the daughter of a minor government official. She was married to a Mr. Grand of the East India Company. When discarded by him for infidelity, she returned to Paris where she eventually became Talleyrand's mistress.

tember 19, 1802. This marriage, which regularized a liaison of extremely long standing, was without issue.

Talleyrand was a man in whom pride of ancestry often found expression in family feeling, and as soon as he returned to Paris in 1796 he began to take an interest in the welfare of his brother's children. Archambauld de Périgord had been among the first *émigrés* to leave the country; his wife, Sabine de Sénozan, last remaining descendant of Sully, had gone with him, but in 1793 returned in order to see her children and to oppose the threatened confiscation of her possessions. She was arrested and, on the 27th of July, was executed. The children—Louis, born in 1784, Mélanie, born in 1785, Edmond, born in 1787— had been placed under the guardianship of a M. Langlois, who took good and faithful care of them, managed their affairs honestly, and left them in enjoyment of a considerable fortune.

Archambauld de Périgord rejoined his family in 1802, and several months later Mélanie married Just de Noailles. The marriage was a hasty one, and its main purpose, if we are to believe Talleyrand, was to avoid a match, desired by Bonaparte, with Eugène de Beauharnais. If we are to believe Sosthène de la Rochefoucauld, however, the unwanted match, in fact desired by Talleyrand, was one with the Duke of Chevreuse.

Whether or not Talleyrand was in favor of his niece's marrying into the old aristocracy, however, the interest he showed in the careers of the two boys could not have been more definite.

Edmond, the younger, was frivolous and happy-go-lucky. In both character and intelligence he took after his father, who had always been more appreciated for his grace of manner than for the qualities of his mind.* In 1805—when Edmond was approaching his eighteenth year—in order to keep the young man out of Paris Talleyrand had sent him to serve his military apprenticeship in Italy, as aide-de-camp to General Pino, the Minister for War. Since he was both the nephew and the protégé of the powerful Minister for Foreign Affairs, Edmond had very quickly been promoted to the rank of Lieutenant, and then, in November 1806, to that of Captain. In March 1807,

---

* Archambauld de Périgord's nickname was Archibeau: he had in fact been one of the best-looking men of his age. The malicious also used to add that he was as stupid as he was handsome (aussi bête que beau).

Talleyrand had him posted to serve under Berthier. At the headquarters of the Prince de Neuchâtel, Edmond found himself back in the company of his elder brother, Louis, once more. The latter was already a Major, and doubtless Talleyrand was hoping that he would prove a restraining influence on Edmond, who was so weak when it came to cards, so weak when it came to women.

Louis's career had been equally as rapid as his younger brother's, but his character was of quite a different stamp; he gave promise of going much further, of eventually becoming one of the army's most distinguished officers, one capable not only of commanding a regiment but also of fulfilling the most delicate diplomatic assignments. Like all the Talleyrand family, Louis was possessed of physical charm and perfect manners, but he also had a quickness and subtlety of mind reminiscent of his uncle's, as well as a strong character and a good heart. He was respected for his honesty, extremely well liked for his generosity, and very much admired for his valor. In short, the proud affection with which Talleyrand regarded this nephew, the heir to whom he was confidently planning to leave the principality of Benevento and his 120,000 livres of income, was entirely justified by the young man's worth.

But before the moment came for this inheritance, Talleyrand wished to assure Louis of a brilliant marriage. Toward the end of the Consulat there had been some question of a match between the young officer and one of the richest heiresses in France. This project, which had been viewed by Bonaparte with a certain amount of suspicion, had remained vague, however, and was finally brought to nothing by the young woman's sudden ruin. Talleyrand had then begun to look for a suitable match outside France.

In 1807, during his long stay in Warsaw, the minister had continued his prospecting in this field. His friend Emmerich de Dalberg, nephew of Charles-Théodore, by then a prince of the Church and Archbishop of Mainz, suggested his great-niece, a Princess of Leyen, as a possible match.* Batowski, on the other

---

* This was undoubtedly the Amélie de Leyen who in 1810 married Count Tascher de la Pagerie, a second cousin to Josephine and later Master of the Household to Empress Eugénie.

hand, having come to Warsaw with Maret and fallen immediately under the influence of Talleyrand, drew his attention to
the Duchess of Courland and her daughter Dorothée. He even
offered to act as go-between.*

In May, Talleyrand had gone to join the Emperor at Finken-
stein, but without allowing his private concerns to languish. On
May 28, Dalberg, who had been extremely well informed of
everything to do with the Courland family by his uncle and his
friend Vitrolles, wrote to the minister: "If it were to come off
[the projected marriage between Louis and his niece Amélie de
Leyen], I should be quite lightheaded with pleasure. The idea
charms me too much for it ever to come to pass. We shall see.
Mademoiselle Batowski, on the other hand, is a gold mine. Can
you afford to take such things lightly? Happiness in this life is
compounded of pleasures; pleasures can be obtained with
money. It is a thing of which it is impossible to have too much,
provided one can acquire it without incurring blame. In a time
of flux such as ours, everyone ought to take whatever circumstances bring within his grasp. Has Batowski received the kind
of answers that remove all hope of success? I should be distressed if that were so. . . ."

The matter was pursued no further at that time, doubtless
because of the tender years of both candidates.

The peace treaty was signed at Tilsit on July 9, 1807. A
month later, Talleyrand relinquished his post as Minister for
Foreign Affairs to Champagny. Then, on August 14, Napoleon
named Talleyrand Vice-Grand Elector, a sinecure that assured
its holder, already Grand Chamberlain, of a yearly salary of
330,000 francs, entitled him to be addressed as Your Serene
Highness, and made him the third highest dignitary of the
Empire, after Cambacérès and Lebrun, the former consuls. The
Minister's retirement was not therefore a disgrace, at the very
most a slight loss of prestige. Talleyrand was not deceived, however. Out of patience with his minister's venality, divining that
his political activities were ultimately directed to private ends,
Napoleon had withdrawn his confidence. In the future, the

---

* The motive was personal gain. "He later complained quite shamelessly
in my presence of having been insufficiently rewarded for his services,"
Dorothée wrote later.

Emperor would do nothing to help Louis find a suitable match in France, and the search for a foreign heiress became a necessity.

Meanwhile, now that the treaty at Tilsit had been signed, Caulaincourt had been named ambassador to St. Petersburg. Napoleon attached a great deal of importance to this appointment, for it was the new ambassador's task to win the confidence of the Russian aristocracy and overcome their hostility to the Tsar's recent political reversal and alliance with France. The task would have been a difficult one for any man, and despite the friendship showed toward him by Alexander it was an even more difficult one for Caulaincourt because the whole of the Muscovite nobility considered him to have been a party to the Duke of Enghien's murder. All the most elegant and attractive officers in the French army were sent in turn to the aid of the new ambassador, all those with handsome faces, all those who danced well, all those who might please the Russian ladies and so appease their ire. Louis de Périgord was one of those chosen to take part in this campaign of seduction.* Since his own ties with Caulaincourt were extremely close, Talleyrand watched the departure of his nephew with satisfaction; the young man would learn a little diplomacy while he was away, and a few months absence would give his uncle all the time he needed to arrange a suitable marriage.

He had counted without fate. On May 23, 1808, Louis de Périgord left St. Petersburg with urgent dispatches for Paris. He arrived at Mittau on the 27th or 28th, already ill. If he had been able to pass on the dispatches to someone else at that point, to stop, to seek treatment, it is possible that he may have recovered, but he was obliged to continue his journey as far as Berlin, which he reached, half dead, on June 4. Once the dispatches were in safe hands, he took to his bed, fought back for two weeks against a bad attack of fever (almost certainly typhoid), and died on June 18, alone and far from all his kin. Two days later he was buried at St. Ursula's.

---

* On April 28, 1808, Caulaincourt asked to keep Louis de Périgord for a while longer and also requested the services of Charles de Flahaut, Talleyrand's son. He was expecting marvels from the latter in the way of making "a few young women more outraged than the rest" see reason.

Talleyrand, who was at that time acting as escort to the captive children of the King of Spain, received the news of this catastrophe at Valençay. It was a hard blow for this man who never showed emotion. On July 1, he wrote to Osmond, once his secretary and still a friend: "You are so much one of us that you will have felt the terrible loss recently inflicted upon us as much as we ourselves.

"Go to see Forel, I beg of you, and, however painful the details, send me word of everything that happened after our poor Louis's arrival in Berlin.

"Farewell.—My heart is full of grief, I can promise you.—I saw him, when I was gone, head of my family, and a head assured of universal esteem and affection.—And now, there is no one."

Talleyrand tried to shift his hopes onto Edmond, but he had no illusions where that young man was concerned, and his first evaluation of the family's position, made in the initial moments of grief, was to remain the only valid one. He did not regard Edmond as his true heir even for a moment. And it was this disappointment, this feeling of regret, that lay at the root of the disdain Talleyrand displayed towards his nephew in later years when the latter had fulfilled the only duties his uncle had ever required of him: to marry and have children.

❖　❖　❖

Spain had not accepted the rule of Bonaparte: even before Joseph Bonaparte had crossed the Pyrenees, the Peninsula was ablaze. 100,000 French troops marched down into Spain under Moncey, Reille, Bessières and Dupont to pave the way for the country's new king. On July 14, 1808, Bessières won an overwhelming victory at Medina del Rio Seco; on the 20th, Joseph entered Madrid. But three days later, just as Spain appeared to be on the verge of surrender, Dupont, after an imprudent advance into Andalusia, was forced to capitulate at Baylen.

The effect of this event was tremendous. A French army capitulating to a band of rebels in open country! All Spain went mad with joy; Joseph, his ambition not matched by his courage, fled from Madrid; and Germany quivered with hope beneath its conqueror's yoke. Napoleon decided to go avenge the defeat at Baylen himself. But before disappearing into the depths of the Peninsula, the Emperor resolved to meet the Tsar once more at Erfurt, with the intention of strengthening their alliance and persuading Alexander to prevent any encroachment by Austria during his own absence.

"The part I had played in the negotiations at Tilsit, the marks of particular kindness bestowed upon me by the Emperor Alexander, the embarrassment in which the Emperor Napoleon continually found himself with regard to M. de Champagny, who, as the Emperor himself remarked, used to arrive every morning bursting with a zeal that was intended to excuse all the blunders of the day before, my personal connection with M. de Caulaincourt . . . all these motives caused the Emperor to overcome the strain that he had recently introduced into our relations," Talleyrand writes in his *Mémoires* when offering an explanation of Napoleon's decision to pass over the Duke of Cadore and give the responsibility of negotiating with the Tsar to his Grand Chamberlain.

There is no doubt that Talleyrand, after ten years as Minister for Foreign Affairs, knew the diplomatic map of Europe better than any man alive, and it was certainly true that he had personal connections or business with a great many rulers or their agents. He could be a very valuable collaborator in difficult transactions, Napoleon knew, but would he be a faithful collaborator? Placing so much trust in the minister removed from office only a year before seems now to have been a strange aberration. Not content with underestimating the grudge that Talleyrand bore him, Napoleon also overestimated his patriotism.

Talleyrand arrived in Erfurt on September 24, 1808. On the 28th, the two emperors met; the meeting was a cordial one and offered hopes of happy results from the negotiations. But that same evening, Talleyrand and Alexander were brought together at a reception given by the Princess of Tour and Taxis, sister of Queen Louise of Prussia, and the betrayal began. The form it took is well-known: the Tsar receiving a day by day account of Napoleon's secret plans, the Vice-Grand Elector of the French Empire revealing every chink in France's political armor to the Emperor of Russia, predicting Caesar's fall, and casting Alexander, almost despite his own wishes, as the savior of Europe.*

Thwarting Napoleon's designs brought Talleyrand a definite intellectual pleasure, but he had more tangible satisfactions in mind. Louis de Périgord's death had brought the question of Edmond's marriage to the forefront of his uncle's preoccupations, and the young man found himself heir to the young women previously envisaged as matches for his brother. Having been informed by Batowski that the Duchess of Courland, since she depended upon the Tsar for the payment of her settlement, would yield to pressure on the subject of her daughter's marriage, Talleyrand seized the opportunity offered by his visit to Erfurt of bringing this scheme to a satisfactory conclusion.

"I had often heard the Duchess of Courland spoken of, both in Germany and in Poland. I knew that she possessed all the distinction that nobility of sentiments, excellence of character, and the most amiable and brilliant personal qualities could bestow. Her youngest daughter was of marriageable age, and it was a choice that could not fail to please Napoleon. It was one that would not deprive any of his generals of a match, since they would all have been rejected in any case, and it was even likely to flatter his vanity by proving that his fond belief in his power to attract all the greatest foreign families into France was justified. . . . I therefore resolved to ask for the hand of Dorothée of Courland on behalf of my nephew, and in order to prevent Napoleon from rescinding his approval at a later date, whether upon reflection or in a moment of caprice, once it had been given, I requested the Emperor Alexander, a personal friend of the Duchess of Courland, to ask that lady for her daughter's hand on my nephew's behalf himself."

After the "extraordinary service" (the expression is Chancellor Pasquier's) he had just rendered to Russia, Alexander could refuse Talleyrand nothing. In the course of their final

---

* "I was struck by the way in which his journey to Erfurt, and his relations there with M. de Talleyrand, had increased Alexander's self-confidence," Princess Louise Radziwill noted shortly afterward. She also added: "It was upon him [Talleyrand] above all that he [Alexander] based his hopes for our future."

interview he not only promised his help in the matter of Edmond's marriage but even gave a guarantee of success.

❖ ❖ ❖

Once settled at Tannenfeld, Dorothée was rarely to be seen at Löbikau. This is not surprising, since the château had been invaded by a band of indigent German princes, Hohenlohe, Solms, Mecklenburg, Reuss, who had been attracted there by the young Princess's tender years, by her excellent education, by her even more excellent dowry, and were now all offering themselves as prospective husbands.

Rejecting none of the attentions that these men paid to her, though offering encouragement to none, the Duchess of Courland herself insistently repeated that her daughter was free to make her own choice. However, since this choice had not yet been announced, she did sometimes take certain of the would-be husbands over to visit at Tannenfeld. Although Dorothée received them all coldly she was unable to dissuade them from their enterprise. Luckily, however, she found this parade rather amusing and was not in any case averse to Adam Czartoryski's knowing that she was so much sought after. Perhaps a little jealousy would lend spurs to his somewhat faint-hearted love?

It was now a year since they had met at Mittau. Still under his mother's imperious thumb, the Prince had not steeled himself to make a formal offer even yet. Early in the summer of 1808, he had written to Piattoli, by then back in Saxony, to say that he was expecting to go with his mother to one of the spas in Bohemia and then to continue his journey as far as Löbikau in order to make a formal request for Dorothée's hand. But the old Princess had contrived to delay that visit. Autumn was already on its way, bringing no sign of either mother or son, when a Russian courier rode in from Erfurt with a letter from the Tsar: it informed the Duchess of Courland that the Emperor Alexander would be pleased to dine with her on October 16.

The Tsar arrived at Löbikau at five in the evening, accompanied by the Prince Troubetzkoï, his aide-de-camp, Caulaincourt, who was on his way back to St. Petersburg, and a young French officer. The Duchess had two of her daughters, the Princess Hohenzollern and the Duchess of Acerdenza, staying with her at the time, and had insisted that Dorothée be present as well. The Grand Duke of Mecklenburg, a brother-in-law of the Tsar, was also present, together with several of Dorothée's would-be husbands and a number of curious visitors.

Though affable to all present, Alexander paid particular attention to Dorothée. After telling her how much taller and prettier she had become since Mittau, he teased her about the number of her suitors. Unaware of the meaning of all this, the young girl replied to all his remarks without any hint of embarrassment.

At dinner, Dorothée and Alexander were separated by the Duchess and Caulaincourt. Apropos of nothing, the Tsar suddenly asked the young Princess whether she had not been struck by a sort of resemblance between the Prince Czartoryski and M. de Périgord.

"Whom does your Majesty mean?" Dorothée answered with a blush.

"Why, that young man sitting down there, the Prince of Benevento's [Talleyrand] nephew who is accompanying the Duke of Vicenza [Caulaincourt] on his way to St. Petersburg."

"You must pardon me, Sire, I had not remarked upon the Duke of Vicenza's aide-de-camp, and my eyesight is so poor that it is impossible for me to distinguish his features clearly at this distance."

The Duchess looked displeased, while Caulaincourt proceded to make it clear that Edmond de Périgord was not his aide-de-camp but was on temporary assignment to the St. Petersburg Embassy. Dorothée did not find the matter interesting and hardly listened to this explanation.

After dinner, the Tsar asked the Duchess to accompany him to a private drawing room. As she left the salon, the latter said to her youngest daughter: "Be polite to the Duke of Vicenza, talk to him, you know the Emperor treats him as a friend. I've not been able to persuade your sisters to address a single word to him. . . . I want you to take care of M. de Caulaincourt for me, because I don't want him to go away with a bad impression of us."

Dorothée went over and sat down beside the ambassador, leaving her sisters to chatter to the German princes. "The conversation of a very young girl . . . with a general in Bonaparte's army could hardly prove very satisfying to either party; yet it was so to me; I thought M. de Caulaincourt very noble in appearance and well versed in the ways of society." Caulaincourt was also favorably impressed with Dorothée. He was perfectly acquainted with Talleyrand's wishes with regard to the young princess, and wrote to him next day from Leipzig: * "The beautiful Dorothée is fifteen years old and appears to have been extremely well brought up. We found the château teeming with hopefuls, but the number one rival was not there."

Once alone with the Duchess, the Tsar came straight to the point. He had the greatest obligations toward the Prince of Benevento and he wished to fulfil them. The only favor the Prince had asked of him was his help in bringing about a marriage between his nephew Edmond and Dorothée of Courland. He, Alexander, had granted this request, and he had now come to ask for the Duchess's consent to the match also. He was counting on her help in giving "to a man who was dear to his heart, and whom it was important to him to satisfy, the only proof of friendship that he seemed to desire."

Opposed from the start to the Czartoryski match, feeling slighted by that Prince's hesitation and his mother's hostility, anxious to take up residence in France and flattered by Talleyrand's interest, for he was the third greatest personage in the French Empire and of ancient and aristocratic stock, only too well aware of the debt she owed to Alexander and of the extent to which she was dependent upon the good will of that very changeable monarch, the Duchess immediately became a supporter of the Périgord match: but although she assured the Tsar

---

* Caulaincourt notes in his *Mémoires*: "I accompanied the Emperor Alexander to Weimar, then to Löbikau, where we visited the Duchess of Courland. It was during this visit that I arranged the marriage between the latter's daughter and M. Edmond de Périgord, thanks to the honorable intervention of the Russian ruler."

of her own obedience and devotion to his person, she expressed some uneasiness.

"You know, Sire, how violently anti-French some Germans are in their ideas, and my daughter subscribes to them all; she is a very strong-willed girl, her position makes her independent, and her sisters, her relatives, her friends, the Prussian court, all Germany will protest against this marriage. Though I have no reason to complain of Dorothée's conduct towards me, still I am aware that I have very little influence over her thought; and besides, I must admit to you quite frankly, Sire, that there has been question for a long time now of my daughter marrying one of Your Majesty's former friends. The Prince Adam Czartoryski is the man whom she has favored with her choice; I have no reason of any weight with which to oppose the match, and I can see no means of preventing the marriage taking place within the year."

"Do you yourself desire this marriage?" the Tsar asked.

"No, Sire. The great differences in their ages, the difficult character of the old Princess, and the ill grace with which she has behaved in this matter until now all rather combine to make me oppose it."

"In that case," the Tsar replied, "I cannot accept any of your other objections; Dorothée is only fifteen, she cannot have formed any proper notion of political matters at so early an age; as for the gossip you seem to fear, that may be avoided by delaying the announcement of the marriage I desire until the last possible moment. The young Princess has been far too well brought up for me to believe that she would remain unmoved by a mother's influence, should you consent to employ it. As for Adam Czartoryski, I can assure you that he has no desire whatsoever to marry anybody, and that he will always allow himself to be ruled by his mother, who is a dangerous and conspiratorial old woman, even for a Pole. . . . In short, my dear Duchess, I can accept no excuses. I have given my own word and I must now ask you for yours; I ask it as a proof of that friendship which you have promised to me and of which I believe myself to be deserving."

The situation could not have been clearer: though still employing a mask of courtesy, the autocratic monarch had expressed his will. The Duchess bowed before it and gave her promise to obtain Dorothée's consent. She returned to the salon with the Tsar; shortly afterwards he left.

Next day, the Duchess asked her daughter what impression Edmond de Périgord had made upon her. Somewhat astonished, Dorothée admitted without hesitation that she had not even looked at him. The Duchess then questioned her other daughters; neither had paid any attention to the young man in question. She then sent for Piattoli and remained closeted with him for a long time. When they emerged from this interview, the Duchess was wearing a preoccupied expression and the Abbé was looking downcast and sad; neither of them spoke a word.

Regina Hoffman, offended at not being taken into their confidence, told her pupil that it was high time they both moved back to Berlin. Oppressed by the heavy atmosphere prevailing at Löbikau since the Tsar's visit, uneasy at Piattoli's sudden silence on the subject of Czartoryski, Dorothée agreed. Early in November, she returned with her governess to No. 7, Unter den Linden, where they were to stay for three months. In January 1809, when Dorothée of Courland left the house of her birth again, it was, although she did not know it, a final leave-taking.*

❖   ❖   ❖

When he left Löbikau, the Tsar had taken the Duke of Vicenza with him in his carriage as far as Leipzig. On the way, Alexander gave Caulaincourt an account of his conversation with the Duchess and told him of the promise he had obtained from her. Upon their arrival in Leipzig, the Ambassador dispatched Edmond to Paris with letters for Talleyrand.

"Edmond has arrived, my dear Caulaincourt," Talleyrand wrote on October 26. "I shall ask the Emperor to send him back to you. You have shown kindness to both uncle and nephew; he has told me what pains you took to show him in a good light."

* In 1839, at a time when she had not yet decided whether or not to settle definitely in Prussia, Dorothée sold the palace of the Courlands to Russia for 95,000 thalers.

Talleyrand wanted this matter concluded with all dispatch. Within three days he had obtained the necessary permission, and on October 29, the very day on which Napoleon left Paris for Spain, he was writing to Caulaincourt that Edmond would be leaving for St. Petersburg within the week. "I must ask you to keep a somewhat fatherly eye on him. . . . I invest you with all my powers in this respect. The family are extremely happy about this whole matter and the way in which it is being managed."

Although obedient to his uncle's imperious wishes, Edmond no doubt felt some measure of regret at being forced to leave again so soon for so distant a country in order to conclude so precipitate a marriage. Two weeks had elapsed before he finally set out again.

"Edmond has received his authorization to leave, my dear Caulaincourt, and I am sending him off immediately. The leave of absence Berthier has sent him allows him to be away three months; that is more than enough time in which to set on foot and conclude the negotiations, potentially so advantageous to him, that I have undertaken under your auspices. Batowski is accompanying him; he is a man of affairs and extremely well aquainted with the Duchess of Courland's way of life. After he has spent a week with her, he is to write to me exactly what we should and can do. Edmond, when that week is over, will continue to St. Petersburg, place himself under your orders, and remain there until we have come to some definite decision. If that decision is the one I hope it will be, Archambauld will leave for Löbikau and draw up all the necessary agreements with the help of his business agent. Then Edmond will arrive at the same time as his father, and after that everything should move very quickly. . . ."

Next day, November 15, Edmond de Périgord left Paris with a letter from Talleyrand to the Duchess of Courland.* The

* "Madame, Edmond will have the honor of delivering this letter to Your Highness. You have been [good] enough to treat him with some kindness; he is proud of the attention you paid him, has spoken of it to me with great warmth, and would willingly spend his life attempting to become worthy of it. I told him that the undertaking would be no light one, that, being a man not entirely unacquainted with the affairs of Europe, it was impossible for

Duchess received the young man kindly and invited Batowski to stay with her in Saxony for the rest of the winter, an offer that he accepted. The Duchess also replied in very encouraging terms to Talleyrand's letter. "You may also be assured of my approval. Only that of my daughter is now lacking, and I do not wish to interfere with her liberty of choice."

Talleyrand did not miss the hidden meaning. If they wanted her to force Dorothée into this choice, the Duchess must be provided with the necessary weapon. On December 16, Talleyrand sent off a letter to Caulaincourt requesting him to obtain that weapon from the Tsar.

Alexander had not lost his interest in the Périgord marriage. Back in St. Petersburg once more, he wrote to Talleyrand, and his courier was riding toward Paris as Edmond rode away from it. On December 26, Talleyrand thanked the Russian monarch and informed him of all that had been done in the matter. "Your Majesty's advice has been followed. Edmond must by now have left Löbikau. . . . I sent a letter by him to Madame, the Duchess of Courland, in which I was even audacious enough to hint that Your Majesty was not far from approving the request I had been so bold as to make."

That same day, assured of Alexander's good will, and determined to strike while the iron was still hot, Talleyrand sent Caulaincourt his plans for the battle ahead. "I have today written to the Emperor thanking him for the letter he did me the honor of writing to me. I want Edmond to leave for Löbikau so as to arrive there on February 3. This will be convenient to the Duchess since it is her birthday and there will be a great deal

---

me not to be aware how entirely Your Highness's beauty, grace and elevation of mind have given you the right to be difficult in such choices; his answer is that he himself is even more aware of that truth than I, who have never had the good fortune to visit at Löbikau, but that goodness of heart, gentleness, a rectitude of conduct tested by the most trying circumstances, and an unfailing desire to please must also count for something in the matter. Emperor Alexander has been kind enough not to reprove his audacity, it would be wrong of me to exceed him in severity, and I trust, Madame, that you will not find it in you to display more than me. If Your Highness were so good as to give me some assurance of this, you would be making my nephew eternally happy and earning the lifelong devotion of all my family."

of other company there. He is to stay there for whatever period Batowski deems advisable and will then continue on to Paris. If he were to arrive at Löbikau with a letter for the Duchess from the Emperor, and if, in that letter, the Emperor were kind enough to insert a word or two in his favor, I think some good would be done by it. The Duchess seems to me very willing to fall in with our wishes. I am sending Edmond a letter that I have written to the Duchess in reply to the one I have received from her."

These letters, the one from the Tsar and the one from Talleyrand, were to be shown to Dorothée of Courland on the morning when her mother informed her of Edmond de Périgord's request for her hand.

◇   ◇   ◇

The Duchess insisted that her daughter come to Löbikau for her mother's birthday celebrations. Piattoli, now sick and living at Altenburg, perhaps in order to be near to his doctors, was sending Dorothée letters whose confusion betrayed his embarrassment. He spoke of vanished dreams, of "hope that cannot die without also bringing those desires to an end." The Duchess's letters were insistent, Piattoli's enigmatic. Dorothée decided that some attempt must be made to dissipate the oppressive mystery of the situation, and toward the end of January 1809, Mlle Hoffmann and she left for Löbikau.

They stopped at Altenburg to visit Piattoli. Dorothée found him so changed that she scarcely dared to ask him if he had news of Czartoryski.

"No, I have none. And this silence ought to prove to you, dear child, that our dreams were only idle fantasies."

"God forbid such a thought!" Dorothée cried.

"Let us not talk about it," the abbé begged, "it is a subject that causes me so much pain."

Dorothée reached Löbikau with an anxious heart.

The Duchess greeted her most tenderly. "My mother received me with more joy and more grace than I had ever seen her display before. She told me that I must not think of going to my summer house in winter, that she had had a suite of rooms got ready for me, and that she absolutely insisted on keeping me with her."

An amazing display of affection, and one to which the unexpected presence of Batowski lent a disturbing significance.

Three or four days went by. Dorothée was just beginning to feel reassured when one evening, while all the others were finishing letters before the courier left and she was alone in the salon making the tea, she heard the sound of the hunting horn heralding the arrival of a stranger. A few minutes later a servant came in looking for the Duchess. A French officer, the one who had been there with Caulaincourt, was asking for her.

The veil was ripped aside—Dorothée understood. Terrified at the idea of being left alone with Edmond de Périgord, she crossed the hallway at a run, climbed the stairway two steps at a time and hurled herself into the safety of her own apartment.

Regina Hoffmann was there. Dorothée told her about the young Frenchman's arrival and burst into tears, "I'm sure he's come to marry me." The governess reassured her; the Duchess had never gone against her daughter's wishes before. Dorothée was insistent:

"Because none of the marriages I refused mattered to her; but you know how she loves France and wants to go and live there."

"She can't force you to marry anyone," Regina replied. "Calm yourself down or you won't be in a fit state to go down to dinner."

A little calmer, her eyes dried, Dorothée went back down to the salon. While Batowski bustled about, "delighted, intolerable," the Duchess, "radiant and embarrassed," holding several letters in her hand, presented Edmond de Périgord to her daughter who, this time, looked at him.

Tall and well-built, Edmond was also elegant and distinguished in his appearance. His face was oval, his brow wide below the dark hair; eyes red-brown and not very expressive; a straight, delicate nose; a laughing mouth, still the mouth of a child. In short, a pleasant, kindly countenance with no sign of either character or intelligence.

Dorothée retired early and slept scarcely at all.

⬦ ⬦ ⬦

Early next morning, the Duchess sent for Mlle Hoffmann. At the end of an hour the governess returned, wearing a troubled expression. Refusing to explain, she said to Dorothée: "You must go to your mother. She is asking for you."

With drawn features and a beating heart, Dorothée made her way down the staircase and into her mother's room. The Duchess was still in bed, letters lying scattered over it. She gave her daughter an account of the conversation she had had with the Tsar on October 16, then added: "You know of course that in Russia the sovereign's favors are always precarious, that everything depends upon his caprice, and that it is of the very greatest importance to me that I should retain his good will. I have promised him that I will do everything in my power to persuade you to the marriage he desires. I therefore beg you not to refuse without carefully weighing the advantages that would result for all your family from this alliance. First, read these letters I have just received."

The first, dated January 10, was from the Tsar; it contained a firm expression of his wishes. "M. de Périgord, during his stay here, has further increased the esteem in which I had already held him! He is a charming young man, filled with excellent qualities and lacking in nothing to make any woman happy. I very much desire to hear that Your Highness and the young Princess share my opinion of him, and that this union, which is so much desired, is to take place."

The second, dated December 26, was from Talleyrand. It was a perfectly judged piece of work, and full of feeling. He spoke with tenderness of the joy this match would bring to his old mother—the mother whom the articles of his marriage, six years previously, had declared deceased. "My mother, with whom I shared all my hopes the very day I dared to conceive them, to whom I showed Your Highness's letter, my mother, whose advancing years seem only to increase the extreme goodness of her heart, says that happiness is always an urgent matter; that she would still like to devote a few more years of care and caresses to her granddaughter; that when one has satisfied oneself that all the moral, physical, and social conditions on both sides are such as must produce a worthy alliance and, above all, a happy household, then there would be a kind of barbarousness in depriving oneself of a part of the sweet and happy life thus offered for one's enjoyment.

"I think and feel as my mother does. I can only express my ardent wish that the Princess Dorothée will decide in Edmond's favor. . . ."

Dorothée read through the two letters slowly. The Tsar's revolted her; the one from Talleyrand she found interesting. She handed the sheets of paper back to her mother without a word.

The Duchess then continued to pursue the subject while the fifteen year old girl strove valiantly to defend her happiness. She reminded the Duchess of her long attachment to Czartoryski. She could have resigned herself to all the rest, marrying a stranger, leaving her own country, going to live at the court of Bonaparte, saying good-bye to all her friends, but she would not break the promises she had made. Despite Prince Adam's delay, she had no doubt that he still valued her. . . .

Imprudent words: they were to be exploited against her.

The Duchess lost her temper, then complained of her daughter's ingratitude. "At least show M. de Périgord some courtesy; and in order not to make you appear ridiculous I shall let two or three days go by before I give the Prince of Benevento an answer, for it must at least appear that you have thought the matter over. I also wish you to be more polite to M. Batowski; he knows everything there is to know about M. de Talleyrand and you can at least agree to listen to what he has to tell you about so illustrious a family."

Dorothée, by then in tears, returned to her own rooms, where Regina Hoffmann was waiting for her. There was no help to be expected from that quarter. The Duchess had demanded the governess's word that she would not try to influence her pupil in any way and Mlle Hoffmann, subservient by nature, was already deserting to the stronger cause.

While Edmond, not knowing where to put himself, retreated behind a barrier of reticence and hardly spoke,* Batowski took the center of the stage and began to intone his eulogy of the Talleyrands. The Prince of Benevento himself was an easy subject, and Batowski was able to vaunt his great talents without referring to his semi-disgrace. Edmond's bravery was dazzling, his father amiable, his sister full of graces. There remained the Princess of Benevento. Till then, Batowski had been painting in the brightest colors; now, a certain obfuscation became apparent. Catherine Grand appeared as "a person of such nullity and insignificance that she could not be regarded as a drawback." Dorothée listened to him, then replied simply: "If I were still free, all that you have told me is such as would tend to destroy my repugnance; but I consider myself already engaged elsewhere; I have told my mother so, and I have nothing to add."

Since Dorothée would not yield, a scheme was devised to deceive her: if she could be brought to believe that she had been betrayed, scorned, then her pride would drive her into the Périgord marriage.

Batowski left for Altenburg, stayed there a day, then returned with a letter extorted from the failing Piattoli, by now too weak to resist. "All our hopes are destroyed; I have at last had news from Poland. The letter came, not from Prince Adam, but from a common friend, who tells me that a marriage has been arranged between the Prince and Mademoiselle Matuschewitz, that all Warsaw is talking of it, and that the old Princess is delighted." †

After one glance at these lines, Dorothée called for horses and drove directly to Altenburg. Piattoli, almost on the brink of death,‡ refused to see her. She insisted and went in. "Be

* "It was impossible to divine what qualities of character or mind he might possibly possess, since no one has ever been so lavish with his . . . silence," Dorothée wrote in her mémoirs.

† In fact, it was not until 1817 that Adam Czartoryski married the Princess Anne Sapieha.

‡ He died on April 12.

happy," the old man murmured, without paying any attention to her questions, then added, "Forgive me for having tried to decide your future and place it from now on in the hands of Madame, your mother." After speaking these few words Piattoli relapsed into a stubborn and unshakable silence.

Upon her return to Löbikau, Dorothée observed the presence of a new arrival, Countess Oguinska, a Polish lady already well rehearsed by Batowski and the Duchess. The next day, at a moment when the whole party was present, the Countess announced that she had just received letters from Warsaw: they contained news of Adam Czartoryski's marriage.

Dorothée disappeared into the next room. Her mother followed her. Blinded with anger, no longer feeling love for anyone or anything, Dorothée agreed to marry Edmond de Périgord. "I spoke hurriedly, with tears in my eyes and voice, but my mother seemed not to notice anything; she kissed me in transports of delight, praised me, applauded my pride, stirred up my resentment to further heights and, without losing a second, told me that she must go and tell M. de Périgord the good news. I didn't want her to. . . ."

Dorothée spent that night weeping. Next morning, the Duchess came to her room, "coaxed her a great deal," and told her that she must perform what she had promised with good grace: she was to go downstairs and behave graciously towards Edmond.

Downcast and red-eyed, Dorothée made her way to her mother's rooms. The Duchess was a woman of experience, she had lived a great deal, she had loved a great deal; she could have helped those two self-conscious children to overcome their embarrassment and their anxiety. Yet she made not the slightest attempt to do so. She simply disappeared and left them alone.

Sitting face to face, Edmond and Dorothée both maintained a long silence. Dorothée was the first to break it:

"I hope that you will be happy, Monsieur, in the marriage that has been arranged for us. But I am obliged to tell you myself what you doubtless already know: that I am merely complying with my mother's wishes, without repugnance I may truly say, but certainly with the most complete indifference where you are concerned. Possibly I may be happy, I should like

to believe so, but you will, I think, find my regrets at leaving
my own country and my friends simple to understand, and you
will not, I hope, dislike me for the sadness that you may, in the
beginning at least, have occasion to observe in me."

"That seems to me only natural," Edmond replied. "And
anyway, you know, I too am only marrying because my uncle
wishes it, for at my age one much prefers a bachelor's life. . . ."

Edmond left Löbikau with Batowski the following day, without any further words having passed between the two young
people.

⬦   ⬦   ⬦

By the time Edmond arrived in Paris, at the end of February 1809, Talleyrand's situation had undergone a startling
change. Still in the depths of Spain, Napoleon had learned
that Archduke Charles was making hurried preparations for
war in Vienna, and that Talleyrand was conspiring with Fouché
in Paris. The Emperor lost not a single instant in returning to
his capital where, on the 30th of January, after a violent scene
on the 28th, he removed Talleyrand from the office of Chamberlain. This time the disgrace was indisputable, even though
Talleyrand remained Vice-Grand Elector.

On February 24, Talleyrand wrote to inform Caulaincourt
of Edmond's return. Keeping his head high, even with such an
intimate friend, he added: "His affairs, thanks to you, are now
flourishing. There remains only to obtain an order of transmissibility, which I shall ask the Emperor for tomorrow. . . ." The
Emperor did not grant it.

Disturbed by his brother's disgrace, Archambauld de Périgord waited almost a month before writing to Clarke, the Minister for War, requesting the indispensable authorization. Clarke
referred the matter to Napoleon on March 22, and the Emperor
granted his consent on the 23rd. "I have the honor to inform
you that the Emperor has approved the marriage of M. Edmond,
your son, with Mlle Dorothée, Princess of Courland," wrote
the future Duke of Feltre on the following day.

Talleyrand uttered a sigh of relief and immediately passed

on this news to the Tsar. "The negotiations that Your Majesty permitted me to undertake under your kind auspices on behalf of Edmond's happiness have now been concluded to the satisfaction of both parties. Agreements have been drawn up. Everything has turned out perfectly, Sire, as one was bound to believe it would when two such great powers as yourself and Love had taken pains to use their influence in the matter."

Love? One wonders what Alexander thought of that.

The authorization of the Emperor once obtained, Edmond set off on the road to Löbikau once again with his father and Batowski. He found a sad and apathetic fiancée waiting for him. Terrified at the prospect of a future she could not understand, weeping at the thought of leaving Germany, completely ignorant of Paris and of the family into which she was about to enter, Dorothée was living as though in a nightmare. The people who surrounded her were mere shadows, and the most unreal of them all was undoubtedly the man who was soon to be her husband.

On April 22, 1809, in Frankfurt, the Archbishop of Mainz, Charles-Théodore de Dalberg, gave his blessing to the marriage of Edmond de Périgord and Dorothée of Courland. The old man knew a great many things, and he guessed a great many more. As a wedding present, he gave the aloof and melancholy little bride a bird that beat its wings inside a golden cage.

Part Two

AT

THE

IMPERIAL

COURT (1809-1814)

❖

WHILE Dorothée was pledging her future to Edmond de Périgord in Frankfurt, the cannon were thundering at Eckmühl. A dazzling victory: it cost the Austrians 60,000 men and opened the way to Vienna. On May 8, Napoleon was "moving back" into Schoenbrunn, where he was to plan the Wagram campaign.

The Countess Edmond de Périgord had scarcely ever seen her fiancé, and she was to see very little more of her husband, who departed to rejoin his regiment almost the day after their marriage leaving his wife to be taken care of by the Duchess of Courland * and Talleyrand, more particularly the latter.

Talleyrand had not made the journey to Frankfurt. It was a prudent and understandable omission at a moment when he was compounding his previous betrayal to the Russians with his present betrayal to the Austrians and using the imperial city as a meeting place for his own and Metternich's spies. The child his greed had wrested from the land of her birth, perhaps from her happiness, was therefore a stranger to him when, toward the end of April 1809, she arrived in Paris and took up residence with her mother and governess in the great Hôtel de Monaco on the Rue de Varenne.†

Dorothée was presented to a fair-complexioned man with a strong chin and disdainful mouth that gave him a sarcastic and haughty air. Despite some difficulty in walking, the Vice-Grand Elector was not without elegance. The pale and impassive countenance, the clear, cold eyes, half hidden by their heavy lids, produced an impression of tranquillity and power in the beholder.

Talleyrand for his part was disappointed. He was accus-

---

* On April 25, in Strasburg, the future General de Reiset noted: "The Duchess of Courland passed through, having just married her daughter to Count Edmond de Périgord in Frankfurt; she stayed only a short while."
† Now the Hotel Matignon, which Talleyrand had bought from Crawford.

tomed to the full-blown charms of maturity and, having no taste for unripe fruits, found Dorothée skinny and underdeveloped. He liked women with a bloom on them, and as Charles de Rémusat so uncompromisingly put it, Dorothée was a "prune" with a "tiny, tense, angular face given to grimaces," softened only by her admirable eyes, which were full of sadness and disquiet in those days. Talleyrand valued simplicity in women, and Dorothée seemed to him affected, possibly intelligent, but above all pedantic.

"I am thoroughly contented with the young niece I owe to your kindness," he wrote unenthusiastically to Caulaincourt on May 9, 1809; "I am doing my best to make the first moments of her husband's absence tolerable for her; the mother is quite charming . . ."

Young in appearance, despite being well over forty, with a skin of dazzling whiteness, and eyes full of vivacity and caressing glances, the Duchess did not fail to attract Talleyrand. The great lord recognized her immediately as a woman after his own heart, this great lady whose experience in the intrigues of love was only equaled by her experience in the intrigues of contemporary politics, and who had been occupying all Europe with her various adventures for the past twenty years.

The Duchess too did not take long to succumb. She had been wholly entranced by the idea of the French court before her arrival, and was not Talleyrand, in Napoleon's absence, one of its most important personages? He was, in any case, certainly one of the most attractive, and so highly regarded by Alexander.

A tender intimacy sprang up between them; * this soon developed into a long liaison, one full of passion and jealousy on the Duchess's side, for this was possibly the last love affair

---

* On June 15, 1809, Talleyrand was already writing to the Duchess, who was then at Rosny: "I received your kind letter yesterday. . . . Even had I not been so entirely alone and in so melancholy a spot as Bourbon-l 'Archambault, it would still have brought me the greatest pleasure. You appear to be pleased with Rosny; I had hoped as much. . . . I do not know why all my thoughts are so black. I feel the need to be surrounded once more by all my family, and you must permit me now, thanks to Dorothée, to consider you too a member of it. . . ."

of her life, but mainly sensual with Talleyrand, to whom this woman's weight of experience afforded both physical and intellectual pleasures. One strange result of this intimacy with Talleyrand was that the Duchess's admiration for Napoleon was transformed into a profound hatred, which, in its turn, lent an even greater impetus to Talleyrand's treachery. And finally, it must be added that the hostility existing between mother and daughter, though concealed beneath an outward display of affection, had the effect, now that the Duchess had formed so close a tie with Talleyrand, of creating a rift between the latter and his new niece, at least during the first years of her marriage.

❖   ❖   ❖

On May 17, Talleyrand announced to Caulaincourt: "Having introduced Edmond's wife to my whole family, I shall now take her to Rosny and from there go on myself to Bourbon-l'Archambault."

The only member of the family that Dorothée had seen was her father-in-law, first at Löbikau, then at Frankfurt. A swift appraisal had disclosed both his urbanity and his insignificance.

Mélanie de Périgord might perhaps have afforded her young sister-in-law some pleasure by her company, and a measure of help too; but the barrier created by an eight year difference in age was made even more insurmountable by the dissimilarity of their characters. The Countess Just de Noailles, a woman of fashion, happy in her home, concealed beneath the most exquisite veneer of courtesy a total indifference of heart. Her caustic wit was quick to seize upon the absurdities of others and she mocked them unmercifully. Doubtless she exercised this vivacity of mind at the expense of the awkward and bewildered Dorothée. Mélanie lived in terror of boredom: fearing that she would encounter it only too often in the company of this pedantic little German girl with her still unassimilated education, she made no attempt to win Dorothée's affection and no intimacy was ever established between them.

Talleyrand's youngest brother, Boson, had married upon his return to France after the Revolution. He had only one daughter, Georgine, a little girl of eight. Since they had no wealth of their own, Boson de Périgord and his wife lived on Talleyrand's charity.

Rather colorless, avid eyes fixed upon the Vice-Grand Elector's present liberalities and future legacies, their pride satisfied by Edmond's marriage, too lazy of heart and mind to undertake the task of making Dorothée feel at home, to make her love her new family, her new life, and her new country, the Talleyrands as a whole merely formed a neutral tinted background from which, sparkling with color and making a most astonishing figure, there emerged Mme de Talleyrand herself, that woman whom Batowski had described as "of such nullity and insignificance."

It is true that all intimacy had long since ceased between Talleyrand and his wife, but they still lived beneath the same roof, and it was his wife who ruled over the salons of the Hôtel de Monaco. She had made it her task to bring up as her own daughter the ten year old Charlotte, who bore such a striking resemblance to Talleyrand, as well as to Charles de Flahaut.

Catherine Grand immediately sensed a rival in the Duchess of Courland, and with equal immediacy she displayed every sign of an unshakeable antipathy toward the Countess Edmond de Périgord, whether because some instinct warned her of what was to come, or whether simply because she was her mother's daughter.

About fifty kilometers outside the capital, not far from Mantes-la-Jolie, Edmond de Périgord had inherited from the Sénozan family a large château, constructed all of pink brick, that had originally been built for Sully. Rosny stood high above the light-drenched beauty of the Seine valley, at a spot where the river swung in a great curve across the valley floor. The huge park contained an English garden, which soon became Dorothée's favorite walk.

Dorothée spent many quiet months at Rosny. They were certainly amongst the happiest of her life, as were those she spent later at Valençay, at Rochecotte above all, and later still in retirement at Sagan. In the country—provided she was not too much alone—Dorothée, a creature with great depths of soul, felt herself drawing nourishment from the moist earth itself; she grew calmer there, she soaked herself in peace. When she was with humble country people she shed her affectation and showed the simplicity of heart that lay beneath it. When she was with poor people she rediscovered the human warmth within her that was masked in society by an armor of detachment and aloofness, as though to protect herself against attacks and painful bruises.

❖   ❖   ❖

While his wife was acquainting herself with France and the Talleyrands, Edmond had returned to his post on Berthier's staff. The evening before Essling (May 22, 1809), as Napoleon advanced towards the bank of the Danube, he waited with watch open until it chimed eleven o'clock. Turning to the major-general, the Emperor said: "It is time to write out the order for retreat." Edmond de Périgord then had a torch lit and held it up firmly, despite the wind, so that Lejeune, by that fitful light, the paper pressed against his sabretache, could write the two lines ordering Masséna and Bessières to retire at midnight onto the island of Lobau and take up their positions there. Six weeks later came the battle of Wagram.

Several days after the battle, Edmond visited Oblass, Masséna's headquarters. Marbot, the Marshal's aide-de-camp, had been charged with a mission that entailed an interview with Berthier. He therefore accompanied Edmond when the latter set out on his return to Zukerhandel, where the Emperor's chief of staff was encamped. As they were following a narrow path beside the Taya, they suddenly found themselves in the midst of a violent bombardment. Both young officers urged their mounts to a gallop, but Edmond's horse stumbled and fell. Edmond's leg had been trapped beneath the horse's body in such a way that he could not wrest it free. Marbot rushed to his aid. There was no time to lose; the cannon balls were flying more thickly every moment. At last the horse struggled to its feet. Edmond leaped into the saddle and set off again with

Marbot at top speed. Back in Zuckerhandel, after his interview with Berthier, Marbot found himself the toast of the entire general staff, for Edmond was extremely popular.

Though brave, exemplary in his conduct under fire, a good companion, and much loved by his fellow officers, young Périgord did not, alas, enhance his reputation in times of peace. Once the armistice had been signed at Znaïm on July 12, Napoleon moved into Schoenbrunn with his general staff while peace terms were being hammered out. The struggle had been a hard one, the losses heavy, and the young French officers now hurled themselves with a kind of fury into every kind of amusement, as though haunted by the thought that their pleasures might have no tomorrow. The Viennese women were charming, and it was a fact that did not go unnoticed. But there were amusements other than women. Edmond de Périgord, rich in his own right and richer still after his marriage, was liberal in his entertaining; there was a great deal of gambling at his house. Too much. And besides the women and the gambling there were also other follies that appealed to a young hothead anxious to throw his money about.

Edmond had the most breathtaking cape made to wear with his uniform. "From each braid frog there hung as many bullion fringes, themselves forming as many epaulettes; never had such a gloriously gilded hussar been seen before," Castellane wrote. The gilded hussar made a triumphant entrance into the mess. His success was total but of brief duration. Berthier took one look at him and said: "What is that, Monsieur? It is not the uniform of my aides-de-camp." And Edmond was obliged to lay aside his beautiful braided cape.

Berthier was on the closest terms with Talleyrand, which was why the latter so frequently placed his protégés on Berthier's staff. Louis had been one of Berthier's aides-de-camp. Charles de Flahaut had held the same post since 1808. It was from Berthier no doubt that Talleyrand learned before long of his nephew's follies. Doubtless the aristocratic eyebrows were raised, the thin and arrogant lips compressed in disdain.

Dorothée, on the other hand, must have sighed at the knowledge that political considerations had thus provided her with a

husband who, though certainly not bad, nevertheless offered
her no hope of either protection or fidelity.

❖   ❖   ❖

Once the peace had been signed in Vienna, on October 14,
1809, Napoleon left for Fontainebleau, which he reached on
the 26th. Berthier and the general staff followed closely on his
heels. While the Emperor was reconciling himself to the necessity for divorce and an Austrian marriage, Edmond de Périgord
and Dorothée were settling down to married life together. For
two years they continued as an apparently happy and united
couple.

To begin with they set up their own establishment in the
town house, No. 2, Rue de la Grange-Batelière, that Edmond
had purchased shortly after their marriage. Built during the
reign of Louis XV, this house had belonged first to the financier
J. J. Laborde, then to a Fermier-Général named Laage. (Under
the July monarchy it became the Jockey Club.)

Edmond was a good-natured young man; he was also very
good-looking and extremely well-mannered. He was by no means
a disagreeable companion, and for several months Dorothée
seems to have accommodated herself to her new life without
too much difficulty, without too many regrets. It was a life
devoid of complications, one that stilled the uneasiness in her
heart, so that marriage gradually brought a fullness, a bloom
to the skinny "prune" who had so disappointed Talleyrand, and
transformed her into a child-woman who was already pretty and
gave promise of becoming even more so.

The Austrian, Clary, came to spend three months in Paris
at that time on the occasion of Napoleon's marriage. He moved
a great deal in society and frequently encountered the Edmond
de Périgords, who always attended social engagements together
at that time, like any normal married couple. He decided that
Edmond "looked like a young man," which was a term of dis-
paragement in his vocabulary, and that Dorothée, though rav-
ishing, was "not agreeable."

Early in May of 1810, the Edmond de Périgords gave a ball. As was only proper in a household with claims to elegance, Julien, the famous Negro, conducted the orchestra. Clary was present. He enjoyed himself hugely and left, long after most of the other guests, at half past four in the morning. The following day he wrote an account of the evening to his mother, then devoted a great deal of space to the young couple. During the two months he had been in Paris his opinion of them had become more definite: "Mme Edmond de Périgord has really achieved an astonishing success when one thinks of the reservations that people must necessarily have entertained about her. Everyone is fond of her and full of her praises. She—Mme Edmond—still has a slightly pinched air, a manner of speaking that one might be inclined to think affected; well, she overcomes all that with her pleasant manner, her tasteful appearance, her behavior. . . . Her eyes are magnificent, and in five or six years, when she has had a few children, she will be one of the prettiest women in Paris. She is extremely sensible for a girl of sixteen, has an aversion to being idle, and is as orderly in the running of her house, they say, as her husband is the opposite. At bottom, I suspect her of having more head than heart. M. de Talleyrand is affable with her but does not love her, because he loves no one. . . ."

Though Talleyrand may have been affable with his niece without feeling any great love for her, his liaison with the Duchess of Courland on the other hand was now becoming public knowledge. The charming Countess Alexandre Potocka, Charles de Flahaut's tender and affectionate friend, also came to Paris in the spring of 1810. She remarked upon the intrigue and found it amusing. "M. de Talleyrand, by no means insensible to this lady's charms, had procured her a place amongst Mme de Laval's most intimate circle, and it had become quite customary for all the members of that salon to admire everything that the Duchess did. . . . Her aging worshipper gazing at her meanwhile with a degree of admiration well calculated to make his entire seraglio die of jealousy, my Aunt Tyszkiewicz being among their number."

Clary too furnishes us with some piquant details of the behavior prevalent in this seraglio, where the former favorites had all, or almost all, remained friends with the sultan even after they had served their turn. "When M. de Talleyrand leaves, these ladies [the Duchess of Courland and Mme de Laval] follow him out onto the stairs and remain there with him in conversation for a further half an hour." The Austrian visitor also adds: "They say that the Duchess wants M. de Talleyrand to leave everything to M. Edmond de Périgord, but that M. de Talleyrand, who loves nothing in this world apart from himself, intends to leave M. Edmond only his Benevento title and the very tiny principality that goes with it. All the rest is to go to the little Charlotte whom he and his wife, especially the latter, seem to worship so."

◇ ◇ ◇

Napoleon had retained almost all of Josephine's official ladies-in-waiting to serve in the household of his new Empress, Marie-Louise, but even at the time when he was still only engaged to her, he had decided to appoint "seven or eight further ladies-in-waiting of the same age as the Empress."

During the first months of the marriage, still wholly absorbed by his new conjugal life, the Emperor had not troubled to make these appointments. It was not until September 13, 1810, that a decree was issued from Saint-Cloud announcing the definitive form of the Empress's household, or of her retinue of ladies-in-waiting at least.

The Emperor had decided that from July 1, 1810, onward the Empress was to have a retinue of thirty-six ladies-in-waiting. The decree's fourth article laid it down that attendance was to be by quarterly periods "according to rules laid down by us." (The original wording had been "by the Empress," but Napoleon had corrected it.) There were always to be four ladies-in-waiting in ordinary and four ladies-in-waiting extraordinary. Of the four ladies-in-waiting in ordinary, there had always to be two attending on the Empress, while the other two and the four ladies-in-waiting extraordinary were always to be available in case of extraordinary audiences, receptions, theatrical performances or concerts, church services, etc.

Of the twelve ladies appointed on September 13, the majority were foreigners: apart from the Duchess of Elchingen and the Countess of Beauvau, the only two of French birth, there were Princess Aldobrandini, the Duchess of Dalberg, the Duchess of Bellune, a Dutch woman who had been married to Victor in the year IX, two Belgians, Mmes de Trazenies and Vilain XIII, four Italians, Mmes Rinuccini and Pandolfini Capone, Princess Chigi née Barberini, and Countess Bonacorsi née Braschi, a niece of Pius VI; lastly, there was Countess Edmond de Périgord.

What could all these foreign women do to help Marie-Louise become more familiar with France and the French? Very little. For even had they not been of foreign nationality themselves, they were further handicapped by Napoleon himself, by Marie-Louise's own timidity and aloofness, and by the proprietary character of the Duchess of Montebello, the Empress's maid of honor and their superior. They scarcely saw the Empress, as it were, and certainly never spoke to her. They never entered Marie-Louise's private apartment; they never ate at table with her, except when traveling or by express invitation; they could hardly be said even to wait upon her, and if the Empress left the palace her ladies-in-waiting all rode in separate carriages behind her.

Extremely elegant by now, silent and reserved, careful to conceal the extent of her intelligence and education, Dorothée set out to play her role in the ballet of the Imperial court with passive detachment. Her first tour of duty took place during the fall of 1810, when the court traveled to Fontainebleau.

The imperial couple had spent their summer at Saint-Cloud. On September 22, Napoleon and Marie-Louise came back together to spend several days in Paris, since the Emperor wished to impress on the people of Paris the fact of the Empress's pregnancy. On the 25th, the court reached Fontainebleau after a stop of several hours at Grosbois. Dorothée and Talleyrand both took part in this progress.

The Duchess of Courland had gone back to Saxony, Mme de Talleyrand and Edmond had both stayed behind in Paris, and there was an opportunity for uncle and niece to increase their acquaintance. Being an experienced libertine, Talleyrand must certainly have observed the way in which Dorothée had bloomed, especially now that an easy pregnancy was lending her a new serenity. Throughout the innumerable hunts and entertainments, all chilled by the icy breath of boredom inseparable from official merrymaking, Talleyrand remained, as he wrote to Montrond (who had been exiled several months previously to Antwerp), "what you English refer to as *an indolent looker* [*sic*]. . . . I often talk about you with Mme de Périgord, who is the last person to have seen you. She is an agreeable companion. She talks and listens well. Nor is she too much incommoded by her pregnancy. My lodgings are not far from hers. It would not be easy to find anyone in the whole of the château with whom one could enjoy such good conversation. . . ."

❖   ❖   ❖

Before becoming Stendhal, Henri Beyle pursued a career as an army quartermaster. On January 1, 1811, he put on his full dress uniform and attended a function at the Tuileries. That evening, he noted in his *Journal:* "A fine-looking crowd. During Mass, I enjoyed watching the face of Mme la Comtesse Edmond de Périgord (the Duchess of Courland's daughter); she had such purity of expression. If I were not afraid that I was allowing myself to be carried away by my present taste for German women, I should account for these qualities by the fact that she too is of German birth. . . ."

A piece of evidence made all the more interesting by the fact that several years later Stendhal proved merciless in his opinion of Dorothée.

It is without doubt during this period that the portrait now hanging in the gallery at Valençay was painted. Dorothée is seated; her straw-colored satin dress discloses a high, white bosom. The delicate head is poised on a long, slim neck. Straight nose, dark eyes. The black hair gathered up at the back of the head. She looks very young, very ingenuous, and it is as though she is waiting for something too. Life has flowed by without impinging upon her as yet, without really opening her eyes, without disturbing her depths.

On March 12, 1811, Dorothée was delivered of a son, Napoleon-Louis, for whom the Emperor and Empress stood as godparents. It was a happy event for the Talleyrand family, who now had their longed-for heir, and a happy one too for Dorothée, who would perhaps find compensations in motherhood for the deficiencies of a marriage that Edmond's worthlessness and wild behavior had already begun to jeopardize.

"Heaven had endowed her with both beauty and intelligence," Mme de Boigne wrote later "but as to the moral side of things, all practical education and example had been wanting; or rather, all that a precocious intelligence enabled her to take in of her surroundings was not of a kind likely to give her any healthy notions as to the duties a woman is called upon to fulfill. Possibly she might have escaped these early dangers if her husband had been a match for her own capacities, so that she could have loved and honored him. But that was impossible, the distance between them was too great."

Another invaluable piece of evidence, coming as it does from an objective observer hardly likely to be guilty of any indulgence toward Dorothée.

Edmond was open to blame on a great many scores: the lack of order in his household already emphasized by Clary, his excessive and unintelligent personal expenses—a threat to the young couple's fortune—his gambling, and almost certainly young ladies from the Opèra. They provided the young man with a respite from the excessively intelligent and perhaps contemptuous wife that his uncle had forced upon him.

Though Edmond may have neglected his wife, Narbonne, another experienced libertine, a man in his fifties and, together with Montrond and Choiseul, one of Talleyrand's intimates, suddenly began to take a great interest in her. "I remember," Dorothée recalled many years later, with retrospective rancor, "how he decided to make it his business to dazzle me, and all he succeeded in doing was embarrassing me. One day, during a small dinner party at my mother's, where everyone could hear everything that was said, M. de Narbonne began to pay me a series of very direct compliments, only expressed in the form of opposites, commenting on my tiny eyes, my clumsy and savage behavior, etc. I didn't really understand, and since I was only seventeen I had no way of replying to this language whose vocabulary was an entirely closed book to me. M. de Talleyrand took pity on me, or rather, delighted at the opportunity to use his claws on M. de Narbonne, he broke in loudly with: 'Do be quiet, Narbonne, Mme de Perigord is too young to understand what you're saying and too German to appreciate it.' The mention of my youth was a criticism of Narbonne, the mention of my *Germanness* a criticism of me. He had thus succeeded in winging us both, but even at the expense of the feather or two I lost in the process, I was still grateful to my uncle for having rescued me from my tormentor."

Nevertheless, Dorothée was saddened and occasionally disturbed by the speed with which her new existence seemed to be collapsing in ruins, and one day she resolved to consult Mlle Lenormand, the celebrated clairvoyant. She arranged an appointment with the fortune teller, using an assumed name and address, and on the day appointed, accompanied by her lady's maid, drove to the Rue de Tournon in a hackney carriage.

She was shown into a clean and quite lavishly appointed apartment, where she was confronted by a woman in her fifties with an abrupt manner. Tall, muddy-complexioned, "with tiny, lively eyes like those of an untamed animal," Mlle Lenormand possessed a countenance at once coarse and fascinating.

After a few questions as to the month, day, and hour of her birth, her favorite animal, flower, and color, as well as those she particularly disliked, the fortune teller predicted for Dorothée a separation from her husband, lingering griefs, then a close relationship with "a person whose position and influence would oblige her to play a kind of political role." Dorothée thought the prediction a strange one and paid no attention to it.

❖   ❖   ❖

The Duchess of Courland, having returned to France at the end of 1810 or early in 1811, spent the summer and fall of 1811 in Saint-Germain at the Château-Neuf. Talleyrand and Mme de Laval both went to stay with her for a considerable period, and the Château-Neuf thus became a center of intrigue against

Napoleon. The Duchess kept up an assiduous correspondence with the Tsar, and Talleyrand more or less dictated all her letters.

The Emperor was unaware of his Vice-Grand Elector's treachery, but he did know a great deal about his peculations. Moreover, he also had more than an inkling of the Duchess's conspiratorial activities and had resumed his former mistrustful attitude toward her. Dorothée knew no more about her mother's political intrigues—we have mentioned how little intimacy there was between them, and there was even less between Edmond and his mother-in-law *—than she did about her uncle's money troubles, but she did sometimes suffer from them indirectly at moments when one or the other drove the Emperor to express his exasperation.

On August 13 or 14, 1811, the Countess Edmond de Périgord was in attendance on the Empress at Saint-Cloud. Napoleon suddenly called her over:

"Your husband is really guilty of far too many stupidities. How could he have bought ten thousand francs' worth of cameos?"

"Sire," Dorothée replied, "Your Majesty has been misinformed. My husband is not guilty of that stupidity."

The Emperor then turned to Berthier:

"You ought not to permit such behavior in one of your aides-de-camp."

When Berthier refused to be drawn, Napoleon turned back to Dorothée.

"However, this piece of stupidity is more excusable in the last resort than a great many others that are habitual with him. In any case, as you know, that whole wretched Périgord family ceased to be of any interest to me a long while ago."

Tears were rising into Dorothée's eyes as she answered with a red face:

"Sire, my husband and my uncle have always served your Majesty with the utmost zeal, and as long as it pleases Your Majesty will continue to do so. In any case, their past services

* It was at this time that the Countess of Kielmannsegge, a friend of the Duchess's from Saxony, noted: "I often used to help her during reconciliations with her daughter and son-in-law."

have at least merited that Your Majesty should refrain from mocking them."

Marie-Louise, apparently very agitated, did not dare to intervene and Dorothée, incapable of controlling herself any longer —she was just eighteen—hurried out of the room.

Next morning, the courtiers avoided her. But Napoleon had realized the injustice of taxing a child, perhaps an unhappy one, with her husband's weaknesses and her uncle's malversations. Dorothée was invited to the Imperial table and treated with particular regard. During the hunt, Napoleon himself offered her some fruit. The effect of these attentions was immediate and Dorothée found herself made much of on all sides.

When she was not on duty with the Empress, Dorothée was always glad to go back to Rosny, away from Paris, which she disliked, away from Saint-Germain and her mother. Besides, she was somewhat disturbed in mind, for she was on the brink of a serious decision, and the Countess of Kielmansegge, who went to spend three days with her at the time, has described her as "clinging to the fragment of some wreck, lost and battered by the waves," searching with her eyes for "some promised land that she sensed was just ahead."

It was in fact during that summer, or the following autumn, that Dorothée became a convert to Catholicism. Several weeks after her marriage she had come by chance across a set of Bossuet's works. She had been struck by the soundness of the doctrine given such admirable expression in them, and from that moment had begun to incline toward the Roman faith. Possibly it was the birth of her child, the desire to belong to the same church as her son, or an instinctive need for some sort of spiritual support that had finally precipitated her decision. One day she sent for the parish priest of the nearby village and made an act of abjuration in his presence.

❖   ❖   ❖

"The Duchess, monsieur, who sends you a thousand greetings," the Countess of Kielmannsegge wrote on January 9, 1812, to a still unidentified friend, "Mme de Périgord, who is making good progress in an admirable pregnancy, and myself, who am making good progress in nothing save the raising of my children—which is no small thing—, are all sharing our lives together; we cough together, freeze together, and share all the pleasures and pains that come our way. I am surrounded by a whirlwind of at-homes and important visits. The state of the war, which is opening the door to so many possible future changes of fortune, is the thing that most absorbs my two companions, for the Duchess's entire existence and her daughter's husband are both involved in it."

Meanwhile, however, Napoleon had already passed judgment on that husband's lack of ability: Edmond de Périgord would never make a good staff officer; at most, he was capable of commanding one of the Imperial Army's innumerable regiments.* A colonel before he was twenty-five, Edmond would never have attained any higher promotion as long as he lived, had the Empire survived. On January 19, 1812, therefore, the Count of Périgord was appointed to the command of the 8th Light Cavalry, then stationed at Brescia, and on January 24 the Minister urged him to take up his post without delay. And so Edmond left the world of the staff officers, which he had inhabited for the past five years only because his uncle's influence had kept him there, and until the Empire finally fell his fate was to remain linked to that of his regiment.

The new colonel set out with the best of intentions, resolved, according to a confidence made to Mme de Kielmann-segge, to attempt the acquisition of some personal merit. The 8th Light Cavalry was already on its way to Germany when Edmond caught up with them, early in February, at Trent. He immediately charmed all the officers with his good manners and his generosity, and before long he had also won their hearts with his assiduousness in providing compensations for the boredom of the long journey in the form of balls and parties which he provided in every town they stopped at on the way.

This time, Edmond's departure was also the end of his married life. The marriage itself, of course, still had a few years

---

* Cavalry regiments consisted of from 800 to 900 men in the French army and 1,200 men in other European countries. There were consequently a very great number of them.

to run; there was also to be a third child, Alexandre, born in December of 1813, but the couple were never to resume a genuine life together, that "domestic life" that Dorothée, forty years later, sadly lamented never having known.

As war with Russia became more and more inevitable, the Duchess of Courland began to think of leaving Paris. It was probably a heartbreaking moment for her, since in all likelihood she discovered that Talleyrand was able to accept the separation philosophically. Whatever the reason, the Duchess's mood suddenly turned bitter. In March of 1812, the Countess of Kielmannsegge wrote: "The complaints she is constantly making against her daughter seem on the whole to be producing the opposite effect from the one she intends, and M. de Talleyrand, who certainly cannot be accused of any excessive sympathy for Dorothée at the moment, can scarcely help but come to esteem her in time, even though now, true libertine that he is, he is inclined to wonder whether a young woman of nineteen can really count virtue and strength of character among her endowments. . . .

"M. de Périgord has written me several times from the army to say: 'I hope you will look after Dorothée while I am away. I know that she suffers because she wants to be simple and open. Take care of her for me.' "

Their intimate friends were therefore not ignorant of the fact that relations between mother and daughter were rather strained and those between Talleyrand and his niece none too good either. Yet appearances were kept up—as they always would be—and on April 10, 1812, Talleyrand and the Duchess of Courland stood as godparents at the font of Notre-Dame-de-Lorette to the Edmond de Périgords' second child, a daughter, Dorothée-Charlotte-Emilie.

On that same day, Napoleon bestowed on Dorothée herself a mark of his favor and of the esteem in which he held her conduct and her good reputation. She was given a promotion at the palace, moving up from the category of ladies-in-waiting who received three thousand francs into the category of those whose emoluments were six thousand.

Nor did the Emperor stop there. Before leaving Paris, on May 9, he decided, according to Mme de Kielmannsegge, that

Talleyrand could not dispose of the endowments he himself had received in favor of Charlotte, his illegitimate daughter. At the same time, Napoleon assigned Dorothée to attendance in ordinary upon the Empress during the months of July, August, and September. This was proof of great esteem, for it was simultaneous with his deliberate removal from Marie-Louise's household of the Maréchale Ney, whose behavior had incurred his anger. "It was becoming much too excessive and would have led to trouble," he said to the Duchess of Elchingen one day after summoning all the court ladies to appear before him. He then turned to Countess Edmond de Périgord and added: "As for you, I know you're always very well-behaved; try to see that it continues."

On June 1, 1812, Talleyrand informed Caulaincourt: "The Duchess of Courland is leaving tomorrow . . . for Löbikau, and Mme de Périgord in three days for Rosny with her children. Princess Tyszkiewicz leaves for Warsaw at the end of the week."

The Duchess's farewells were heartrending: she herself was bathed in tears, Dorothée seemed very upset, Talleyrand apparently unmoved.*

◇   ◇   ◇

Talleyrand went to take the waters as usual, then took up residence at Saint-Brice † with all the rest of his family: the Princess his wife, Charlotte, the Bosons and Dorothée, who was waiting for the Empress's return in order to resume her duties.

* The Countess of Kielmannsegge reported that as he walked away, he remarked: "I have organized these ladies' departures in such a way that I shall be accompanying one of them to her carriage every afternoon at half past one for a whole week together. It is really very comic!"

† Talleyrand's financial situation had been extremely difficult during 1810 and 1811. It is said that the failure of the financier Simons in 1810 had cost him fourteen to fifteen hundred thousand francs, and that the Tsar had refused the loan Talleyrand had then requested from him. In 1811, Talleyrand was obliged to make restitution amounting to 680,000 francs to the Hanseatic League. At the end of January 1812, Napoleon extricated Talleyrand from a difficult position and bought his house in the Rue de Varenne for 1,280,000 francs. After paying his debts, Talleyrand then acquired the Hôtel de l'Infantado, 2, Rue Saint-Florentin, and a small country house for the summer at Saint-Brice, just outside Ecouen.

After her return from Dresden, Marie-Louise held her first reception in the state apartments on July 27. "She was very well dressed and displayed no embarrassment. Mme de Périgord attended on her with the other ladies-in-waiting," Talleyrand noted that evening, adding: "I should be glad if Edmond were to do something that ensured his being mentioned in some reasonably outstanding way in an official report. . . ." Several weeks later Talleyrand's wish was fulfilled. On September 4, three days before the battle of the Moskva, the 8th Light Cavalry was involved in an important skirmish with the Cossacks; this action earned Edmond a citation in the King of Naples' dispatches.

The French vanguard entered the ancient capital of the Tsars on September 14; on the 15th, Napoleon took up residence in the Kremlin; on the 16th Moscow was in flames. A month later came the retreat, throughout which Edmond behaved with valor, composure and cheerfulness. Early in 1813, he rode back into his cantonment at Guhrau in Silesia at the head of the seventy-five horsemen still surviving from the regiment of eight hundred that had left Brescia the previous fall.

Talleyrand, however, supposed that the army would be wintering in Russia. He was apprehensive of how his nephew would behave in such an event, and on October 24 he wrote asking Caulaincourt to keep an eye on the young man. "It seems to me, from the preparations now being made in your part of the world, that everyone there is beginning to think of settling down for the winter. The younger men, lacking other forms of distraction, are bound to seek for it in gambling, and I must admit to an apprehension that Edmond, despite the powerful motives he has to abstain from it, will not prove strong enough to resist so protracted a temptation. I hope you will allow me to request your interest on his behalf and even, if need be, your severity in this respect. Please try to make him understand that any further wild behavior, apart from the distress it would cause his family, will do him harm in the opinion of the Emperor, whom Edmond fears and loves."

When the first quarterly period of court attendance came to an end, Marie-Louise had not dared to replace her ladies-in-waiting without referring the matter to the Emperor. The latter, still in Moscow, had sent orders that she should make no change in her attendants until his return. Life at Saint-Cloud was uneventful, bourgeois, and above all dull, with fewer and fewer visitors and only the most occasional diversions during the evenings. But this shrinking court, more and more like ordinary home life, reminded Marie-Louise of Austria; seeing the same faces day after day suddenly made her feel at ease, and she began to bloom. Her attendants, on the other hand, grew steadily more lax in carrying out their duties, for the boredom was exhausting, and they all seized on any pretext to disappear. One lady was worried about her brother, another explained that she must visit her children. Dorothée herself was sick and had withdrawn to Rosny. There were occasions when the Empress was left with only a single lady-in-waiting in the whole palace.

At the beginning of December the court returned to Paris, its numbers increased by the onset of the cold weather. Dorothée settled her own household back in the capital then resumed her duties. On December 18—the XXIXth official report had arrived in Paris the previous day with its admission of the Russian disaster—the Empress had just retired for the night when her lady in-waiting (doubtless Dorothée, since she was one of the first to hear the news) was attracted to the door of the Empress's private apartments by the sound of someone asking to be let in. She rushed into the antechamber and recognized the two men bundled up in thick furs as the Emperor and the Master of the Horse.

Next morning, Talleyrand was awakened by the arrival of a message from his niece: she had sent him news of Napoleon's return.

❖   ❖   ❖

The Russian campaign had done nothing to sober Edmond. Such a close encounter with death, as in Vienna in 1809, merely spurred him on to further follies. After returning to Paris for several days in March of 1813—which explains the birth, at the end of the year, of the third Périgord child, Alexandre—Edmond was posted without delay to Gray, where the 8th Light Cavalry was being reformed. There, he met up with his friend Talhouet, Colonel of the 6th Light Cavalry. Both were rich, both loved to amuse themselves above all else. The period spent at Gray was "a time of pleasure" according to the ingenuous admission of Colonel Combe, then adjutant of the 8th Light Cavalry. In the course of one night's orgy the whole of the furniture disappeared through the window.

Talleyrand learned of these events, Talleyrand was disturbed, and he alerted Berthier. On April 21, the latter informed Clarke, still Minister for War, that he had ordered Colonial de Périgord to Hanau, where he was to take command of another detachment of his regiment. Talleyrand was still not satisfied. "I wish the Prince of Neuchâtel [Berthier] had ordered Edmond to the front. Being in the reserve is not going to get him anywhere in such a campaign," he wrote to Caulaincourt on May 9.

Dorothée's first two pregnancies had been easy ones, but the first months of the third one were difficult. Already unwell, she suffered a fall at Rosny early in May, and there was some fear that she might miscarry. She was obliged to resign herself to life on· a chaise longue, and in June a stubborn cough also appeared to try her. Wretched, she lay counting the days until at last, during the fourth month, her condition improved. Edmond, meanwhile, had taken advantage of the armistice signed at Pleiswitz on June 4 to visit Dresden in search of distractions. "Our stay there was another time of pleasures," notes the forthright Colonel Combe, and goes on to list with satisfaction the various delightful picnics enjoyed in the company of Mlles Mars, Bourgoing, Mezeray, and several others. Mlle George also passed through the town, on her way back from Russia, and was honored with a visit by Colonel de Périgord to her rooms.

On August 10, 1813, the congress that had met at Prague after the signing of the armistice was deliberately broken up by the Allies. On August 11, Austria entered the war in its turn. Two weeks later Schwartzenberg was beaten at Dresden, but on October 16, the Battle of the Nations began outside Leipzig. It lasted four days, after which Napoleon was forced to retreat, overwhelmed by the opposing numbers. On October 30, the French Army crossed the Rhine back into France at

Hanau, but this retreating tide of troops did not include Edmond de Périgord: on September 16, at Milberg, he had been surrounded by the Cossacks, had his horse killed under him, and been taken prisoner with the faithful Combe.

Being a prisoner of war was not, however, a particularly harsh fate if one was the husband of a Princess of Courland and a nephew of Talleyrand. Thanks to Bernadotte, Edmond found himself assigned to residence in Berlin, and he moved into No. 7, Unter den Linden. For the next three months, while Napoleon was mustering the last of his troops in order to defend France against invasion, while Talleyrand was steadfastly refusing to return to the Ministry for Foreign Affairs and working patiently towards the overthrow of the Emperor, if not of the Empire, Colonel de Périgord amused himself in Berlin. He was still in Berlin when Dorothée gave birth, on December 15, to a son, Alexandre-Edmond.

⬧   ⬧   ⬧

For two years, military campaigns and the separations that they made necessary had thrown Edmond back into that bachelor life which, in February 1809, he had expressed so sincere a regret at abandoning. With unconcealed pleasure, he had slipped back into his former habits and resumed the way of life he had known before his marriage. And over the same period of time the same set of circumstances had produced a striking evolution in the relationship between uncle and niece.

Dorothée was too intelligent not to have realized, even at the very beginning of her marriage, that Talleyrand was by far the most interesting person with whom her new life had brought her into contact. She wrote later: "Beneath the nobility of his features, the slowness of his movements, the sybaritism of his way of life, there was a rich lode of fearless audacity that glittered through at moments, revealing a whole new order of faculties, and making him, simply because of the contrast, one of the most original and attractive of beings."

But the antipathy that Talleyrand had shown toward her, as well as his liaison with the Duchess of Courland, had also created a repugnance in Dorothée during her early years. Yet during October of 1810, at Fontainebleau, when the uncle and niece found themselves alone together for the first time, they had enjoyed each other's company. We already know what Talleyrand wrote about her at that time: "She is an agreeable companion. She talks and listens well."

In 1812, the absence of her husband and that of his mistress—the Duchess of Courland had left in June 1812 and did not return until November the following year—and the departure of their friends—the seraglio had scattered by then, and Mme de Kielmannsegge been got rid of *—had left Talleyrand and Dorothée face to face. They came to know one another better, and this further acquaintance had led to a mutual appreciation and affection. A new intimacy had sprung up between them. When she was with Talleyrand, Dorothée experienced those same sensations of security and stability that she had sought as a child in the company of Duke Pierre, while for this now beautiful and self-assured niece Talleyrand had come to feel the affection of a father-in-law, of a father-in-law who often thinks to himself what a fortunate marriage his son has made and at the same time is filled with anger at that husband's escapades.

They often rode together, Talleyrand mounted on a little chestnut, taking Charlotte with them. But this new intimacy was also one of mind. Dorothée had always been drawn to politics; her former interest in Czartoryski had sprung more from the intellect than from the heart, and it had been above all else a desire for involvement in the important events of her time. The same interest was now brought into play when she was with Talleyrand, even in the stagnant days of his semi-disgrace. Was she aware of his treachery? It is impossible to know for sure. Certainly she was able to sense what was on his mind.

The brief appearance Edmond put in during March of 1813 did nothing to interrupt this intimacy. Perhaps it even

---

* "Your great Kielmannsegge is dragging her dreary person to and fro between Paris and Saint-Germain; she has not appeared at Saint-Brice, a thing for which I am extremely thankful," Talleyrand wrote to the Duchess of Courland during the summer of 1812.

drew uncle and niece closer together. They had rather lost sight of him during the long months of his absence, this nephew, this husband, and he must have seemed to them in some way a stranger. Talleyrand perhaps felt some remorse at having imposed upon a being so richly endowed with gifts a husband who had so very few. It perhaps entered his mind that Edmond did not deserve a happiness that he apparently valued so little. And perhaps Dorothée, on her side, judged her husband more severely now and compared him to his uncle. Perhaps she found it offensive, having been appreciated by a man of talent, to be disdained by a fool.

From this moment on, a sort of transposition of interests seems to have occurred. Talleyrand began to worry about Edmond, about his career, less because he was his nephew than because he was the husband of Dorothée, of the Dorothée whose ill health was at that time causing him such affectionate anxiety. Henceforth, it was Edmond's career that he recommended to Caulaincourt's attention, and not, as before, his person and his weaknesses of character. Perhaps Talleyrand was already thinking of passing over the father in the interests of the son, young Louis. Dorothée on her side now displayed a lukewarm, slightly weary interest in her husband, rather like that a businessman might show towards a partner whose lack of ability has finally become only too apparent.

The Duchess of Courland returned to Paris at the end of 1813. Talleyrand resumed his custom of sending her daily messages couched in the tenderest terms. But she was a very experienced woman in such matters and must have sensed that something had changed; the messages were no longer a mark of an exclusive preoccupation with the Duchess herself, for Dorothée's name appeared in almost every one, and almost every day it was at Dorothée's—where the daughter was still recovering from her confinement—that Talleyrand arranged to meet her. He also frequently spoke to the Duchess about her daughter, the happiness she deserved, her health, her children.

Nothing definite as yet, but a growing tenderness, a growing concern for a being who was becoming daily more dear, with whom the understanding reached was already profound. For Talleyrand, his niece was henceforth a constant factor in his

life, in his hopes—in his betrayals too—and on the same footing as his former mistress. It was a strange situation, the mother
and daughter so long divided now reunited by their affection and
admiration for the head of their family. But it was also a situation that hung in precarious equilibrium, one that could be
shattered by a single incident, a single accident.

Napoleon had understood the significance of Talleyrand's
refusal to return to the Ministry for Foreign Affairs in November 1813. Though he had no certain proof, the Emperor
scented treason. And yet he could not make up his mind to
have Talleyrand arrested. Napoleon had valued him once, he
respected the man's intelligence, he knew that he was "still the
man who knew most about the world and society of our times,
about both the governments and the peoples." As before, he
contented himself with harsh words. It was a dangerous half
measure: it increased Talleyrand's desire to do Napoleon harm
and left him in possession of all the means to do so.

On Sunday January 16, after Mass, Napoleon subjected his
Vice-Grand Elector to yet another scene. Those present—
Caulaincourt, Cambacérès, Savary—wondered whether he was
at last about to have him imprisoned at Vincennes. The
Emperor ordered Bassano to be summoned. So Talleyrand's fate
was sealed. The Duke was not to be found. Napoleon's anger
waned, and Talleyrand was permitted to withdraw.

"Dear friend," he wrote to the Duchess next day, "I shall
go to Dorothée's at about four o'clock. Nothing new this morning. So the storm has blown over; but that is no reason not to
take precautions."

On January 25, Napoleon left to undertake his prodigious
French campaign, the most glorious since the days of Arcole and
Rivoli, and Talleyrand, breathing more freely, was able to pursue
his treasonous activities in greater comfort. He had the assist-
ance of the Abbé de Pradt, Dalberg, the spies of the Count of
Provence, Bourrienne, a former secretary of Bonaparte's dismissed for malversation, Jaucourt, and the Abbé de Montesquiou.
For several days he kept Dorothée and the Duchess well
informed of his activities. "I have just been in to kiss the children, who are all bursting with gaiety and health.—Happy
age!—I shall go to Dorothée's this morning, dear friend, to talk

over our affairs with you," he wrote on February 1. Next day, the day before the Duchess's birthday, he sent her his best wishes, then added: "My hope is that Dorothée will finally attain all the happiness that she has the right to ask for and to enjoy."

When events began to move more rapidly, Talleyrand needed more room to maneuver. On February 9, he sent all his dependents, the Duchess, Dorothée and her children, his wife and Charlotte, to Rosny. The messages to the Duchess continued, and those to Dorothée as well, without Talleyrand's ever omitting to include in the former a kiss for Dorothée, for big Dorothée, as opposed to her little daughter, his godchild.

❖   ❖   ❖

Early in January of 1814, Colonel de Périgord had visited Bernadotte in Lubeck and received permission from the latter to return to France on parole. Accompanied by Combe, for whom he had obtained the same concession, Edmond immediately set out, crossed the Rhine at Cologne and reached Rheims. Since the French campaign had already begun, the two French officers were detained there by Wintzingeronde. They moved into the Hotel de la Poste, and Edmond made a dutiful attempt to communicate with his family. Thanks to Caulaincourt, who was negotiating with the Allies in Châtillon at the time, there was no difficulty. On February 21, Talleyrand wrote to the Duchess of Courland: "I am sending Dorothée a letter I have received for her via the Duke of Vicenza [Caulaincourt]; he takes it to be a message from Edmond." Dorothée immediately replied to her husband's letter, and on March 2 Talleyrand noted with satisfaction that her reply had been received safely. "It will bring Edmond a great deal of pleasure, for he has been so far away from us all for so long." A normal enough tone for an uncle talking about a nephew. Next day, the prince added: "I imagine that Edmond is being held up on his journey because the enemy does not want a soldier to come back here giving us reports on the state of their health and reserves." Talleyrand supposed that the Allies were detaining his nephew because they were apprehensive of the information he might pass on to Napoleon. Meanwhile, Talleyrand himself was having no hesitation in passing on information to them, and information of the most damaging kind. Having left Paris on March 6, Vitrolles reached Allied headquarters on the 10th. He was the bearer of a message from Dalberg to Nesselrode, a message that Talleyrand had refused to write but had nevertheless inspired. Forgetting that he was a Frenchman, Talleyrand, the Prince of Benevento, Vice-Grand Elector of the Empire, was demanding that the Allies advance on Paris; * clandestine support was promised if they did so.

Talleyrand was angered by Edmond's delay as well as that of the Allies. "I cannot understand why Edmond is still in Rheims. It seems to me that he could wait to be exchanged just as easily at Rosny . . ." he wrote on March 14. He was unaware that on the 13th Napoleon had crushed Saint-Priest at Rheims, or that Edmond and Combe must have left the city several days before for Laon. There they had hidden, hoping for a French advance. Their expectations were not realized. The news of their escape was passed on and a search instituted for the fugitives. They concealed themselves inside two barrels in a cellar, then waited for an opportunity to continue their escape. It was provided by two charcoal-burners, who sold the officers their passes, their smocks, their cloth caps and their thick boots. Blacking their faces and hands, Edmond and Combe made off through the woods towards Soissons and, after several adventures, including an unpleasant encounter with some Cossacks, arrived at Edmond's house on the Rue de la Grange-Batelière on about March 20.†

What did Edmond do then? He must have visited his uncle, since his name is not mentioned in any of Talleyrand's subsequent messages. Perhaps, like an honest soldier, young Colonel

---

* "You are walking on crutches; use your legs and attempt what is within your power."

† On March 19, Talleyrand was still writing to the Duchess: "Everyone brings me news of Edmond except Edmond himself. I know that he is in good health, but I can't understand why he doesn't write. I am told that he is negotiating his own exchange. I am extremely glad to hear it, but it should not be difficult to get a few letters through to us. I can see that Dorothée is becoming impatient at not hearing from him."

de Périgord rejoined his regiment? * In any case, he does not appear to have gone to Rosny, unless it was merely in passing.

The previous twelve months had finally succeeded in loosening the bonds between Edmond and Dorothée that the births of their three children had never succeeded in providing with any true solidity. Distant with each other from the first, they had now become vaguely hostile strangers; Dorothée, assured henceforth of Talleyrand's support, was angered both by Edmond's infidelities and by his follies: after ruining himself he was now going on to ruin her as well, thus compromising the future of their children. Edmond, warned perhaps by a family jealous of its heritage, was disturbed by the rumors that were already current on the subject of Dorothée's relations with Talleyrand. The difficulties in the way of their achieving a life together based upon a mutual tolerance and understanding were already great; they were rendered insurmountable by a sudden misfortune—the loss of a child—which precipitated a rupture between them, and by the political events—the collapse of an Empire—that took Dorothée to Vienna.

* Since he had been detained in Rheims by Wintzingerode, Edmond was no longer bound by his promise to Bernadotte.

Part Three

LIFE

WITH

TALLEYRAND

(1814-1838)

"VIENNA!
MY WHOLE
DESTINY
IS IN THAT WORD"
(1814-1816)

O N March 31, 1814, the Allies marched into a Paris that had surrendered the day before. The next day, a provisional government was set up with Talleyrand at its head; on April 2, a minority of senators, prebendaries of the Empire hand-picked by Talleyrand, voted the downfall of the Emperor.

On that same day, despite the cares of office, Talleyrand organized Dorothée's return from Rosny which she was very anxious to leave: "There will be a detachment of Cossacks waiting at midnight at the Saint-Germain coach stage to escort Dorothée into the city. To reach Saint-Germain she must take the route through Aubergenville, Flins, and Fresnes. Take particular note of this, because the other road is bad. . . ." *

Meanwhile, at Fontainebleau, Napoleon had not given up all idea of continuing the fight. And in Paris, Talleyrand had not been able to convert the Tsar into a supporter of Louis XVIII. It was a period of terrible suspense for Talleyrand. He invited the Duchess of Courland to dinner every evening, and every evening he asked Dorothée to be present too. There is no doubt that he needed the mother's aid in order to increase his chances of winning over the Tsar, who had taken up residence in the Rue Saint-Florentin, but perhaps he had an even greater need, for himself, of the presence and the passionate attention of her daughter.

---

* We must take this opportunity to emphasize in our turn, as Lacour-Gayet has already so pertinently done, that this letter of Talleyrand's completely invalidates the imputation made by Vaulabelle and several other Restoration writers, and revived later by Houssaye, that Countess Edmond de Périgord took part in the Allied march into Paris riding pillion behind a Cossack horseman. We should also add that when the German historian Gervinus reiterated this false rumor in 1855, Dorothée made a protest to Frederick-Wilhelm IV against the allegation. Finally, we ought not to forget that there were two other de Périgord ladies in Paris in 1814, the Duchess and Countess Elie. There is also reason to think that Vaulabelle, and Houssaye later, was by no means displeased at an opportunity of attacking Talleyrand through his niece.

On April 4, at Fontainebleau, his marshals succeeded in extracting Napoleon's agreement to abdicate in favor of his son. On the same day, won over—tricked, almost—by Talleyrand, Marmont betrayed the Emperor and announced that he no longer wished to "serve Bonaparte against his country." Early on the afternoon of the 5th, the Tsar was informed that Marmont's troops were abandoning Essonnes. So the army was not so very attached to the Emperor after all, Alexander thought; and from that moment on Napoleon II was doomed. Next day, a Senate in which regicides and royalists were strangely intermingled summoned Louis-Stanislas-Xavier to the throne. On that day too, detached from everything, Napoleon signed his unconditional abdication.

Talleyrand breathed again. Once more he had won every trick. After contributing to the downfall of the Directoire, he had now overthrown the Empire. Once more he was going to be indispensable to the new regime.

In celebration of this success, a "family dinner," which is to say a dinner that included the Tsar, was given in his house on the Rue Saint-Florentin. "I am inviting Archambauld, and I wish Dorothée to take precedence at this event because Archambauld is eating with us. It is she who receives him in my house." Sibylline phrasing that perhaps indicated a reconciliation between Talleyrand and his brother or between Dorothée and her father-in-law, but which indicated above all the growing importance that his niece was assuming for Talleyrand.

The day after this "family dinner," Caulaincourt signed the treaty of Fontainebleau, which decided the fate of Napoleon, and on April 12 the Count of Artois arrived in Paris to take up the duties of Lieutenant General of the Realm. The provisional government was dissolved and replaced by an equally provisional Council of State.

Talleyrand was a product of the Ancien Régime, he was satisfied with the France that he had known under the monarchy, and the conquests of the Revolution were of no interest to him. Besides, he loved money too much to care for glory. In short, it was with a light heart that Talleyrand subscribed on April 23, 1814, to the agreement that deprived France of fifty places still occupied by French troops in Germany, Danzig and

Hamburg to the east of the Rhine, and also the towns along the Rhine valley itself, from Antwerp to Mainz. Talleyrand was thus anticipating the future peace treaty; he was committing France's future even before the arrival of the king.

Louis XVIII had delayed in England. He did not disembark in Calais until April 24, where he found a message waiting for him that had been composed by Talleyrand, though it was signed by Dayot, a straw man. Via this mouthpiece, Talleyrand assured the new sovereign of his devotion and requested certain favors: "He believes his presence to be necessary at the Ministry for Foreign Affairs, and asks to be placed at the head of that department. . . . He entreats the King that he will graciously deign to grant M. Edmond de Périgord the title of first aide-de-camp to his royal person, and to Mme Edmond de Périgord that of lady-in-waiting to the Queen, a post of which her conduct and piety render her eminently worthy. He also recommends M. Edmond de Périgord to His Majesty's attention when His Majesty deigns to undertake his first creation of Dukes and Peers."

Though Talleyrand's appointment to the Ministry for Foreign affairs was an indisputable necessity—he moved back onto the Rue du Bac on May 13 for the third time—the favors granted by the king in other areas, though prompt, were not excessive. On April 26, Edmond was promoted to the rank of Brigadier-General. No further mark of royal favor followed.

The king arrived at Compiègne on April 29th. His first meeting with Talleyrand took place in the middle of a press of people. The greeting he extended was apt and somewhat cold: "Monsieur le Prince de Bénévent, I am charmed to see you. So many things have happened since last we met."

The new charter was granted at Saint-Ouen on May 2, and the next day, Louis XVIII made his entry into Paris to the sound of acclamations whose fervor was already waning. "The troops lining the route from the Pont-Neuf along the Quai des Orfèvres as far as Notre-Dame were a regiment of the old Foot-Guards," Chateaubriand notes. "I doubt whether any human faces have ever expressed anything so menacing and terrible."

❖   ❖   ❖

"A child with measles needs to be kept warm," Talleyrand wrote to the Duchess of Courland from Compiègne on May 2. He was referring specifically to little Dorothée, Edmond's daughter, then two years old. He added, "Don't spend too much time in her room. I am sending Dorothée a kiss. Don't let her visit the sickroom."

The illness seemed to be following the normal course. But suddenly there was a change for the worse. "I am very worried about our little Dorothée," he wrote on the morning of May 10. "I went there yesterday evening after leaving you, and I was told that her illness is beginning to look serious. M. Nicod, who spent the night there, is worried about it. I beg you to keep Mme de Périgord with you * and to prevent her from going to the child; it is essential for her health . . . besides, her presence there can be of no use; if there were something that she alone could do for the child I would say nothing. . . ."

Talleyrand's uneasiness was justified: the child died that day.†

At no point, either in her *Souvenirs* or her *Chroniques*, or in any of her letters that have been published, did Dorothée ever make any reference to the little girl who died in 1814. It is impossible to believe that this was the result of indifference, since she was an attentive mother. In all likelihood the wound was too deep ever to be probed with impunity, the shock so brutal that it modified the mother's whole subsequent behavior.‡

The Duchess of Courland, after a brief period of acute sorrow, was able to find distraction without too much difficulty in the arrival of her other three daughters and did not fail to

* The Duchess of Courland had rented the town house of Général Walther's widow, No. 24, Rue du Faubourg-Poissonière.

† We find the following entry in the Register of Deaths of Notre-Dame-de-Lorette: "On May eleventh eighteen hundred and fourteen was presented in this church the body of Charlotte-Amélie-Dorothée de Talleyrand-Périgord, aged about two years, deceased at No. 2, Rue Grange-Batelière in the presence of André Osmond and Jacques-Parfait Tollay, who have signed with us below."

‡ Dorothée wrote to Vitrolles in 1818: "I never try to offer consolations, since I should detest any that were indiscreetly offered to myself; there are some sorrows that one must leave to time, without permitting it to destroy the regrets that it is sweet, that it is good to preserve. . . ."

attend a party. Edmond too, shallow in his emotions as always, quickly forgot a child he had scarcely known.*

Talleyrand, on the other hand, because his feelings for Dorothée were already growing deeper, had a far greater understanding of the grief and also of the rebellion in the heart of this passionate creature. Despite his political worries and the burden of his negotiations for the peace treaty, Talleyrand went to visit Dorothée almost every day. If his niece refused to see him, then he came back the next day. He recommended that she should not be thwarted in any of her wishes, and later, after a few days had gone by, he invited himself to dinner, taking Charlotte with him, and tried to distract Dorothée from her grief.

The death of their child deepened and rendered finally impassable the rift that the difference in their characters and Edmond's excessive absences had set between Dorothée and her husband. On the other hand this same misfortune drew her still closer to the understanding uncle who displayed such compassionate affection towards her, and who wrote at that time, with heartfelt emotion: "Dorothée, whatever anyone may say, has the prettiest face it would be possible to possess." A new note from the pen of this old Epicurean. . . .

◇ ◇ ◇

More concerned with overcoming Louis XVIII's antipathy towards himself than with defending the rights of his country, Talleyrand had made no difficulties about permitting the king to grant a charter rather than to sanction the constitution voted by the Senate. Similarly, having already signed the territorial agreement of April 23, he accepted without too many regrets the

---

* Combe tells us that Edmond appointed him his aide-de-camp and provided him with a lodging on the Rue Grange-Batelière. He adds: "There was always a place laid for me at my father's as well as at my general's, and I used to accompany the latter to his beautiful place at Rosny where the very best company used to gather." Not a word about the death of the child. Yet this excellent man would not have failed to give an extensive account of it if Edmond had ever spoken to him of it.

fact that France was reduced by the Treaty of Paris to its frontiers of 1791.*

What was to be done with the vast spoils of this ruined Empire? The Allies—England, Austria, Prussia, and Russia—decided to convene in Vienna what they euphemistically termed a congress, but which in fact was simply an auction sale during the course of which, with the smaller nations in attendance as impotent and resigned onlookers, they intended to remodel Europe to suit their own best interests. France was invited to fulfil the role of a spectator at this sharing out of its former conquests, and Talleyrand was appointed to represent her.

The Prince of Benevento, whom Louis XVIII had just created Prince de Talleyrand, picked his staff with great care. He chose Dalberg for his connections with everyone who counted for anything in Germany and Austria and La Besnardière for the serious work. He resigned himself to the presence of two royalists whose job it was to keep an eye on him—La Tour du Pin, who was to sign all passports, and Alexis de Noailles, whom he knew to be moderate in his opinions. He also took Neukomm, his usual musician, Rouen, his private secretary, and also Carême, who was to provide the French Embassy with the best table of the whole congress. Above all, Talleyrand decided to take Dorothée.

"It appeared to me too, that it was necessary to combat the prejudices that the high and influential society of Vienna had formed during the French Empire," Prince de Talleyrand wrote in his *Mémoires*. "In order to achieve this, it was necessary to make the French Embassy an agreeable place; I therefore asked my niece, Mme la Comtesse Edmond de Périgord, to be so good as to accompany me and to do the honors of my house. The superiority of her mind and her tact enabled her to attract and please Viennese society, and she was very useful to me. . . ."

There were a great many motives for this decision, and some of them were obvious enough. For one thing, Talleyrand could not have taken his wife to Vienna with him even if he had

* The Tsar, "having passed from his former trustful benevolence toward the Prince [Talleyrand] to the most ill-disposed mistrust," wounded at seeing his generous intentions towards France ignored and almost scorned, wrote on June 1: "This man's actions constitute a wilful sacrifice of his country and his friends to his own ambition."

wished to do so. Furthermore, Dorothée was by birth and education one of the greatest ladies in Europe and had the right of entry to any social gathering on that continent. Many doors that would have remained closed to the Prince of Benevento would be opened for Dorothée of Courland. Then again, she was the sister of the Duchess of Sagan, at that time Metternich's mistress, and also of the Princess of Hohenzollern and the Duchess of Acerenza, both of whom were to be present in Vienna.

But these reasons, however real they may have been, were not sufficient to have justified so serious a decision. It was one that implied, in fact, a public admission of the break between Edmond and Dorothée. Was there not a possibility that this admission would provide justification for rumors and provoke a scandal? Nevertheless, Talleyrand, the past master in amorous intrigue, the great diplomat, made no attempt to gloss things over. Neither the Duchess of Courland, whose presence in Vienna would have been quite normal, nor Edmond, for whom some excuse could have easily been found,* accompanied him to Austria.

Both Talleyrand and Dorothée were too intelligent, however, too experienced in the ways of the world, to underestimate the gravity of this decision. The secrecy in which they at first cloaked it, a secrecy that gave their departure the air of an elopement, proves that they wished to avoid all discussions with anybody, all recriminations from whatever source, whether wife, husband . . . or mistress. . . .†

---

* A Talleyrand was in Vienna at the time fulfilling the duties of Government courier, and it has sometimes been supposed that the person in question was Edmond. His rank could not have permitted his employment in so lowly a function however, and the Talleyrand in question was in fact Alexandre, the husband of the young Charlotte.

† Mme de Boigne writes: "I was with Mme de Talleyrand on the day M. de Talleyrand left, and I was present when she learned that Mme de Dino, then Countess Edmond de Périgord, was to accompany her uncle to Vienna. They had arranged to meet in a country house outside of Paris. The fact was passed on to Mme de Talleyrand quite innocently, though indiscreetly, by someone to whom it meant nothing.

"Mme de Talleyrand was not deceived as to the importance of this meeting that had been so secretly arranged; she was unable to hide her disturbed feelings, or to overcome them. Her predictions have not been proved false: she has not seen M. de Talleyrand again since that day, and was shortly afterwards driven out of her house."

This decision had become a necessity then, for Dorothée as well as for Talleyrand.

⟡ ⟡ ⟡

There was a period of four months between thé death of little Dorothée and the departure of Talleyrand and his niece for Vienna. What had happened during those weeks? What transformation had her ordeal brought about in the young woman's heart and mind? No direct testimony has survived, but there are certain facts that provide us with some evidence.

Until that time, Dorothée had never been separated from her children for any length of time. Yet after the loss of her two-year-old daughter she did not hesitate to put 875 miles— and an eight day journey—between herself and her sons, the youngest of whom was no more than a few months old.

Never, during a period of five years, despite both the absences and the infidelities of her husband, had Dorothée provided any excuse for gossip on her account. No other man's name had ever been linked with hers. Yet now she was accepting a situation of the most delicate kind, one that could be construed in the most equivocal way.

Rather shy, aloof, and reserved, she was a young woman who had often avoided society altogether. Yet now she was hurling herself into the heart of a social merry-go-round that became the most extravagant that age had ever seen.

Strange metamorphosis. A butterfly finally emerging from its chrysalis? Possibly. A being at last finding her true direction in life? Hardly, for Vienna was merely a long transition. More simply, a being in revolt. What had life brought her? An unhappy childhood, an unwanted marriage, the loss of a child. Now, her ambitions kindled, her mind matured, she intended to wrest some satisfaction from life.

When Dorothée set out with her uncle for Vienna in September 1814, she was also setting out on the conquest, perhaps not of happiness, but certainly of an important social and political position. What better place to establish such a position than in Vienna, which was to become for the next few months the meeting place of all Europe? Who could better guarantee success in attaining it than Talleyrand, that amazing conjuror who had just whisked away an empire and put an ancient dynasty back in its place?

Here was a young woman turning a new page in her life. Whatever the outcome of the adventure, she was never to turn back, she was never to resume the former cold and passive life she had endured beside her husband. Stendhal was never again to see that "purity of expression" that had so charmed him a few years before.

It is impossible to believe that this will of Dorothée's to make a change in her life had gone unnoticed by Talleyrand. His own ecclesiastical career had at one time imposed a constraint upon him quite as serious as the one Dorothée had experienced through her marriage, and it was that constraint that had made him what he was. Because he was a cripple, his parents had forced him to enter the Church when he was faced with the only really important question in a man's life: his choice of career. Because she was rich, he himself had forced Dorothée to marry Edmond when she was faced with the only really important question in a woman's life: her marriage.

He had been enabled to escape from the Church by the Revolution. How was Dorothée to escape from her marriage?

Perhaps it was then that Talleyrand discovered he could no longer envisage an existence that did not include his niece. He had had a great many love affairs. But though a libertine, Talleyrand was not fundamentally a very sensual man * so that almost all his mistresses had been mature women with sufficient experience to kindle his ardors. Whether it was Mme de Brionne, who had educated him in his youth, the Princess of Vaudemont, "who asked above everything else that she should always drink her tea with the most powerful men of the day," Mme de Flahaut, the mother of his son Charles, Mme de Staël, who served him so well, Mme de Laval, whom he used to visit every day under the Empire, or, lastly, the Duchess of Courland, who helped him to forward his plots with the Tsar, most of his mistresses had also been—one might almost say, had

---

* Gouverneur Morris, on the authority of confidences made to him by Mme de Flahaut, is categorical on this point.

all been—women of distinction whose houses were elegant, whose salons were agreeable, and whose conversation was witty. It was in the company of such women, in their tranquil "chambers," that he found the atmosphere in which he was at home. It was in such places that he had reigned, serenely moving his pawns across the European chessboard.

"Women are politics," he said several years later to Thiers.

And now, into this circle of women whose ages and minds bore such a similarity to his own, a much younger woman had suddenly glided, at first, no more than a presence. Mutual discovery had come in the years 1812 and 1813. Two minds, two ambitions had recognized their kinship. Then the difficult months preceding the fall of the Empire had drawn Talleyrand and Dorothée into an even closer understanding. The latter, being a German at heart, had been able to accept without difficulty a betrayal that overthrew the Empire—for which she had no love—but also damaged France itself—to her a matter of indifference.

The almost feminine subtlety of Talleyrand's intelligence had drawn strength from the robust understanding of his niece, and his cautious audacity had become more vigorous as it fed upon the young woman's swiftness of spirit. They had come to feel a mutual esteem for each other's profound delight in politics and innate sense of intrigue. The man of sixty, charmed and dazzled, had found in this woman of twenty a disciple, and perhaps one day a partner in the new career that would be his under a new regime.

Dorothée had it in mind to escape from a husband whose absences alone had enabled her to bear with him. Talleyrand wished Dorothée to remain a member of his family and close to him. The better to keep her, he himself provided her with the escape that she was seeking.

In 1812, Mme de Kielmannsegge, whose remarks are frequently tendentious, accused Talleyrand at one and the same time of lacking sympathy for Dorothée and also of having attempted to seduce her. Marie de Bunsen, who has made a perspicacious study of Dorothée's life, dates the beginning of her liaison with Talleyrand from the spring or early summer of 1814, before their departure for Vienna, claiming that Talleyrand's feelings had by that time reached a pitch of intensity that would have made cohabitation under any other conditions impossible. The hypothesis is acceptable in itself, even though it is based on a somewhat naïve premise and is difficult to reconcile with Talleyrand's letters expressing impatience at his nephew's prolonged absence. It is more likely that it was Edmond's return, followed by little Dorothée's death, that drove Dorothée into the arms of an uncle who loved her and understood her so much better than her husband did. There are also certain details of Talleyrand's behavior in Vienna that run counter to Marie de Bunsen's hypothesis.*

Why should we not accept the probability that although Talleyrand already felt the most profound predilection for his niece's person and an overwhelming passion for her mind, that although her presence had become indispensable to him and although, in a word, he was heart and soul as much in love with her as it is possible to be, this statesman so heavily laden with political responsibilities, this ambitious schemer who was about to play one of his most difficult hands, this libertine accustomed to women with much physical experience, had still not attempted to introduce to the pleasures of the senses a young woman who until that time had remained pure and perhaps even frigid? Is it not permissible to suppose that Talleyrand's passion did not reach physical expression until the moment when he became certain, and this would have happened in Vienna, that Dorothée was, after all, the Duchess of

* On October 9, 1814, Jean-Gabriel Eynard, the Swiss representative, noted: "We have just returned from the house of M. de Talleyrand, who had arranged to grant us an audience at noon. Apparently, however, the Minister was still in bed, since some attempt was made to delay us as we made our way up to his apartment, and at the very moment we were entering his first drawing room we caught sight of a young tart rather hastily leaving an inner room; she appeared to be very scantily clad. We were struck by such edifying conduct in a former Bishop. What then confirmed us in our suspicion that Talleyrand had not yet risen was the sight of various valets and menservants walking in and out, obviously in the process of aiding Monseigneur with his toilette. After we had waited for three quarters of an hour, the Minister finally came in to us; he had on all his orders and was in full Ambassadorial dress."

It is scarcely believable that if Talleyrand was already his niece's lover at the time he would have permitted himself to indulge in an adventure of this kind. And we should add that from the day when Dorothée took up residence on the Rue Saint-Florentin, in March, 1816, no other name than hers was ever again linked with that of Talleyrand.

Courland's daughter, the Duchess of Sagan's sister, and shared their capacity for physical ardor?

❖   ❖   ❖

What the Congress of Vienna was from the diplomatic point of view is only too well known. A four-handed game, the cards all dealt originally to Castlereagh (England), Metternich (Austria), Hardenburg (Prussia), and Nesselrode (Russia), into which Talleyrand (France) had insinuated himself within very few days, which he soon came to dominate, and which he eventually disrupted. On January 3, 1815, Austria, England, and France agreed to disallow the cession of all Saxony to Prussia and all Poland to Russia. Then came Napoleon's return, which banded all the erstwhile allies together again, in theory against the Emperor, but in fact against a France guilty of greeting this new flight of the imperial eagles with excessive joy. While the sovereigns returned to their respective States in order to muster their armies, the five ministers labored on for three more months—clarifying and hammering into final form the decisions sketched out between October of 1814 and March of 1815.

On June 9, 1815, the final act of the Congress of Vienna was signed. Russia was given the lion's share of Poland, even though both Prussia and Austria were thrown a few scraps. Austria was given control of Italy. England at last saw the constitution of the Kingdom of the Netherlands (Belgium and Holland) that she had always dreamed of as a bastion against French threats. Lastly, Prussia was permitted to absorb a large section of Saxony and occupy the Rhineland. All these great powers were satisfied. Talleyrand and Louis XVIII were satisfied also. Twenty years of exile had made the new King of France forget the needs of France. The ambitions he betrayed in his instructions to his Minister were not patriotic ones but dynastic ones: save the Kingdom of Saxony, since the King was a relation of his; expel Murat from Naples and restore the Bourbon rule.

With a savage determination to pay off the mortgage that

Louis XVIII's hostility was putting on his future, Talleyrand directed his efforts to the satisfaction of these egoistic desires before all else. In order to save Saxony he allowed Prussia to occupy the Rhineland. Whatever fine phrases Talleyrand may have used in his attempts to deceive himself and cozen posterity, one indisputable fact stands out: France, forced back into its frontiers of 1791, was facing a new Europe. The balance of power had been broken, and to France's detriment.

From the social point of view, the Congress of Vienna was a prodigious carnival, an enormous fair at which all Europe, after twenty years of war, rediscovered its forgotten joie de vivre. Imagine a town, still provincial in many ways, encircled by ramparts that could be walked around in three quarters of an hour. In the middle, the Hofburg, a vast and somber edifice composed of many disparate blocks of buildings and courtyards. During the autumn of 1814, it was being occupied by two Emperors, Alexander and Francis, their two Empresses, four kings, those of Prussia, Wurtemburg, Bavaria and Denmark, the Queen of Bavaria and a good dozen assorted princes and archdukes. Each one of these had his or her personal household of attendants and also a guard of honor provided by the Austrian court and more or less responsible for surveillance of the potentate to whom they were attached.

All day, and sometimes all night, if we are to judge by the detailed reports made to Hager, the Austrian chief of police, there were idle bystanders—and spies—waiting in front of the palace gates in the hope of seeing one sovereign or another emerge. The Tsar was usually escorted by only a single officer when he left on his visits to the Duchess of Sagan or Princess Bagration. Almost every day, he was also to be seen walking with Eugène de Beauharnais. The Emperor of Austria drove his modest carriage himself, whether he was merely going to the Prater or whether he was visiting Marie-Louise and the King of Rome at Schoenbrunn. Frederick-Wilhelm III was frequently to be seen entering the residence of the beautiful Countess Julie Zichy.

Then there were the palaces of the Austrian nobility, grouped around the Hofburg along a dozen or so dark, narrow streets and overflowing with German princes, European diplomats, English lords, great Hungarian landowners and Russian boyards. There were also a good many women: great ladies in search of some prestigious or merely agreeable affair, hostesses only too happy to open their salon doors to kings and princes. The pro-Prussian contingent was grouped around the Princess of Tour and Taxis; the Duchess of Sagan's salon was of the same tint as her amorous inclinations, either Austrian or Russian, invariably anti-French. Talleyrand made a practice of being there every evening in the hope of surprising Metternich's secrets. Finally, at the Kaunitz Palace were to be found all those who favored France, drawn in part by the charm, the beauty, and the wit of Countess Edmond de Périgord.

❖ ❖ ❖

Talleyrand and Dorothée arrived in Vienna in late September. It had been a hard journey from Paris, with only two stops, at Strassburg and at Munich. This haste was necessary; the sovereigns, the Tsar and the King of Prussia were also on their way, and the newly created Prince de Talleyrand meant to have his forces marshaled in battle order before their arrival.

La Tour du Pin had reached the Austrian capital earlier in the month. He had moved into the Kaunitz Palace, 1029, Johannesgasse, which had been rented for the French Embassy, and set about putting that vast building, as massive and primitive as a Florentine palace, into some sort of order. Scarcely lived in since the death of Maria Theresa's Chancellor, it had the most magnificent salons, all decorated in the purest Viennese rococo; there were enormous clocks and gigantic lusters supported by putti and cherubim. The furniture too was rich, and the carpets sumptuous. Every mattress in the place, on the other hand, had been devoured by moths.

Then La Tour du Pin moved out to make room for Dalberg, who moved into one of the suites. Later, Talleyrand and Dorothée occupied two of the other suites with their servants, Neukomm, the musician, and Rouen, Talleyrand's secretary.

On October 1, Adam Czartoryski arrived in Vienna. He

had regained his former influence over Alexander * and was there to defend Poland's claim to be reconstituted as an autonomous kingdom under the Tsar. He swiftly became a regular visitor at the French Embassy. On October 9, he dined with Talleyrand and that same day sent a message by hand to Dorothée.

Prince Czartoryski had hardly changed at all since 1807. On the other hand, the woman with the great, enigmatic eyes, the self-assured bearing, and the bold, original mind who greeted him in the gilded salons of the Kaunitz Palace no longer bore any resemblance to the thin and taciturn child he had observed so closely at Mittau.

Did he now feel regret at having shown so little eagerness in the past? It is possible. Were there the beginnings of an affair between them? It is unlikely. Both of them were intent on their ambitions, and those very ambitions were a barrier between them. Czartoryski's only thought was to serve the Kingdom of Poland; Dorothée's was to serve Talleyrand, and Talleyrand was wholly opposed to the existence of that kingdom.

One thing is certain: they talked about the past, and it is without doubt from Czartoryski that Dorothée at last came to know the whole truth about the secret plot that had precipitated her marriage. In February of 1809, when the Duchess of Courland had sent the Prince a hurried announcement of her daughter's engagement, she had at the same time sent back certain letters written by Czartoryski to Piattoli. In them, he had told the Abbé that he had at last overcome his mother's hostility to the match; that, having learned of the Emperor Alexander's interest in another marriage for Dorothée, he was making all haste to wind up his affairs and would arrive at Löbikau within a few weeks. There could therefore have been no further doubt as to his intentions, and the Duchess of Courland had knowingly told her daughter a deliberate lie in order

* In May 1831, while he was French Ambassador in London, Talleyrand wrote a note to Count Walewski that constitutes an amazing commentary on Alexander's sudden changes of mood: "For my part, I have known what he was since Erfurt. Others have done him the honor of thinking him subtle and treacherous, but they were entirely mistaken: he was merely weak and changeable, his opinions never remained the same for two days together. . . ."

to extort from her the promise to marry Edmond de Périgord.

There was truly something in the Viennese air that autumn of 1814 that drove its inhabitants to commit all kinds of follies. The entire town had become one vast trysting place. Dorothée was presented with the spectacle of her sisters, Princess Hohenzollern and the Duchess of Acerenza, both making public acknowledgment of their lovers. As for the Duchess of Sagan, her lovers' quarrels with Metternich were a constant and universal topic of conversation.*

Upon Dorothée, who had had scarcely any contact with the elegant and gamey international society of her day until that point, who had moved without transition from Mlle Hoffmann's little circle in Berlin to an Imperial court at which, since his remarriage, Napoleon had insisted upon a certain austerity of tone and manners, this scene of nonchalant debauchery had a liberating effect. She had arrived a bruised and rebellious young woman; Czartoryski's confidences then increased her bitterness, and she allowed herself to be invaded by the prevailing atmosphere of amorality all around her.

Visiting Vienna again, in 1841, Dorothée wrote: "It was in Vienna that I first began to acquire that wearisome, albeit heady, celebrity that is so much more a trial to the spirit than it is a flattering unction to the soul. I amused myself prodigiously in this place, and shed abundant tears as well; the complications of my life began here, and the first of those many storms that have rumbled for so long around me. Of all those who had some part in turning my head, exalted and bewildered as I was here, not one now remains."

⬦ ⬦ ⬦

* When the subject of Saxony was first mooted, a report was sent to Hager setting out the Prussians' complaints against Metternich, who was "mad with love, pride and vanity, idling away all his forenoons—not rising until ten, then running to the Duchess of Sagan's and spending the rest of the morning sighing at her feet." Frederick von Gentz, the Secretary to the Congress, who loved women sometimes, men usually, and money always, noted for his part: "Went back to Metternich's and had some conversation with him—alas!—about the unfortunate Windischgraetz liaison [that of the Duchess of Sagan with the prince of that name] which seems to be of more interest to him than world politics. . . ."

"Not one now remains." When she wrote those words, Dorothée was doubtless thinking of Tsar Alexander, who died in 1825, of Talleyrand, who died in 1838, of her sister Sagan, who died in 1839, and of many other companions. Perhaps, too, she was thinking of Count Clam-Martinitz, who had died the year before, almost without warning.

In April 1814, when Napoleon set out for Elba, he was escorted as far as Fréjus by Allied military representatives. The Austrian representative was Field Marshal Koller, and with him he had Major Clam, then a twenty-two year old officer.

Provence was royalist. In Orgon, Napoleon was greeted with cries of "Down with the tyrant!" and his escort of Allied officers was obliged to ride in tight formation around him as a shield. The Emperor changed into a courier's uniform and galloped for several miles on the back of a post horse. In Aix, the threat was renewed. His escort became alarmed. Crushed by his fatigue and disgust, Napoleon gave way to them: on Major Clam's suggestion he changed into an Austrian uniform.*

When Schwarzenburg went to London in June-July 1814, Clam accompanied him as an aide-de-camp. This elegant and worldly man, a member of a very ancient family, was not only a courageous soldier but also possessed a lively, open intelligence and a mind well equipped for diplomacy, which was the field into which his career soon lead him.† He quickly won the favor of the Tsar, and when Alexander arrived in Vienna Clam was posted to serve in his guard of honor as an aide-de-camp.

It is possible that the young officer had met Dorothée in Paris during the spring of 1814. In Vienna, at all events, they met quickly and they met frequently. In early November, Gentz,

---

* A year later, in March of 1815, Humboldt said sourly to Reichenbach that "Count Clam, and it was a great misfortune, had saved Napoleon's life."

† Promoted to Colonel in 1821, then appointed to special missions in Russia during 1824 and 1826, Major-General in 1830, then appointed to further special missions, one of them to Prussia in 1832, Clam became a Field Marshal in 1835 after the death of the Emperor Francis, and general aide-de-camp to the new emperor, Ferdinand, head of the military section of the Council of State, and, in fact, Minister for War to the Monarchy. We should add that this brilliant military career had also enabled him to display outstanding statesmanlike qualities, that he was considered by many as Metternich's only possible successor, and that his death at the age of forty-eight, on January 30, 1840, was considered an irreparable loss.

a close acquaintance who much appreciated Clam's intelligence and amiable temper, had a long conversation with the young officer about his passion for Mme Edmond de Périgord.

Shortly thereafter, at Rennweg on the outskirts of Vienna, Metternich gave a masked ball, "by common consent one of the finest entertainments ever seen," according to Gentz. Clam certainly saw Dorothée there. Did she flirt with him? Did he ask Gentz to plead his cause with her? It is possible, for the latter had a matchmaker's soul and kept an unwinking and avid eye upon each and every one of the innumerable amorous intrigues then flourishing in the city. In mid-November, the Secretary to the Congress dined at Talleyrand's and later engaged Mme de Périgord in a lengthy conversation.

There was no end to the balls and entertainments, and "Mme Edmond," according to Dalberg, was at that time "one of the busiest people at the Congress." She was also one of the most wooed. By Lord Charles Stewart, who became the lover of her sister Sagan; Lord Charles presented Dorothée with a horse—a dangerous gift: the beast took the bit between its teeth and ran away, almost breaking Dorothée's neck. She was also wooed by Clam, who seems to have loved her sincerely. And by the Master of the Horse, Count Trauttmansdorff who, despite his liaison with Petite Aimée (one of the dancers who had come from Paris for the festivities), was paying the Countess of Périgord assiduous court and chose her as his lady for the tournament given on November 23.

For this entertainment, which was exciting every imagination, every rivalry,* the "fair damsels" participating had been divided into four quadrilles. The costumes were of the Renaissance period, emerald green for Hungary, turquoise blue for Austria, crimson for Poland, black for France. Dorothée, who led the French quadrille, wore an enormous skirt of black velvet held

---

* The ladies in the quadrilles wore thirty million francs' worth of jewels. Princess Paul Esterhazy, née Tour and Taxis, wore six millions' worth of diamonds alone. The female spectators also joined in this contest of finery. The Duchess of Sagan's dress was embroidered all over with precious stones. "She broke up M. de Metternich's order of the Golden Fleece in order to extract the diamonds from it," wrote J.-G. Eynard, a Swiss delegate. "There were enough jewels to cover the cost of three military campaigns," said the Prussians, avid-eyed as ever.

open at the front by diamond and ruby clips to disclose a further skirt of white satin. The costume had wide slashed sleeves, and an extremely low-cut neckline. At her neck, three rows of pearls.

On November 23, to the accompaniment of an antique air, the twenty-four ladies, veiled in white gauze, entered in procession and took their places in the stand reserved for them at one end of the lists. They were escorted by their knights, whose François I costumes were of the same colors as their ladies' dresses. Scarcely had these ladies taken their places when a fanfare heralded the arrival of the sovereigns. Raising their veils, the ladies signalled for the jousting to begin.

This was followed by a supper, then by a ball, to which more than three thousand people had been invited. The pièce de résistance of the evening was the quadrille danced by the fair damsels and their knights. All that evening Dorothée drew every eye with her dazzling beauty, the elegance of her costume, and the liveliness of her conversation.

Several days later, a report made to Hager informed him that: "There is much talk of the Countess of Périgord's liaison with Count Trauttmansdorff."

❖ ❖ ❖

Talleyrand had been observing the changes in Dorothée with a perceptive and no doubt anxious eye. A new woman was becoming apparent in her, a young, ardent passionate being, abandoning herself to life with a violence made commensurately greater by the length of time it had been suppressed. Could he keep her, this new woman? Might some attraction of the heart or flesh not impel her into a choice from which there was no turning back? Were his prestige, his intelligence, his tolerant passion, the full life he was offering her, and his experience as a seducer sufficient to keep her by his side?

The hand he held contained so few trumps; he could afford no mistakes. But what did it matter? With powdered hair, slim in his plum-colored coat that glittered with decorations, poker-faced and cold-eyed, Talleyrand moved through the salons of

Vienna, leaning with one hand upon his cane and radiating an air of tenacity and power. It was on one of those days that the Archduke John remarked of him: "A wormeaten heart, but a perfect brain." And on another, when questioned about his attitude between the retreat across the Rhine and Napoleon's abdication, that the Prince quietly replied: "I limped." Dorothée admired the skill with which he subjugated all Vienna, and she respected the will that made friends and enemies alike all bow to his desires.

Every evening at the Kaunitz Palace, seated upon a sofa beside his niece, Talleyrand was surrounded by the Ministers of the victorious powers, who all remained standing as they conversed with him. "In fact," La Garde-Chambonas noted, "seeing almost all the diplomats in Vienna crowding around M. de Talleyrand, one might well have supposed that his house was the place officially appointed for the Congress meetings." For Dorothée there was a profound satisfaction in being so closely associated with her uncle's brilliant position.

But Talleyrand did more than merely allow his niece a share in the dazzling surface of his life—he also shared his work with her, revealed all his hopes and fears to her, and asked her for help. "One evening, he had occasion to dictate a long dispatch to her. The Countess, already dressed for the evening, was throwing frequent and impatient glances at the clock. At last, the Prince reached the end: she thought she was free to rush off to her ball. 'And now,' her uncle said, 'we have to fight our "battle with the words."' And indeed, there then followed the necessary process of revision, the weighing of every expression, the erasures, the substitutions, which went on until the terrible censor finally deigned to announce that he was satisfied. Then, and not until then, she was able to withdraw and seek the pleasures that were awaiting her." Dorothée was too intelligent not to be deeply interested by such intimate contact with a mind of such quality.

More than once too, Villemain was to write in 1855, "this support [Dorothée's], or this diversion, came most happily to the aid of M. de Talleyrand's consummate knowledge, smoothed away apparent contradictions for him, helped him to avoid obstacles, and won over possible helpers to his opinions before he had made them fully clear to others, or even perhaps formulated them precisely to himself." A profound remark—and Villemain had interrogated a great many eyewitnesses, we might add. Talleyrand was aware of Dorothée's need to dominate. In order to keep her, he allowed himself, or appeared to allow himself, to be dominated by her; he bowed, or appeared to bow, to her young and imperious will.

Those were Talleyrand's cards. Backed by that profound need for security and order instilled in Dorothée by her troubled and scattered childhood, did they constitute a winning hand?

Trauttmansdorff gave him no cause for anxiety. The Austrian Count was merely a frivolous man whose favors could be won by any lady of birth or demi-mondaine who sought them; he was too much like Edmond for the latter's wife to remain interested in him for long. She was amused, her vanity flattered, by a courtship that brought her into social prominence. Perhaps, following her sisters' example, she might engage in an "affair" with him; but it could not last.

Clam was a different matter. Attentive as always to any matter that concerned his niece, Talleyrand had sensed the deep, abiding interest that Dorothée had conceived in the young officer. However, the Prince had a great knowledge of women and a great knowledge of his niece. Apart from the reasons imposed by family considerations and her own position—Talleyrand alone could guarantee her custody of her children—he knew the strength of the intellectual bonds with which he had bound her to him over the past year. He also knew that this woman, though young in years, was not so in mind or heart, and that Clam must appear childish in her eyes. Lastly, he thought that Dorothée's head would always prove stronger than her senses. In short, he hoped that his young niece would become bored, make comparisons, arrive at a verdict. . . .

When did it begin, this liaison between Clam and Dorothée? The young Countess seems to have come to her decision early in the December of 1814. On the 7th, Gentz spent the evening with Dorothée at the Duchess of Sagan's and then left with her. Gentz underlines this fact. There is little doubt that they discussed Clam that evening. Four days later, the entry in Gentz's *Journal* makes things clear enough: "Dined at Talleyrand's. Long conversation with Mme de Périgord.—Home at eight.—Visit from Clam." Good matchmaker that he was, Gentz must have passed on the results of his "long conversation" to Clam, and the information was not long in bearing fruit. On December 31, 1814, ᵃnd on January 1, 1815, Gentz in fact mentions two further dinners at the Duchess of Sagan's. The guests at both of them included Windischgraetz, the Duchess's favorite at that time, the Duchess of Acerenza and her lover Borel, and Countess Edmond de Périgord with Clam, who had doubtless by then become hers. For many successive weeks afterwards, their names were to be linked again and again in the diarist's pages.

❖   ❖   ❖

One of the greatest pleasures of the Austrian Empress, Maria Ludovica, was to give theatrical performances in her apartments. Undaunted by the difficulties inherent in the role of impresario, she had recruited a troupe of society actors, and Dorothée was one of its comedy stars. Talleyrand wrote to the Duchess of Courland quite seriously that Dorothée was acting "as well as Mlle Mars," then added: "There is nothing that Dorothée attempts to do that she does not do well."

On March 5, 1815, one of these theatrical performances was taking place at the Hofburg; the festivities were at their height when a dispatch was brought in from Metternich: Napoleon had escaped from Elba.

During the night of March 24-25, the Duchess of Courland arrived in Vienna and took up residence in the Kaunitz Palace. Doubtless she did not take long to grasp the situation: Talleyrand in love, Dorothée engaged in a liaison. She must have found these facts extremely unpleasant and very difficult to accept. Did she attempt any form of protest? If she did, it is probable that Dorothée in her turn took advantage of the confidences made to her by Czartoryski and reminded her mother of the lie with which she had been inveigled into marriage.

On April 3, Montrond arrived to represent Napoleon. Talleyrand greeted his friend amicably enough, but since Montrond was there to plead the cause of the King of Rome he quickly passed the newcomer on to his niece.

"You already know the kind of entertainment she has to offer you: music, cards, plays, the whole repertory of the Comédie-Française; though they do very few of Voltaire's tragedies, and never *L'Orphelin de Chine.*" *

The staff of the French Embassy was shrinking daily and money was becoming scarce. Nevertheless, Talleyrand decided not to leave for Ghent, despite Louis XVIII's requests that he should do so.† Possibly he was hesitant about throwing in his lot irrevocably with the Bourbons and contemplated switching his allegiance to the Orléans faction. But it is equally probable that he did not wish to leave Vienna before knowing what Dorothée would do.

In fact, she seemed unable to make up her mind. She had no desire to rejoin her husband and children in France or Brussels, even though the former, according to one anonymous opinion, had been "behaving wonderfully." ‡ Clam had rejoined Schwarzenberg's staff at Heilbronn early in May; on the

---

* It is possible that Talleyrand later regretted not having listened to Montrond. Arsène Houssay tells us that immediately after the revolution of 1830 the Prince expressed the following opinions: "Diplomacy, you know, is a fencing school where one is often wounded in play. Every word is a sword and one must have a perfect aim; I knew my trade well enough, but my aim has not always been perfect. For instance, I made a mistake in 1815. . . . A nation like France needs prestige. Louis XVIII had no prestige. Since France was acclaiming Napoleon, war had to be prevented; in fact, I fanned the flames. . . ."

† Ghent, April 22, 1815: "I am extremely anxious, especially in the present circumstances, to have you here with me. . . ." May 5, 1815: "It is a matter of little moment which of my plenipotentiaries in particular signs the treaty; but it is extremely important to me that you should be here with me. . . ."

We may also add that Durant de Saint-André, one of Talleyrand's subordinates who was extremely devoted to him, informed his employer on April 24: "The Congress is drawing to a close and it is much more important that Your Highness be here with the King, a fact of which Blacas himself and the Duke of Berry are aware." Blacas and the Duke of Berry were to be among Talleyrand's most determined enemies a few weeks later; Saint-André's words, disguised as mere information, were in fact a warning.

‡ When the news of Napoleon's landing was announced, Edmond de Périgord had asked Soult to be put back on the active list. On the 14th, he made the same request again to Clarke, the new Minister for War. The Count of Périgord's brigade formed part of the Kellermann division that was sent to Essonnes with the intention of barring the Emperor's route. As soon as Napoleon appeared, the soldiers all drew their sabers and ran forward to acclaim him. Edmond did not follow his men's example but returned to Paris. On April 7, by Imperial decree, he was stripped of all his possessions.

19th, however, he returned to Vienna for several hours and doubtless paid a visit to Dorothée. Whether at his instigation or for some quite different reason, the latter made her decision shortly afterwards: the first week of June, she left for Berlin and her properties in Silesia.

A week later, Talleyrand left Vienna for Ghent. He rejoined Louis XVIII at Mons on June 23, five days after Waterloo.

⬥   ⬥   ⬥

The day after his return to Paris on July 8, Louis XVIII resigned himself to appointing Talleyrand Premier of a cabinet that included Fouché.* The Prince moved back into his house on the Rue Saint-Florentin, which his wife had by then vacated. Upon receiving the news of Napoleon's return, the Princess of Talleyrand had succumbed to a strange aberration of judgment and left Paris for London instead of Vienna.† Delighted at being thus rid of her, perhaps in compliance with what he sensed to be Dorothée's wishes, or with the latter's

---

* Talleyrand's disregard of his summonses and delay in leaving Vienna had lost him Louis XVIII's favor for good. The King accepted him henceforth as a necessary evil of which he was resolved to disencumber himself at the first opportunity. The opportunity presented itself on September 24, 1815, when the French sovereign became convinced that the Tsar's hostility toward Talleyrand was very likely to make the conditions for peace more onerous. Whereupon his dismissed his Minister in the twinkling of an eye, to the great astonishment of Talleyrand, who found himself outmaneuvered by someone even more skillful than himself.

† Though reputed to be stupid, the Mme de Talleyrand may have been less so than was generally thought. In 1816, she said to the Marquis d'Osmond, Mme de Boigne's father: "I am expiating my error in yielding to a mistaken impulse of vanity. I knew what Mme Edmond's position was in M. de Talleyrand's household in Vienna, but I did not wish to be a witness to it. It was my sensitivity in this respect that prevented me from going to join him, as I ought to have done, when the return from Elba forced me to leave Paris. If I had gone to Vienna instead of coming to London, M. de Talleyrand would have been obliged to take me in. And I know him so well, he would have done so with perfect grace. The more my arrival vexed him the less he would have permitted it to show. I knew all that; but I have a horror of that woman and I allowed it to influence me. I was wrong. My mistake was in believing that his weakness would prevent him from ever daring to cast me off. I underestimated the courage cowards can display when the danger is a distant one! . . ."

already clearly formulated request, Talleyrand saw to it that this exile in England continued. The way thus cleared, when Dorothée returned in mid-July, she moved into her uncle's house on the Rue Saint-Florentin with him. She also met Clam again in Paris.

Molé has left us a sly sketch of one typical morning in the Talleyrand town house during that summer of 1815 when the destiny of France was being haggled over yet again. "Between eleven o'clock and noon, rising from his bed, M. de Talleyrand would walk through into his private drawing room where he would be greeted by a display of all the English and French newspapers, at which he did not deign to glance, by Mme Edmond de Périgord and Mme Alexandre de Talleyrand (Charlotte), by whom he permitted himself to be embraced, by two or three menservants, his surgeon, and such of his intimates as had managed to rise before him. . . ."

It is an idyllic picture, albeit somewhat surprising when one thinks of the crushing weight of responsibilities then resting on the aging Talleyrand's shoulders.

But it is above all a false picture.

The Duchess of Courland was "eating her heart out with jealousy over her daughter's success" with the Prince, and Edmond de Périgord was apparently not behaving in any way like a complaisant husband. In August, a note to Hager reported: "An Austrian major has fought a duel with Count Edmond de Périgord, nephew to Talleyrand, the same one that married the youngest Princess of Courland and defied the King [*sic*]. I cannot discover the reasons that led the major to fight, but I know that Périgord was given a great saber wound across his face and that the Courland family, his wife included, are delighted by the fact. She is known to have been seeking a separation from him before this occurrence." An Austrian major? Clam was a major at that time. The police files contain no allusion to this duel, but we may be allowed, I think, to consider the fact that Fouché was Chief of Police at the time, and Talleyrand the Premier.

In any event, their separation seems to have deepened Dorothée's feelings toward Clam. She was considering moving permanently to Vienna; Talleyrand was aware of this and could not conceal his emotions at the prospect. This is attested to by three witnesses whose testimony can scarcely be dismissed: the Chancellor Pasquier, Charles de Rémusat and Mme de Boigne.

The first writes: "As for M. de Talleyrand, it is difficult to believe, unless one was a witness to it, that the very moment when he should have been exclusively occupied with affairs of state, affairs so onerous and fraught with responsibility that they would have been a cause for alarm to even the most consummate and self-confident of statesmen, should have proved to be precisely the one at which, now past his sixtieth year, he chose to yield to a sentiment whose all-devouring ardor entirely deprived him of all presence of mind. . . . When he realized that the lady whose presence is so precious to him had left him in order to go and live in Vienna he fell into a state of moral as well as physical prostration that it would be impossible to describe."

The remarks of the second are equally precise: "Talleyrand had returned from Germany very much in love with his niece, Mme Edmond de Périgord. It was said that this desperate, slightly senile passion completely dominated him, obsessed him, drove him mad. . . . Whatever the date at which she had first inspired this passion in him, it was during the Congress that it became apparent. Nor, be it said, was it without stormy interludes.

"The infatuated uncle was generally thought to have been deceived; he was certainly jealous. This jealousy, it was said, had led to scenes, to separations. . . . Mme de Périgord was in love with someone in Germany whose name was known, and it was his regret at her absence, his need to see her again, the torments of desire and jealousy that were the cause of M. de Talleyrand's seming so much off his usual form during the last few months. . . ."

Mme de Boigne for her part remarks briefly: "She [Dorothée] had formed a passionate attachment to an Austrian, the Count of Clam. And almost as soon as the legitimate wife had left the town house on the Rue Saint-Florentin vacant for her use, she escaped from it under the escort of the Count. Her departure drove M. de Talleyrand out of his mind."

❖   ❖   ❖

"Mme de Périgord is journeying to Italy, where the Duchess of Sagan is already. She will arrive in Vienna with her other sister, the Princess Hohenzollern, and then continue on her way. She is still Talleyrand's favorite." *

It tore at Talleyrand's heart to see Dorothée go. Though his pain did not destroy his hope of the fugitive's eventual return, he patiently set out to mend the threads that her departure seemed to have broken. He wrote to Dorothée.† It is possible that he asked the Marquis of Giamboni, who was traveling to Naples to join Blacas, to visit her and urge her to come back. Above all, he entrusted Gentz, with whom he was "on perfect terms," to negotiate for Dorothée's return.

Gentz arrived in Vienna on December 21. He went immediately to see the Duchess of Sagan, "whose three younger sisters are all staying with her." During the next few days he saw a great deal of Mme de Périgord and no doubt of Clam also. On January 21, Gentz gave a tea party followed by a little supper. The guests included the Princess Hohenzollern and General von Wallmoden, the Duchess of Acerenza and Borel, and also Dorothée and Clam.

Had Gentz failed in his mission then? Had Dorothée irrevocably said good-bye to Talleyrand and France? On the contrary, her liaison with Clam was on the brink of dissolution.

Next day, January 22, Clam paid Gentz a farewell visit before leaving that night to rejoin Schwarzenburg's staff in Milan. Four more days went by, then Gentz noted in his diary: "Spent two hours conversing with Mme de Périgord on the subject of her family affairs." The conversation was renewed on January 30 and continued for an equal length of time.

Was it then that Dorothée came to her decision, or was it only finally precipitated by something her sister the Duchess of Sagan said to her after the latter's arrival from Milan on

---

* This note was sent to Hager on November 5, 1815 by an unidentified spy.

† On November 24, Talleyrand sent Durant de Saint-André a letter that he was to deliver himself to Mme de Périgord "who is in Venice." If she was no longer there when the Emperor (Francis of Austria) left, then it was to be sent on to Vienna.

February 15? * Only one fact is certain: after having given a ball on the 19th, thus making her adieus to Viennese high society, Dorothée, three days later, set out on the road back to Paris. The previous day she had had a final conversation with Gentz. In his diary we find what is a very severe comment coming from a man who was himself both dissolute and an admirer: "A woman as remarkable for the subtlety of her mind as for her depravity of heart, she has been for me an object of much study and amusement."

Let us pause for a moment to consider those February days in 1816 during which Dorothée arrived at her life's decision. To go back to France was to go back to Talleyrand. She knew that, accepted the fact, perhaps desired it. Despite the amorous liberties that she took in the future—liberties to which Talleyrand always turned a blind eye—"this singular, this unique relationship" was never imperiled again. It lasted until Talleyrand's death. For twenty-two years Dorothée showed him absolute devotion, a devotion that often took the form, in this strong-willed and imperious woman, of a conscious and willing submission.†

How can this strange choice be justified?

Ambition alone is insufficient as an explanation. Even though he had been appointed to the post of Grand Chamberlain in February of 1816, Talleyrand was in complete disfavor. True, he was still one of the foremost persons in France, but his

---

* Did Wilhelmine perhaps inform Dorothée of some infidelity on Clam's part, one of those infidelities of the flesh and not the heart that are of so little consequence in a man's eyes and yet so wounding to a woman? Twenty years later, the Dorothée wrote: "The danger for a woman when she discovers that her lover has been unfaithful is that she will yield to a desire for vengeance, that she will lose those illusions that are her protection, not against error, but against hardness of heart and coquetry proper. . . ." Words full of disillusion that in part sum up Dorothée's own story under the Restoration.

† In 1834, Dorothée said that her life, her habits and her whole existence had long ago been absorbed by Talleyrand's needs. Eight years later, she added: "The thing I have least forgotten from my past life, it seems to me, is my capacity for submission." To this can be added the testimony of an observer, Mme de Laval's grandson Sosthène de Rochefoucauld, who wrote: "In her role as an old man's right hand she was always able, while he lived, to conceal her own importance and personal ambition.

"Her life was fused, as it were, with that of another."

chances of ever returning to power seemed very slender, at least while the elder Bourbon branch retained the throne, and the star of the Orléans had not yet risen.

The hope of an inheritance then? But Dorothée had never loved money for money's sake. Besides, despite the inroads that Edmond had made into her fortune, she was wealthy, and would grow daily wealthier now that peace had been restored.

To avenge herself on her mother? That might have held true in 1814 and 1815 for an affair lasting only a few months. It could not be true now, not when applied to a decision that would commit her for life.

It could therefore only have been a choice of the man for the man's sake, with all his defects as well as his good qualities.

The difference in their ages was a matter of no more than relative and trifling importance to the future Duchess of Dino. She herself is categorical on this point: "If, in the course of my life, there appears any cause for astonishment that a great difference of ages has never seemed to me anything more than a slight inconvenience in the various relations of society, it is only necessary to cast the mind back to that period when, though little more than a child, I was accustoming my mind to the idea of marrying a man who was twenty-five years older than myself."

Aging, infirm, Talleyrand still possessed an indisputable attraction. Aimée de Coigny, mistress at one time to Biron and at other times to many others, as well as Montrond's wife for a fleeting instant, spoke of "the inexpressible charm that M. de Talleyrand knew so well how to radiate when he did not choose to cloak that quality in a disdainful silence." "In spite of everything, Talleyrand has a great attraction," the Marquise de la Tour du Pin was to say in her turn. "He fascinates one the way a snake fascinates a bird."

Dorothée doubtless felt this power too, but the presence of its possessor also produced in her a pleasurable sensation of security. Though endowed with a mind of such virility, she was very feminine in many of her reactions. She was easily frightened, and wept with fear while crossing the Rhine in the dark as also on certain mountain roads. She felt a need for reliable masculine protection, and Talleyrand was able to provide her with it where the weak Edmond and the too-youthful Clam had failed.

Lastly, there was the heady knowledge, for this possessive woman whose childhood and youth had been unhappy and somewhat scant of love, that she was sole and absolute ruler of Talleyrand's heart and mind. For with his great experience of women Talleyrand had not miscalculated on that score. He knew that his dependence and his weakness would guarantee him victory far more surely than his prestige, no matter how great that might be. "It is so rare," he said later when talking to Dorothée of the affection she inspired in him, "to have someone who is entirely one's own, without any mental reservations, without secrets from one, without divergent interests. . . ."

Yet all that was almost of secondary importance. What really bound Talleyrand and Dorothée together, what linked them to one another so indissolubly, was the attraction that their minds had for each other; it was the kinship of their souls.

Talleyrand was able to say to his niece: "With you one can simply skip over the intermediate ideas. Your mind never puts its brakes on, and in that way you've ceased to be German. You've remained so in all your habits except those of the mind; that has no more of an accent than your speech." Equally, Talleyrand's conversation was for Dorothée a constant joy and pleasure, and she later said, with melancholy: "My long acquaintance with M. de Talleyrand's expressive powers have made me difficult to please where the rest of the world is concerned. The minds I encounter now seem to me slow, diffused, too easily distracted by trivial details; they are forever putting their brakes on [exactly Talleyrand's own expression] like people going cautiously downhill; I have spent my life with the feeling that we were urging the wheels to go faster, like people climbing a hill." Talleyrand was aware of how valuable and important this deep harmony between them was. He said to Dorothée when she was still a young woman, and perhaps wrote it to her when she was in Vienna: "You must agree that it would be very wrong of us to deprive ourselves of one another since I should forfeit my agility and you your repose."

Kinship of soul as well. Talleyrand and Dorothée had both suffered from restrictions of the same kind, they had both been scarred, one might even say mutilated, by their experiences in the same way, with this one difference—and it is a considerable one—that Dorothée, always more upright, never lost her lucidity of conscience despite the errors she committed, whereas Talleyrand often tried to ignore his. "His conscience was weak because it lacked enlightenment," Dorothée said in 1840. She returned to the subject in 1849 when discussing the newly published *Mémoires d'Outre-Tombe:* "I would not attempt to deny that my poor uncle was a great sinner, but I should prefer to face my eternal judgment with his weak conscience than with this man's, full of pride and malice, spleen and envy. . . ." This kinship of soul led to the creation between Talleyrand and Dorothée of an unwritten pact. Talleyrand was closer to Dorothée than any of her own relations ever had been or ever were to be. They could converse in the most darkly veiled of hints, yet they never hid anything that was in their hearts.

"What people term friends seem to me extremely inadequate," the uncle said to his niece. "It is you who will remain the dominant interest in my life, firstly because you have all that it requires to retain a man, and secondly because there is nothing I fear in your thoughts. You know all my advantages and disadvantages; you have weighed them against each other in the scales; the balance, the difference, is in my favor."

F OR FOURTEEN years, during which Talleyrand was constantly
angling for the power that as constantly eluded him, Dorothée
led an existence half in shadow, half in sunlight.

The sunlight was her life with Talleyrand, entirely occupied
by her devotion to the uncle who was always in the center of
the stage. The supporting cast: a confidante, Countess Tyszkiewicz; a few friends, the Baron de Vitrolles, Prosper de
Barante, Royer-Collard; her relatives, the Duchess of Courland,
Edmond, who reappeared for a few years before the final
scandal; and finally, her children—Pauline, born in 1820, Alexandre, and Louis.

The shadow was Dorothée's personal life. Morally, the
stormy interlude in Vienna had laid her waste. Emerging from
the numbing influence of her unfortunate marriage, Dorothée
had discovered her true self. This new woman, despite the profound affection for Talleyrand that her few impulsive and
short-lived attempts at independence were never able to shake,
was also a prey, often a pitiable one, often against her will,*
to her own imperious inner necessities, and perhaps to her
curiosity. Both led her inevitably into amorous adventures.

There can be no doubt that Dorothée's life under the
Restoration was traversed by a series of ephemeral and almost
furtive figures, figures whose meaning one can only guess at
without being able to give them names, who flitted across the
luminous screen of her existence on the Rue Saint-Florentin like
so many blurred and indistinguishable silhouettes. Then there
was the long liaison that rumor hinted at with Piscatory. These

---

* Of the Duchess of Broglie, and of a letter written by that lady to
Schlegel, Dorothée wrote in 1857: "The Duchess has obviously suffered from
a lack of affection, but she has not been swayed by the claims of her physical
constitution, and the extreme frigidity that governs her every phrase is proof
that she was able to content herself with abstractions. God was very merciful
to her! Such aridity, or at least imperviousness, is sometimes a great aid to
virtue."

brief encounters, and possibly a long attachment, left on Dorothée's soul, only a little drying foam as the ebb tide leaves a line of wrack along the beach. Though still young, her expression became harder, overcast. Her social position was precarious; her great name and her great wealth could not have saved her from the corrosive tongues of a hostile world had Talleyrand not been there to keep her folded in his protective cloak of passionate and indulgent tenderness.

On March 23, 1816, Miss Mary Berry attended a musical evening at Talleyrand's house "that is to say chez la Comtesse Edmond de Périgord, his niece . . . whom he has separated from his nephew . . . and has taken her to live with himself *dans toute l'étendue du terme à ce qu'on dit. Figurez-vous* that she is not five and twenty and has a head more like a pretty little serpent than anything I ever saw. . . ."

Miss Berry was an acid-tongued old maid. But her remarks do contain something confirmed by Charles de Rémusat, who says that Dorothée "was henceforth to be mistress of the Talleyrand household, that she was all-powerful there, that she was decidedly a woman of intelligence, and that she had extremely fine eyes."

The prune of yesteryear had not filled out very much, he continues, "but nevertheless she now had a grander and more imposing manner, a supple and noble bearing, and the face of a bird of prey. Her complexion was still dark and sallow, her eyes, ringed with dark circles, were in fact of a fairly light blue, but so brilliant that one imagined them to be a most beautiful black. Her nose, delicately modeled into an imperious prominence, and the two vermilion patches on her cheeks would have given her a hard look had not the bold and haughty lines of her face been contradicted by a gaze of velvety gentleness and a slow, caressing mode of speech that produced quite the opposite impression."

Apart from these accounts left by contemporary memoir writers, there is also the evidence of the painters. Prud'hon painted Dorothée's portrait in about 1816. It shows us a woman, clothed in furs and white satin, with diamonds in her hair and at her ears, asserting her recent rebirth in Vienna. The tempests of life have swept away the candor, the innocence, the air of hope and expectation seen in the Valençay portrait. The face is gracefully sophisticated. The large, sad eyes are full of intelligence, their expression knowledgeable, determined, and above all inscrutable. A disquieting tranquillity. A tough fragility. An unyielding pliability. In short, a woman who has made her choice, and one who will henceforth continue along her chosen road without fear of the obstacles she may meet.

This was the woman who moved into the house on the Rue Saint-Florentin if not ostentatiously—she had too much good taste for that—at least without any attempt at concealment. And once settled in there she adopted the tone and the bearing that befitted the mistress of such a house.*

There was no way of glossing over the fact that Countess Edmond de Périgord was living under her uncle's roof and not under that of the husband from whom she was in no way legally separated, not even financially,† but the house on the Rue Saint-Florentin was sufficiently large for the preservation of appearances.‡ On the mezzanine, in the right wing giving onto the Rue de Rivoli, were Talleyrand's apartments consisting of six rooms. On the floor above, the great drawing-rooms facing the Tuileries; on the opposite side of the courtyard, Dorothée's apartments. The house also contained a whole little world of permanent guests: Perrey, the secretary, Neukomm, the musician, Bertrand, once the resident friend of Mme de Souza, but who had opted for a more comfortable berth in 1814. Lastly, Alexandre de Talleyrand and his wife Charlotte were still staying in the vast house that was the birthplace of all four of their children.

Once this new situation had been imposed on the Talley-

---

* Dorothée had already been a resident of the Talleyrand town house in 1815, but her stay then had been only of a temporary nature from the start, quite unlike her return in 1816.

† Edmond was still living on the Rue de la Grange-Batelière.

‡ This same concern for keeping up appearances was the reason for Countess Tyszkiewicz's becoming Talleyrand's and Dorothée's perpetual chaperone. The Countess accompanied them on all the journeys they made together under the Restoration, whether to Bourbon-l'Archambault, Cauterets, or to the South of France. She was also a more or less permanent guest at Valençay. Dorothée always retained very grateful memories of this woman who had been so good a friend and sometimes so very helpful a one.

rand family, accepted by the Duchess of Courland,* and recognized by society, Talleyrand and Dorothée left at the end of April or during early May 1816, for Valençay. There was nothing to keep Talleyrand in Paris, and he was aware of his niece's preference for country life, with its independence and its almost feudal relations between château and village. For his sake, Dorothée gave up the idea of living at Rosny, or at any of her properties in Prussia; instead, she accepted his offer of Valençay, a vast 45,000 acre property in the heart of Berry, far from any stagecoach or post horse route, and a twenty-hour carriage journey from Paris.

Dorothée had never been to Valençay. Talleyrand had not been back there since 1808. Everything would have to be repaired, everything needed refurbishing from top to bottom. Yet they liked living there from the very first. "With a little trouble," the Prince wrote to Besnardière soon after their arrival, "Valençay can be made one of the finest places it would be possible to live in," and the Prefect of the Indre, a visiting spy, remarked that Talleyrand was apparently preparing for a prolonged stay there.

For ten years, until the time when Rochecotte also began to claim a share in their existence, it was at Valençay, in the immense Renaissance château with its twenty-five main suites of rooms, beneath the shade of the great covered avenue, "wonderful during the heat," that Talleyrand and Dorothée lived their sweetest moments. And it was there, too, that they showed themselves in their best and perhaps their truest light.

After several weeks at Valençay, Talleyrand was obliged by his duties as Grand Chamberlain and the marriage of the Duke of Berry to return to Paris. Dorothée, however, remained in the country, happy to be free of Paris. This separation, the first

* After the first moments of acrimony in 1815, the Duchess of Courland had resigned herself, perhaps consoled herself, and the harmony between herself, Talleyrand, and Dorothée was never to be broken again.

since Dorothée's return from Vienna and the decision on both sides to spend their lives together, was the occasion of numerous messages between uncle and niece. One of Dorothée's letters to Talleyrand, written on June 4, 1816, has been published. It sheds a great deal of light, not only on what she thought about her liaison with Clam and about the feelings and mutual trust now uniting her with Talleyrand, but also on the undisputed sway she now intended to hold over the Prince's life.*

" A thousand thank yous for your letter of the 2nd. I need the knowledge that every day will bring me a proof of your affection. The two thick letters you sent on to me were from M. de C.; one was written on May 16, fresher by six days than the one I told you all about in my previous instalments, the other is only an envelope containing a portrait I had written to ask him for. . . . Not content with simply returning it, he seized the occasion to write a big letter at the same time full of the same unpleasant things contained in his previous epistle. At all events, I am glad to have the portrait back again, and also he offers me a generous assurance of the profoundest forgetfulness on his part, adding that he is trying to erase from his mind the memory of all the humiliations he has suffered and which are still being inflicted on him daily. He tells me he has read the letters I wrote to my sisters and to Gentz, so that he now realizes how enchanted I was to come back and is himself very angry at my not having taken the step much more speedily, thus rescuing him even earlier from a dream that was still making him a daily amusement for all the world. . . .† His conclusion is an eternal farewell, which I echo with all my heart. That is a

---

* It seems that there were once as many as three thousand letters and short messages in the Sagan archives written to one another by Talleyrand and Dorothée. When Lacour-Gayet was writing his monumental work he was unable to obtain access to them. What happened to all these records of a twenty-five year intimacy? The Sagan archives were still intact at the end of the last war, and were removed from the chateau at that time by two men, one in the uniform of a French officer, the other in that of an American officer. They took everything, except for four boxes containing documents pertaining to the property, and since that time, which is to say for twenty years, no one has so much as heard of any of the material they removed.

† On March 29, 1816, Gentz noted: "Clam arrived with Prince Schwarzenburg; we had a painful discussion of his relationship with Mme de Périgord. . . ."

précis of the principal contents of his latest letter. It is now quite clear that my sisters must bear a very large responsibility for all this ranting and raving. The satisfaction I expressed at my return to France has wounded them deeply. There is one section of this letter that I must translate for you, since it will prove to you the truth of what I wrote yesterday, which is that Wil [the Duchess of Sagan] has made Gentz recant.

" 'Despite the changeableness of Gentz's character, which caused him to pay you a great many tributes for a period of time, he is too much my friend for his advice not to be identical now with that of all the other persons who have my interests at heart. The illness was too serious for the cure to be an easy one, but it is already too complete for me not to deplore the shame of having been no more than the instrument of a caprice.'

"This last letter proves to me that the only proper reply now left to me is the profoundest silence. . . . But how many sad reflections for the rest of my life! You have often enough blamed me for not resenting certain offenses acutely enough; if you knew how much the indelicate behavior of all those creatures makes me hate them you would be pleased with me indeed. . . .

"I have thought a great deal about Mme de T . . . 's reply; it makes me more and more apprehensive that she is suddenly going to walk into your room one of these days.* She will then begin by telling you that she means to stay only a few hours, but that she wants an explanation from your own lips; all this in the hope of extracting a little more money from you. The only suitable course, both from her point of view and from yours, is to make her stay in England. . . . Since money is the only real motive for all of Mme de T . . . 's actions . . . one must always start from that premise in any dealing with her, and I shall now make bold to offer you a piece of advice along these lines that will spare you a meeting both painful and repugnant from your point of view. Here it is. Send someone to her straight

---

* Mme de Talleyrand, finding England tedious, had taken up residence at Pont-de-Sains, a property that Talleyrand had legally made over to her. There was reason to fear that she might indeed return from the north to the Rue Saint-Florentin.

away, not anyone devious like Roux, but make M. Perrey go to
her with a kind of letter of credit; let him be instructed by you
to tell Mme de T. . . that she shan't get her hands on another
farthing of the allowance you make her until she's back in
England, and that she's not going to get another penny out
of you other than that. Let M. Perrey escort her as far as Calais
or Ostend and not leave her until he has seen her onto the ship.
It is very good advice I'm giving you, I assure you, and you
would be wrong not to follow it.*

"The Princess [Countess Tysziekiewicz, née Princess Ponia-
towska] is making me take ass's milk twice a day; I didn't spit
any blood last night and limited myself to a few coughs; the fine
weather is a good medicine, but you are my best doctor. Alas!
the date of your return to me is put off again. It is no longer
the end of the marriage festivities but Charlotte's confinement
I must wait for, and it seems to me that she is determined never
to conclude that tremendous affair! . . ."

Charles de Rémusat went to visit the *curé* † on June 18,
1816, a few days after this letter was written, and noticed that
the usually taciturn Talleyrand was in a state of exuberant
delight. "He is both enchanted and enchanting; he laughs at
everything and is pleased with everything; it's impossible to
make him find a fault anywhere. He claims that he is going
back into the country."

◇   ◇   ◇

Made happy by Dorothée's presence and the existence they
had now established together, Talleyrand was able to forget his

---

* Mme de Talleyrand was not lacking in common sense, as we have
already said. She bowed before the inevitable and declared herself "extremely
willing to avoid anything that might increase the scandal." Talleyrand consequently continued to pay her an annual allowance of thirty thousand francs,
which was doubled in 1826 when the Princess gave up Pont-de-Sains. Mme
de Talleyrand's exile in England did not last long however; she soon returned
to Paris, but never again crossed the threshold of the house on the Rue
Saint-Florentin.

† Mme de Rémusat's nickname for Talleyrand.

ambitions for several weeks. But the desire for power was too strong in both of them for this respite to be of very long duration. For six successive years, until Villèle's rise to power in December of 1821, Talleyrand constantly believed himself to be on the verge of being made Premier again. Like an animal seeking to start its quarry, he zig-zagged from one opposition party to another, at one moment a Liberal, at another an Ultra. And only when every path to power had been definitely closed to him did he finally settle for freedom from all political affiliation.

Talleyrand's wavering allegiances, and Dorothée's broadness of mind—for she had no prejudices about birth where her friendships were concerned—left the drawing rooms on the Rue Saint Florentin without any particular political tinge. As well as Frenchmen of various backgrounds, professions, and opinions, one also saw a great many diplomats and foreigners there. This latter group did at least succeed in raising the tone of a circle that, in the eyes of the Faubourg Saint-Germain, and even in those of the Faubourg Saint-Honoré, seemed sometimes a little too mixed. Dorothée held impartial sway over all alike with imperious grace and a restrained ardor, although that ardor was not without its element of violence. She was angered by the restored government's neglect of Talleyrand. And her advice, though it did not yet carry sufficient weight with Talleyrand to restrain him from any action, had she desired to do so, could on occasion incline him to take a strong stand against the government.

Vienna had shown Dorothée the power she could command. In Paris, still timid where her admired and beloved uncle was concerned, uncertain of her exact position in a society to which she always remained a foreigner and was for much of the time an object of hostility, she used that power without forethought, with a kind of fever. Not until her London years, by which time she had attained a genuine confidence in her influence with Talleyrand and in her own social pre-eminence, did she display the full measure of mental stability and serenity of which she was capable.

A diatribe against the French government, delivered at the British Embassy during November of 1816, earned Talleyrand an injunction against appearing at the Tuileries. When the prohibition was rescinded, in March 1817, he walked back into the royal presence as though nothing had happened. Appearances were deceptive. His stock of favor with the sovereign of a regime that was already intent on passing him over had dwindled even further on account of the incident.

In January 1817, during the period of his deepest political disgrace, Talleyrand had approached Metternich with an offer to sell the Emperor of Austria all the correspondence addressed to Napoleon between his return from Egypt and the end of 1806, Napoleon's own correspondence with the Duke of Cadure in 1807 and 1808, and Napoleon's correspondence with the Duke of Bassano in 1813, all of which documents Talleyrand had "taken with him" at the time of his most recent departure from the Ministry for Foreign Affairs. Metternich had seemed interested in the offer, and Talleyrand's return to favor did not interrupt the negotiations. As his final price for these documents, Talleyrand asked the Austrian Chancellor, in March of 1817, for five hundred thousand francs in the form of money orders made payable to bearer and cashable on a fixed date, together with "an authorization from the Emperor in person for myself and my family to take up residence in Vienna, or in some other part of his dominions selected by us, should circumstances in France ever become such as to render my departure from that country imperative." *

Shameful bargains of this sort were nothing new to Talleyrand, and we cannot attribute this one to Dorothée's influence.† Yet there is something unprecedented here all the same: together with the usual preoccupation with money, this new desire for a safe retreat outside France, away from Paris. Such thoughts could scarcely have been strangers to Dorothée.

International by birth, German by education, Dorothée loved neither France nor the French. Nor is it difficult to understand her lack of attachment to the country that had given her

* These letters were published in the *Revue de Paris*, December 15, 1933.
† Dorothée was nevertheless aware of the transaction. Talleyrand ended his letter to Metternich written on March 6, 1817 with the words: "Madame de Périgord asks me to send you a thousand kind thoughts."

Edmond de Périgord. But she should have had some feeling for a country that was, after all, her children's home.*

Talleyrand was thus preparing a retreat in Austria. Meanwhile, in France, he was attempting to take advantage of his return to favor in order to have Valençay decreed an hereditary dukedom transmissible to his brother Archambauld and then to Edmond.† The reason for this rise in rank was to have been the services rendered by the Prince of Benevento to the King of Spain. Louis XVIII prudently replied that he would consult His Catholic Majesty. Early in July of 1817, Ferdinand VII let it be known that he would prefer not to have his captivity commemorated by the creation of a dukedom.

Talleyrand and Dorothée spent that summer at Cauterets. They had just left the Pyrenees with the intention of traveling for a few weeks through south-east France when a decree signed by Louis XVIII on August 31, 1817, made Talleyrand a duke. A further decree, issued on October 28, authorized him, after the institution of an entail, to transmit his rank, title and dignity of Hereditary Duke and Peer of the Realm to his brother Archambauld.

Aside from this, the King of Naples had already granted Talleyrand, on November 2, 1815, the title of Duke of the Kingdom of the Two Sicilies, together with a yearly revenue of sixty thousand francs.‡ A decree issued two years later added to this title the name of a property in Calabria, or more precisely, that of a royal island in the Gulf of Policastro. The decree also authorized the title to be transmitted immediately to Edmond de Périgord. Several days later, Talleyrand wrote with satisfaction

---

* Dorothée later recognized her error on this score. In 1859, she wrote to her granddaughter, Marie de Castellane, who had become a German through her marriage to Prince Antoine Radziwill: "Princess Victoria, since she has a husband and a child, should try to forget her English ways a little. One must belong body and soul to the country of one's husband and one's children on penalty of becoming a burden and cause of unhappiness to oneself and an object of displeasure as well as a cause of unhappiness to others." Dorothée must certainly have been thinking back to her own past life.

† It is worth recalling that until this time it was for Edmond alone that Talleyrand had sought the transmissibility in 1809, then the dukedom in 1814.

‡ This was Ferdinand's way of buying back the principality of Benevento. Talleyrand's help in ousting Murat had already been rewarded with a sum of six million francs.

to the Duchess of Courland: "Today, Dorothée enters into enjoyment of all those advantages at court pertaining to the title of duchess." We can suppose that a desire to gratify the wishes of the new Duchess of Dino, to assure her during Archambauld's lifetime of a title sufficient to flatter any vanity and with which all Dorothée's older sisters were already furnished, was one of Talleyrand's major motives for his concern with achieving this family promotion.

It was in 1817, then, that Dorothée assumed the title of Duchess of Dino, by which she has always generally been known in France. This same year was also the one in which her life took on the rhythm that was to characterize it for some time to come. Resentful at his exclusion from power (Castellane claimed that the very sight of a Minister for Foreign Affairs made Talleyrand ill), increasingly influenced by Dorothée, this man in his sixties who had been exclusively a city dweller for so long, of whom no one under the Empire would have believed it possible that he could spend his evenings anywhere but in an atmosphere such as that provided by Mme de Laval or the Princess of Vaudémont, this salon-dweller suddenly discovered in himself the soul of a great landowner. He began to take a growing interest in Valençay, in possible improvements, in planting trees and laying out the park, and several months of every year were now given over to these new pursuits.

Talleyrand and his niece would leave Paris in April or May, taking Countess Tyszkiewicz and the Dino children with them, and accompanied each year by an ever-growing retinue. Besides Neukomm and Perrey, there were Thierry, Louis and Alexandre de Périgord's tutor, Andral the doctor, and of course the innumerable members of the domestic staff.

This vast caravan would descend on Valençay and stay there several weeks. The Prince and Dorothée then went to take the waters during July and August, still accompanied by the Countess, the children, the tutor, the doctor, and a full complement of personal servants. September would find them back in Berry surrounded by a host of ever-changing guests.*

* On October 21, 1818, Dorothée wrote to Vitrolles: "It is eleven in the evening and I must leave you now to go make tea for the twenty or so people who are still with us here . . ."

Finally, and regretfully, they would tear themselves away in November, when his duties at court and the opening of the Chambers once more made the presence of the Grand Chamberlain and Peer of the Realm necessary in Paris.

For four or five months, Talleyrand then received in his salons in town. During the winter of 1817-1818, he gave a reception every Monday, and on some evenings five hundred people passed through the great drawing rooms on the Rue Saint-Florentin. The succession of great dinners continued even through Lent. Then Easter came; it was time for the exodus to Berry, and the cycle began again.

◇ ◇ ◇

Because of his hostility towards Richelieu, who was attempting to follow a moderate if not exactly liberal political line, Talleyrand had moved closer to the Ultras. One of the members of this latter group was the same Baron de Vitrolles who had made the acquaintance of the Duchess of Courland and Batowski in 1797 and who, in 1814, had delivered the letter to Allied headquarters conveying Talleyrand's demand for an advance on Paris.

A new European congress was scheduled to take place during the autumn of 1818 at Aix-la-Chapelle, and Richelieu was counting on this opportunity to achieve an evacuation of the territories still occupied by the Allies. The Ultras, on the other hand, were anxious to use it as an occasion for airing their views on the internal situation in France before the Holy Alliance. Vitrolles, by then a member of the Privy Council and the cabinet of Ministers, composed a note, on Monsieur's orders, that he would apparently have liked ratified by Talleyrand.

He was well aware of Dorothée's influence over her uncle: "She possessed over him both *the rights of a mind strong and firm in its power of conception* and also those accruing to her from a long acquaintance with the intimate conversations and long nights of discussion that the Prince liked to prolong sometimes until two or three o'clock in the morning. Her quick and lofty apprehension could accommodate itself to any subject; she helped M. de Talleyrand to think and forced him to crystallize and complete those thoughts that, without her, would have remained vague and useless. More, she often inspired him. Her mind was swift and took huge strides, so that she needed fewer words to understand things than other women."

Vitrolles went to see Dorothée and entreated her to obtain a promise from her uncle that he would be the Ultras' spokesman. "The Duchess of Dino transfixed this idea with her eagle glance without discussing it, without approving it. She asked me to apply directly to M. de Talleyrand, saying that she would speak to him in favor of the request after it had been made. Whereupon a meeting was arranged for the following day."

The negotiations came to nothing. Vitrolles, having been compromised shortly afterward by certain intrigues against the government, was disgraced in July of 1818 and ceased to be a member of both the Privy Council and the Cabinet. Nevertheless, that first meeting was the origin of a long intimacy between Vitrolles and Dorothée that continued throughout the Restoration, and the letters written by Dorothée to this friend—who would have liked to be more than that—constitute a very interesting commentary on the period between 1816 and 1830. Thanks to them, the veil is lifted for a moment. We are given a glimpse of Dorothée as a being very much alive, with her affection for Talleyrand, her intelligent concern for her sons, and her fits of anger, her passions, and her moments of repentance as well.

The guardianship that Talleyrand had managed to obtain over Edmond's estate had not been able to palliate the effects of his nephew's riotous living. In November 1817, the Prince had dismissed the idea of selling Rosny; in August 1818, he was forced to resign himself to it, and the château of Sully became the favorite residence of the Duchess of Berry.

Nothing now remained of the three millions that the Duke of Dino had inherited from his mother, and his continued prodigality had already made large inroads into his wife's fortune as well. But that was not the worst: Edmond also had unpaid debts, and his creditors now had him at bay. Dorothée asked for a legal separation of their estates and received it in March of 1818, after a full court hearing—the latter being a prudent measure that Talleyrand must have approved of if not himself suggested.

Their financial affairs once settled in this way, a *modus vivendi* without any trace of bitterness seems to have been reached by both parties, who had been separated in fact for several years already. The Duke of Dino was now living on the Rue d'Aguesseau, the Duchess still on the Rue Saint-Florentin, but they occasionally found themselves beneath the same roof. In October 1818, Dorothée wrote to Vitrolles: "M. de Dino, my father-in-law, and a great many others have arrived [at Valençay] without your having sent me a word by any of them. . . ."

Indeed, if one were to follow blindly the entries in the *Almanach des 25,000 Adresses,* one might even be led to believe that the Duchess of Dino spent the years 1820 and 1821 living with her husband on the Rue d'Aguesseau. Whereas in 1822 and 1823, Edmond de Périgord seems to have migrated to the Rue Saint-Florentin.

The information is of course erroneous, but the errors may have been deliberate, though there was in fact a reconciliation between the two in 1820. The Duke of Dino accepted an invitation to move into Talleyrand's house,* and on December 29 of the same year the Duchess gave birth to a daughter, Pauline. Six months later, Edmond de Périgord left for England.† When he returned, in September 1821, he moved back into the house on the Rue D'Aguesseau.

The couple's decision to live together once more, then the

* We may be certain that Dorothée did not go to live on the Rue d'Aguesseau. Firstly we know that Gustave Parthey, a young German archeologist who had been Dorothée's playmate at Löbikau, came to Paris in 1820 and dined at the Talleyrand house. After the meal, the Duchess's sons recited passages from *Iphigénie,* and extremely well too, for children of seven and nine. Secondly, on May 9, 1821, Edmond wrote to Latour-Maubourg, the Minister of War, asking to be made a Grand Officer of the Legion of Honor, reminding him of the promise Talleyrand had extracted from him on November 8, 1820. The heading of Edmond's letter gives his address as Rue Saint-Florentin.

† When the War Office expressed astonishment, on August 7, 1821, at the Duke of Dino's absence from his post as a Commanding Officer, the Minister replied, on August 17, that the General had been in London since July 5 on official business. (The last few words were later erased.)

birth of Pauline de Périgord, created great astonishment, so great in fact that there were attempts to discover hidden reasons, and rumors began to circulate attributing the paternity of the child to others than Edmond, and above all to Talleyrand.* These rumors were given substance by the separation in the autumn of 1821. Ought we to believe today that they had any real foundation?

The problem still remains impossible of solution. None of those concerned—Dorothée, Talleyrand, or even Edmond— ever made any comment, and since the last two were uncle and nephew all speculation as to the child's resemblance to Talleyrand is pointless.†

One can do no more than set out a certain number of facts that bear upon Talleyrand's and Edmond's behavior at the time, note certain reactions at court and in society, and recall several veiled confidences made by Dorothée herself.

From the time of Edmond's appointment on September 8, 1815, to his command of the 2nd brigade of the 1st division of the Royal Cavalry Guard, Talleyrand had not once asked for a favor specifically for his nephew. In October or November of 1820, he asked that the Duke of Dino be made a Grand Officer of the Legion of Honor.

At about the same time, all Edmond's debts were paid off, apparently by his uncle.

Talleyrand always displayed a tender predilection for Pauline. One may certainly find it natural that he should have felt a particular attachment for the child of a woman that he loved, a child raised under his own roof, and a child, furthermore, whose nature was of the rarest quality. One may certainly think

* In August of 1820, Mme de Souza told her son, Charles de Flahaut, that Montrond had just returned from a visit to Valençay: "Mme Dorothée has turned mystic. Poor Edmond is obliged to play the part of a pitiful spectator to this pregnancy produced by the grace of God." Only we must remember that Mme de Souza had severed all relations with Talleyrand after a quarrel in 1815 and that she disliked Dorothée.

† Pauline de Périgord resembled her mother, according to Rémusat, "but with a turned up nose that was sufficient to lend an air of likelihood to Talleyrand's possible paternity." Marie de Castellane, Pauline's daughter, bore an astonishing resemblance to Charlotte, Talleyrand's daughter.

also that it is difficult to distinguish between fatherly and grandfatherly affection in a very old man. But it should be emphasized nevertheless that Talleyrand's predilection for Pauline was absolute, that he never gave the same degree of affection either to Dorothée's sons or to any of Charlotte's children, all of whom also lived on the Rue Saint-Florentin. We should also add that this predilection took a tangible form in his will. Not content with making the Duchess of Dino his residuary legatee, he also made a specific bequest to Pauline of his property of Pont-de-Sains, which represented an income of about eighty thousand *livres*. Neither Charlotte nor Alexandre, Dorothée's second son, nor his niece Georgine d'Esclignac, his brother Boson's daughter, received anywhere near so much.

The first separation of Count and Countess Edmond de Périgord had taken place without any fuss, and with the consent of both parties; the second required the interference of the law.

In the autumn of 1824, Dorothée presented to the President of the Lower Court of the Seine a request in which, after giving the history of her marriage and emphasizing Edmond's latest move to the Rue d'Aguesseau, she declared: "Our relations and common friends have made the strongest protests to him on the subject of this domestic separation and the consequences that it would have for the honor of his wife and the future of their children. Several times, she [the Duchess] has urged him, both verbally and in writing, to return to his uncle's house; she has also offered to leave that house herself and to go to live with him. He has rejected both of these suggestions. . . ."

The request concluded: "Given this situation, the plaintiff cannot remain any longer under the jurisdiction of a husband who, while refusing to afford her the protection that he owes her, at the same time gives reasons for this refusal that compromise her honor. She requests that she be granted a legal separation of persons and authorized to continue residing with her children in the house of the Prince de Talleyrand, her husband's uncle."

On November 4, 1824, the President of the Lower Court of the Seine issued an order that the Justice of the Peace for the 1st arrondissement, accompanied by a clerk, should question the Duke of Dino. This interrogation took place on November 6 and an official report of it was drawn up. "We proceeded with Mme the Duchess of Dino to her husband's new domicile, No. 20, Rue d'Aguesseau, and upon our arrival and entry into an apartment on the second floor . . . before us there appeared M. the Duke of Dino . . . to whom we then announced the motives of our proceeding thither, while declaring the presence of Madame the Duchess, his wife, outside in his antechamber.

"M. the Duke of Dino, after having listened to the document we read out to him . . . , declared to us that he persisted in the reply by him made to the bailiff who had presented himself at his door on October 30 last, that in consequence he must return an absolute and formal refusal to receive Madame the Duchess his wife into his house, or to go to live with her, for serious reasons that he believed it his duty not to disclose.

"And on the observations and representations that we then made to him that he ought not to restrict himself to such vagueness of expression and that it was proper that he make known to us the motives for his refusal, so that we might judge how far they might have good foundation.

"M. the Duke of Dino once more declared to us that he would not disclose the motives for his refusal, in which he still persisted, and that he would not even see Mme the Duchess.

"Whereat, this report having been by him read, M. the Duke of Dino did set his hand to it."

If we ignore the ludicrous legal jargon in which this report is written and attempt to see what lies behind it, what do we find? The suspicion that husband and wife had entered into a secret agreement for the purpose of obtaining the legal separation they both desired with a minimum of fuss. But what had driven them to such an extremity when they had already managed to live apart in fact for five years without any need for invoking the law? Furthermore, their relations at that time were lacking in the usual forbearance observed by members of high society. Had the reconciliation of 1820 sown seeds of bitterness then between this husband and wife already so ill-equipped to understand one another? * Both these questions must remain unanswered.

Twenty years later, on October 26, 1840, Fortunée Hamelin, who was very well acquainted with all the affairs of the Talleyrand family because of her intimate relationship with Montrond, but who was also extremely hostile to Dorothée, wrote: "Berryer's plan at that time was to take the Archbishop of Paris into his confidence and to win that prelate's support as a means of forcing the Duchess to deal honorably with a husband who had spared her the scandal and the exile that she would have received at the hands on any other."

A detail that should be mentioned, however, is that shortly after her marriage, and again when she became a widow, Pauline went to visit the Duke of Dino in Florence and was received warmly by him.

Louis XVIII and the Duchess of Angoulême had accepted Dorothée's departure for Vienna with placidity. In 1816, the court displayed the same calm when confronted with her occupancy of the Talleyrand house on the Rue Saint-Florentin, and the newly created Duchess of Dino had taken part in a quadrille during the course of a ball given by the Duchess of Berry in January of 1818.

The separation in the autumn of 1821, however, was viewed from the Tuileries without indulgence, possibly because the prevailing temper of the times had changed from one of tolerance to one of greater austerity, possibly because the King wished to demonstrate in this way his sour reaction to Talleyrand's opposition, or possibly because the Duchess of Angoulême and the Duchess of Berry had been influenced by the rest of the Talleyrand family—Countess Just de Noailles was one of the Duchess of Berry's ladies-in-waiting—who had sided with Edmond in this matter, though without actually breaking off relations either with Talleyrand or Dorothée.†

* On July 6, 1826, Dorothée wrote to Vitrolles: "Fire and water sort better with one another than do M. and Mme. de Dino."

† The eyes of the other Talleyrands were fixed with too much interest upon the Prince's inheritance, and their anger at Dorothée's ever-increasing influence over him was too great for them to allow her to do just as she liked. But the fortunes of their house still remained indissolubly linked to those of Talleyrand.

Dorothée scarecely appeared at all at court any more, limiting herself to two brief and shadowy curtsies before the King's armchair every year. The residents of the Palais-Royal displayed less severity towards her, and it was perhaps this kindly attitude on their part that finally decided Talleyrand in favor of the Orléans branch. This "outcry from the Tuileries" (the phrase is Dorothée's own) had repercussions upon society. Certain salons half closed their doors; close social ties were broken.*

This censure on the part of society was a source of pain to Dorothée. The Duchess of Broglie met her at a dinner given by the Duke of Orléans early in 1822 and remarked upon the change in her physiognomy. "She has beautiful features, but one feels that she is being eaten up by some inner anxiety. Her eyes have a piercing blaze to them, and the expression on her face is older than her years. . . ." In her *Souvenirs,* Dorothée speaks with rancor of the severity and injustice of the judgments that French society saw fit to pass upon her at that time. In 1830, after her return from England, she was to return to the subject again, though this time without bitterness: "All the little wounds that one person or another inflicted on me in the past are erased by a single pleasant word or kindly glance directed at Pauline. It is certainly much better not to declare war on society, but when one has committed that error, or suffered that misfortune, it is sweet beyond everything to effect a reconciliation through one's daughter."

Her horror of Paris dates from those uncertain days of the Restoration. Dorothée had never cared for the city. From this time on she was to detest and fear it. "There is a rift between myself and Paris that may never be mended," she wrote to Barante on January 31, 1826. Ten years later, in September 1835, she confessed once more: "It is still a considerable event for me to drive back into Paris. I have passed so many disagreeable moments there: my whole past unfurls before me as I make my way along those streets, across those squares, all of them filled with memories, and mostly painful ones."

* "During the Restoration, Mme de Castellane denied me," wrote the Duchess of Dino in 1834, "and without thinking of the harm it was in my power to do her [Dorothée was perfectly aware of the Countess' liaison with Molé], she broke off her friendship with me. I was bitterly wounded because I loved her dearly."

Whatever her faults, and whatever errors of conduct she may have committed, Dorothée always remained honest with herself and honest with her friends. She never tried to deny that she had been guilty of errors. Thirty years later, in 1852, she noted sadly: "My memories are often very bitter, as all memories must be that one cannot explore without stumbling at every step against an error, a piece of folly, a deception. . . ."

She was no less frank in her dealings with her friends. The Duchess of Courland died on August 20, 1821, and her daughter was deeply affected by the event. Vitrolles sensed the depth of this emotion, and perhaps attempted to take advantage of it. Dorothée was forced to write him a letter explaining the state of her feelings, and in some places this explanation sounds not unlike a confession.

"I am most faithfully attached to you, but I should like to be so only in such measure as will cause neither you nor myself the slightest regret; and it is better that I should treat you a little harshly at present so that we may avoid experiencing in the future the kind of conflicts that are now entirely beyond my strength and could be no more pleasant for yourself, since you have been accustomed to the gentlest, the most even-tempered person in the world [the Countess of Durfort] and not to a demon like myself. The demon has its merits however; it desires always to display them in your company, and it offers you all the best and safest things within its power to give.

"There is nothing in my heart or in my thoughts that is not entirely friendly towards you. . . . My dear, my very dear friend, I entreat you, do not spoil our friendship with the sullen susceptibilities of love."

A short while later she was forced to insist on the same point again. "You are an object of scruples for me; I am extremely grieved at being a source of distress in your life! I have often told you this before, I am an excellent friend to my friends, but fatal to those who harbor any other feeling! I had an encounter yesterday evening that strengthened me even more in my horror of all that might resemble what I have been. I intend to preserve my peace of mind, even though it may appear like lethargy, as long as I possibly can, and my true friends ought not to try to waken me!"

One last confession, this one rather more surprising in that it was made to Molé.* He noted in December 1822: "A memorable three hours spent in private talk with Mme de Dino. An astonishing woman, not of this age. Semi-confession. Her relations with Talleyrand, her devotion to him, the sense of duty and conscience she has developed in herself. Her verdict on Talleyrand and his *Mémoires*. She did all she could to prevent him from lying, to make him confess everything quite openly in fact. . . . She has written an account of her own life in which there is a great deal she has cause to blush for. . . ."

❖   ❖   ❖

For seven years, since 1816 in fact, Dorothée had scarcely ever been parted from Talleyrand. In 1823, not only was there a loosening of these bonds, but a break in the established rhythm of their lives also became apparent. In July, while Edmond was fighting in Spain and behaving very well there, Dorothée decided to spend several weeks in Germany. Her health had been poor for some time: constant colds and fevers and a sullen liver that she was hoping would improve with a stay at Baden. Also her financial affairs had become somewhat tangled as a result of her mother's death, and her presence in Saxony was becoming indispensable.

She did not leave without regrets. At least, that is what she wrote to Prosper de Barante in one of the first letters of a correspondence that was to continue uninterrupted until Dorothée's death in 1862. Though their friendship was sincere and lasting she never displayed herself to the wise and cautious historian of the Dukes of Burgundy with the same lack of reticence

---

* Relations between Dorothée and Molé were stormy for a long time. They appreciated one another's qualities but did not like each other, and for twenty years they continued to alternate between periods of close friendship and periods of estrangement. Eventually, the one's political retirement and the other's departure to Germany seem to have eased them into a kind of cold but lasting amity.

apparent in her letters to Vitrolles during the Restoration, or to Thiers and Molé during the July monarchy.* Intelligent and adaptable as she was, she showed herself to Barante always in the most favorable light, never failing to write exactly those things that were likely to bring most pleasure to this very French Frenchman, who after an extravagant passion for Mme de Staël had by now settled down to being a good husband and a good father. Barante remained to the end one of those who maintained a bond between Dorothée and France after she had become entirely German again.

"I am leaving full of grief at having to go, at having to say good-bye to my children and my friends, and at leaving M. de Talleyrand so very much alone. I am leaving very low in health, in mind, in will, and I find it very difficult to convince myself that in seven weeks I shall be back in Paris, in two months at Valençay, and that in two months also I shall have the real and very sincere pleasure of seeing you again. Everything good, everything pleasant seems to have such difficulty finding a place in my life that I don't dare to believe such things will ever happen. Farewell, monsieur, perhaps I shall return from Germany with a little of the strength that our native air restores to us, but even more certainly with a disposition of mind and heart entirely to the advantage of my second homeland; though forced on me originally, I have since adopted it, and I have no wish to seek for shelter and repose in any other."

Dorothée had been back at Valençay for several weeks and was preparing to spend the autumn wrapped in "a gentle and rather pleasant lethargy," even though the departure of her children had dispelled "the atmosphere of activity and joy with which their games and their freedom from cares had been sur-

* On April 26, 1835, Dorothée confessed to Barante: "You are not the person I have told most about the private details of my life, but you are the one I have always felt has seen most deeply into me; you have never insisted on the things you sensed hidden there, and the extreme delicacy with which you are able to convey things without articulating them makes the exchange of ideas with you singularly easy, soothing, and agreeable. There is a little declaration for you that I am very happy to make and that can scarcely be a source of chagrin to you."

rounding her," when the Rovigo affair suddenly required Talleyrand's precipitate return to Paris.

In October 1823, Savary, the Duke of Rovigo, had published a pamphlet on the subject of the Duke of Enghien's death in which Talleyrand's name was mentioned in a damaging way. Though normally so impassive, Talleyrand was unable to let this pass. His friends, led by Royer-Collard in particular, would not in any case have permitted him to do so.

In early November, Talleyrand left Valençay, followed a few days later by Dorothée. Upon his arrival in Paris, the Prince wrote to Louis XVIII requesting his accuser's arraignment before his Peers. The King refused this request, but he granted Talleyrand an audience and, according to La Rochefoucauld, made him a rather ambiguous little speech: "We have too many obligations towards you, Monsieur de Talleyrand, for us ever to be tempted to forget them, and I know you too well ever to entertain such suspicions of you." Louis XVIII then added—which was better—that he was going to forbid the Duke of Rovigo the Tuileries.

On November 22, Dorothée wrote triumphantly to Barante, "Everything has been settled, and settled for the best." But she had been deeply disturbed, and three weeks later Talleyrand was writing, also to Barante, "Madame de Dino has been rather unwell lately: indignation has a bad effect on her. . . ."

❖ ❖ ❖

The Cardinal de Périgord, who became Archbishop of Paris under the Restoration, had died in 1821. This prelate, always a good priest, had been tortured until the last hour of his life by the thought that he helped to further the ecclesiastical career of his nephew, Charles-Maurice, for purely secular ends. On his deathbed, he entrusted Mgr Quélen, his coadjutor and shortly afterwards his successor, with the difficult task of effecting a reconciliation between Talleyrand and the Church. From that moment on, Mgr de Quélen was obsessed by this responsibility that had been laid upon him.

He was not alone, however, in his preoccupation with this question. As the years went by, bringing the final reckoning ever nearer, there were many others who felt a similar concern. The Protestant Duchess of Broglie offered the opinion that a knowledge of the world was not enough any more, that one must also know how to die. Metternich too, when he visited Paris during the spring of 1825, told Talleyrand that he had a great example to give.

Mgr de Quélen, who was a good man, albeit of rather scant intelligence, began to pay court to the Duchess of Dino in the hope of using her as a means of approaching Talleyrand. The friendship caused some surprise, and malicious tongues began to wag.* The most noticeable result of this premature attempt was that the prelate was persuaded to vote against a scheme for the conversion of incomes that Talleyrand wanted to see quashed.

Dorothée learned of the success of her intrigue on June 6, 1824, while staying with Metternich at Johannisberg, and she made no attempt to conceal her delight. From the Rhine, she continued on once more into Saxony, then to Baden. When the season there ended, accompanied by the Duchess of Ragusa, whose even and jovial temper appealed to her, and by her young son Louis de Périgord, who evinced a schoolboyish delight in the trip, she visited Switzerland.

By the time she returned to Paris late in the August of 1824, Louis XVIII was breathing his last, although the newspapers were not yet admitting the fact. On September 16, the King died. This event was of little concern to Dorothée; the only thing that worried her was the strain being placed upon Talleyrand in his capacity as Grand Chamberlain, which pre-

* In 1829, Mme de Boigne wrote: "A few years earlier, at a time when her heart chanced to be free of any other occupant, urged on by her boredom, by her idleness, and perhaps by a taste for mischief, Mme de Dino had amused herself by turning the Archbishop's head and making him fall passionately in love with her.

"They say, however, that the Duchess had a treacherous woman friend who informed the Archbishop of the game that was being played at his expense and furnished him with proofs of the trickery before he had completely succumbed. Whereupon he betook himself and his remorse to the foot of the altars."

occupied her "to such an extent that I could think of nothing else." But Talleyrand had a strong constitution and emerged from the ordeal unscathed. Despite the burning heat of Paris, which seemed to her almost unbearable after the air in the Alps, Dorothée refused to move out to Etiolles, the home of the Saint-Aulaires. She was determined to stay near her uncle, who was unable to escape even as far as Petit-Andilly, a modest country house on the fringe of the Forêt de Montmorency that he had recently bought from Mme de Duras.

On September 23, Louis XVIII's body was taken to Saint-Denis. Talleyrand and the Grand Almoner carried the heart on a cushion. A month later, on October 25, the official funeral took place. Behind the sarcophagus, the Grand Chamberlain carried the flag of France.

The Coronation of Charles X at Rheims, on May 29, 1825, was a fresh ordeal for Talleyrand. It was succeeded by numerous festivities, and Dorothée, who kept a relentlessly affectionate eye upon her uncle, thought he looked exhausted.

Talleyrand was hoping to be recalled to office under the new King. With an eye to the future, he wished to avoid giving any offense in the present. In order not to disturb anyone's feelings therefore, if only by his presence, he decided to spend the winter in the Midi, and Dorothée too thought that this change in his mode of existence, this respite from court duties, would give him an opportunity to regain his strength. Possibly too, she thought that a long absence from Paris would finally bring about the extinction of certain rumors that Charles X's kindness had already done something to abate. If she herself were less in evidence, then she would be less talked about, and perhaps the envious would at last cease their attacks upon her.

Early in October of 1825, Talleyrand, Dorothée, and Countess Tyszkiewicz made their way down into Provence by short stages. They split themselves up into three groups in order to avoid a shortage of fresh horses and overcrowding when they spent the night at inns, only meeting again in the large towns: Geneva, Grenoble, and eventually Marseilles.

This new experience disturbed Dorothée. "One only sees the full horror of provincial life in France, and it seems to me that we are none of us equipped to cope with it," she wrote. Despite these initial reservations however, the trip was a happy one. For one thing, Talleyrand was soon displaying a "face younger by ten years." In Dorothée's eyes, this meant that the real goal of the journey had already been achieved. And once her worries on that score had been appeased she also found herself able to enjoy the pleasures of being in Provence and beside the Mediterranean. "The sea and the sun reconcile one to everything," she wrote to Barante after they had been in Marseilles two months.

Nevertheless, the Midi did contain "the nastiest and most unhealthy thing in the world,"—in other words the mistral. The Prince, Dorothée, and the Countess had all agreed to escape to Nice or Hyères as soon as it appeared. They tried Hyères first.*

* Ought we to accept the story that Dorothée gave birth to a daughter there? Alphonse Denis, who had adopted Hyères as his home town and was for a long while its mayor, has left a long and amusing account of his relations with Talleyrand during January of 1826. It ends with these words: "This clever man had no idea that, under his own roof, his niece, Mme la Duchesse de Dino, was to be delivered secretly of a daughter, which she entrusted to M. Fleury, the senior doctor at the Hôpital de la Marine in Toulon, all without the Prince de Talleyrand entertaining the slightest suspicion of it."

Starting from this piece of evidence, apparently confirmed by local rumors, M. Emmanuel Davin undertook a long series of inquiries (see *Le Fureteur,* August-September, 1955) which led him to the conclusion that Dorothée was in fact the mother of a child, Julie-Zulmé, born of unknown parents on January 23, 1826, who was registered in Toulon two days later, on January 25, by Doctor Jean-André Fleury.

If M. Emmanuel Davin's study is not absolutely conclusive—it offers no proof, for example, that the child registered in Toulon was in fact born in Hyères where the Duchess was at the time—if the evidence of relations and friends cannot be considered conclusive when it is based on hearsay and when it is a question of so flattering a connection, if the Duchess' letters to Barante and Vitrolles at that time appear to rule out such an event, nevertheless Dorothée's personal life at that time is too obscure and too complicated to justify our dismissing the hypothesis.

Nor is it possible to arrive at any more certain conclusion where the father of the child is concerned. Following the evidence of Julie-Zulmé's descendants, M. Emmanuel Davin attributes her paternity to a Count of Mornay. But does this mean Jules, who married one of Soult's daughters, or his brother Charles, one of the most famous men-about-town under the Restoration? M. Davin has been unable to decide between them, though inclining slightly to a preference for Jules on account of the similarity between the first names.

Well educated, possessed of a sizeable dowry, Julie-Zulmé was eventually married to a certain Docteur Bertulus, by whom she had several children, and died in 1913.

They thought it an agreeable spot, but the sight of so many invalids made Talleyrand melancholy and they moved on to Nice. A plan for a journey through northern Italy was toyed with, then abandoned, and all three returned to Paris in the early spring, even though Talleyrand could not think of the capital without distaste, or Dorothée without fatigue.

Mme de Talleyrand had by this time again relinquished Pont-de-Sains to her husband, and he took up residence there in June 1826, taking Dorothée with him. "Here we are in the oddest place in the world; it is certainly not a château, by no means a country house, and not at all like a farm; it is simply the house of an ironworks owner, quite isolated, standing between a pond and a factory, surrounded by a paddock and ringed all around with vast woods full of the most beautiful trees you have ever seen; no other view except the woods, no other sound except the ironworkers' hammers; aside from that, absolute silence, absolute rest, absolute isolation; M. de Talleyrand works and I daydream. . . ."

From Pont-de-Sains, Dorothée moved on to Dieppe, which had recently been made fashionable by the Duchess of Berry. Dorothée's reason for going there was to try to shake off a persistent rheumatism by bathing in the sea.

❖   ❖   ❖

Over the past eight years, the intimacy between Vitrolles and the Duchess of Dino had grown gradually deeper. The Baron was Dorothée's best confidant, a confidant whose friendship, constantly teetering on the verge of love, never allowed his perceptive and jealous interest to flag for a moment, even though he had a great many other worries to occupy his mind.

The solitary journey to Dieppe had surprised and intrigued Vitrolles, and he sent Dorothée his "interpretation" of it. She answered with a cry of protest: alas! it was not happiness, it was not even amusement that she had gone to the Normandy coast in search of, she had simply wanted a place in which to recover from a very real moral depression. A cry of protest, a cry of anguish: "If you knew how very unhappy I am!"

Back at Valençay, however, Dorothée recovered a measure of mental calm: she had a great deal to do, she felt that she was useful there as well as loved, and lastly, she was able to be more with her children, especially her sons, who were taking up more space every day as they grew up, and according to their mother filling it very well. And yet, all through that summer of 1826 she was a prey to some vague anxiety and began to long for a house of her own, one in which she would really be "the lady of the house." There can be no doubt that Talleyrand's way of life, at once so theatrical and so choppy, weighed on her sometimes. Or that she felt a need, after ten years with him, of shaking off the yoke, of having a life and a home that were really her own. Already, in 1823, she had begun to go on trips alone. In 1824 she did so again; but in 1825 the Prince had not allowed her to escape a third time, and since then they had scarcely ever been apart.

As Dorothée continued to spend her mornings visiting her schools for young girls, learning the part of Rosine for a performance of the *Barbier* on September 22, and reading the mystical works of Fénélon in the evenings, Vitrolles sensed something underneath these day-by-day activities, a growing expectancy of heart that both disturbed and irritated him.

"You have written me a sentence about the vengeance exacted by love that makes me tremble," Dorothée wrote to him on September 13, 1826. "Do you really believe that I am in danger of his furies? I don't know how I should behave if such a thing were to happen, but until it does I shall continue to chant my hymn to friendship."

Several days after this letter was written, an influx of visitors took place at Valençay. Some of them were not at all to Dorothée's taste, such as Montrond; some of them were very much to her taste, such as Piscatory.* The sight of this young

---

* Born in Paris in April 1800, Théobald Arcambal had been adopted by Antoine Piscatory, who was of Greek origin. As a tribute to the memory of his adoptive father, Théobald Piscatory went to fight in Greece at the beginning of the rising against the Turks. He later settled in Touraine, where he put down such strong roots that in 1832 he was elected deputy for Chinon.

man no doubt crystallized the emotions that she had hitherto refused to admit to herself. A letter written to Vitrolles on September 21 betrays her emotions.

"The consolations of friendship become daily more necessary to me; I ask of them that they should take up a great deal of space in my life, fill up a great void in it, and above all prevent me from feeling an emptiness that I no longer wish to see filled by something that has already brought such disquiet and devastation into my life; but I will swear to nothing; and yet there has been nothing in my past to make me favorably disposed towards the sentiment that has been so kind, so helpful to you; to me it has always been fatal, and the worst service it will have done me is to make it so very difficult for me to rebuild my future on peaceful and solid foundations."

While Dorothée was thus confessing herself to Vitrolles, the sage Barante arrived to spend a few days at Valençay, as Talleyrand and the Duchess had been pressing him to do for several years.* Having been born and bred in a poor and rugged part of France, the historian was a little dazzled by Valençay, though without realizing it. He did not perceive what lay underneath the glitter: the bitterness of Talleyrand's thwarted ambitions, Dorothée's unquiet heart. He saw only the pomp, which he described in a letter to his sister, Mme Anisson du Perron, on September 30: "So here I am in this great château where the hospitality is in every way magnificent, and of which there is no longer, or is not yet, such another example in all of France. . . ."

❖   ❖   ❖

Court duties obliged the Prince and the Duchess to be back in Paris by November 4. The Prince no longer had many illusions about the likelihood of his returning to power, and as soon as he decently could he also left Paris and took up residence at

---

* "You must come to Valençay," Dorothée wrote to him on January 31, 1826. "M. de Talleyrand is always at his most charming there, and if I have any merit at all, then it is there too."

Andilly with Dorothée. The latter was once more unwell. She was running a fever, losing weight, developing a muddy complexion, and Talleyrand was worried *—worried enough to allow her complete freedom of movement. Between May and September, she took a cure at Néris, for her nerves, then another at Bagnères-de-Luchon and Bagnères-de-Bigorre, hoping to recoup some of her lost strength.

In all these places she was alone,† since she had left Pauline in the care of Talleyrand, who took the little girl with him to Bourbon-l'Archambault. "Pauline has been my only pleasure. There is a great charm in the gentle attentions of a pretty child," he confessed to Mme Mollien on August 18, the same day that saw his departure for Valençay, where he was to receive the "holidaying horde"—in other words the Dino boys and their tutor.

Mme de Dino left Bagnères early in September, making her way back by short stages to her *lares and penates* "or what pass for them" in Berry. The bitterness of that expression explains Dorothée's decision to purchase the château of Rochecotte near Langeais.‡ There, she would be her own mistress. And perhaps it was also in her mind that she would be nearer to Piscatory and therefore able to see him more easily.

On the way to Valençay, Dorothée stopped at Angoulême,

---

* Vitrolles had gone out to spend a day at Andilly on April 29. The Prince, though he rather disliked the Baron—certainly no more than Vitrolles did him, however—wrote to him next day: "I should like to know what your first impression was when you saw Mme de Dino. It was two weeks since you had seen her last so that her appearance must have left some impression with you. Do write me a word or two on the subject. . . ."

† Was she really so? M. Pierre de Gorsse has recently revealed the fact that on September 12, 1827, Théobald Piscatory registered a child of the female sex at the town hall in Bordeaux. The name was given as Antonine-Dorothée. Piscatory himself was registered as the father, but the identity of the mother was not disclosed. Rémusat, whose invaluable and recently published *Mémoires de ma vie* shed light on so many obscure points, writes: "She [the Duchess of Dino] has had three legitimate children. . . . As for any others, I do know that she had one daughter, Mme Auvity, whose education and dowry were provided by Piscatory."

‡ Mme de Boigne notes, late in 1827 or early in 1828: "She [the Duchess of Dino] had only recently acquired this property in Touraine. Her life there was made extremely agreeable by her personal relations and she finally made it her principal residence."

where the Naval College had been built in honor of the Grand Admiral of France, the Duke of Angoulême. Dorothée's second son, Alexandre, became a student there that fall. Alexandre de Périgord was, at thirteen, a child of lively intelligence whose rather impulsive character was in direct contrast to the gentle placidity of Louis, his elder by two years. While the latter, whom Talleyrand now considered as his heir, was continuing to study hard and well at the lycée Henri IV, Alexandre for his part had decided to become a sailor.

In May of 1827, two certificates had been issued, both bearing official stamps, the first attesting to Alexandre de Périgord's good behavior and morals, as to his good religious and political principles, the second to the progress of his studies. A Docteur Mège had likewise given his word that the adolescent boy was four feet six inches tall, had been successfully vaccinated, possessed a good constitution, and was without physical deformity of any kind.

These formalities once attended to, Alexandre had been authorized to present himself for the entrance examination to the Naval College, and on August 18 the Duchess announced to Vitrolles with unconcealed satisfaction: "In November I shall take Alexandre to his new post, for he passed his examination brilliantly."

Early in November of 1827 therefore, Dorothée accompanied her son to Angoulême.* The separation was a painful one for her. She saw a lot of herself in this lively and intelligent child, capable of the best as well as the worst, and he was apparently her favorite at that time. She had become a mother very early in life, and since she was a woman with more head than heart she had not shown a great deal of interest in her children when they were very young. The death of the two year old Dorothée, followed by her long absences in 1814 and 1815, had even further increased the distance between herself and her two sons. Although she and Talleyrand had given every attention to the

---

* It is also worth remarking that it was Dorothée alone who made all the decisions relating to the child's career, and that it was she, too, who engaged herself to pay "quarterly and in advance, eight hundred francs for her son's education at Angoulême."

boys' education, Louis and Alexandre had not really counted in their mother's life until they were about ten years old. The same held true of Pauline. In 1828, when writing to Vitrolles, Dorothée could find nothing more to say about her than: "My daughter has a sweet nature." Yet when the little girl grew up, her mother's love for her was both tender and profound.

◇ ◇ ◇

Villèle was worn out by his six years of office; when the elections in late 1827 produced a Liberal majority in the Chamber he handed in his resignation. Once more, Talleyrand thought that his time had come; but it was Martignac who was asked to form the new cabinet on January 5, 1828.

While the Prince was spending his winter and spring in Paris, Dorothée, apart from a brief appearance in November to attend Royer-Collard's entry into the Académie Française, had taken up residence at Rochecotte.

The great Louis XVI château, halfway up a hill overlooking the Loire, had won her heart immediately. The tiered terraces looked out over vast blue and gray horizons, the sky was pure, the house full of light. Dorothée decided that Rochecotte would probably be her principal residence from then on, and she undertook a great many improvements: a heating system, double windows, carpets, door-curtains, everything that could contribute to making life warm and comfortable there in winter. She sent for the furniture and porcelain she had inherited from Duke Pierre, and they mingled harmoniously with her newer Boulle commodes. The library was well-stocked, and above all modern, for this house was still a youthful place, although it did also contain the best classics, in particular all the authors of the "Grand Siècle."

In the gardens, laid out in the French manner, there were long pergolas framing rectangles of lawn and tightly massed flowers. Beneath the foliage of these shady walks the air was light, cool, restful to overwrought nerves, and soon Dorothée began to look a little less peaked.

"Yes, it's quite true, I have a veritable passion for Roche-cotte," she confessed to Barante in July of 1828, "firstly because it's mine, that's one reason; secondly because it has the most beautiful view and is set in the most beautiful countryside in the world; and lastly because there is something in the air here that makes me carefree, and then I am arranging it, rearranging it, making it beautiful, taking it over, making it mine. . . . I am living the country life with a vengeance; and you who have lived in the Vendée and given balls for ladies who arrived on horseback, one leg on one side, one on the other, well you won't be shocked when I tell you that I too, with the addition to my costume that modesty requires, ride everywhere like that, no matter what the state of the weather or roads."

With Vitrolles, Dorothée was more honest and drew a less superficial picture of her life at Rochecotte. She was living there quite alone, with a great many workmen who frequently drove her mad with rage and impatience. On Sundays, she had the mayor and the parish priest to dinner, and from time to time —quite often even—neighbors as well, to whose houses she went in her turn. She rode, she breathed, she looked, she read, she wrote, she did needlework—for she had always been nimble-fingered. In short, she was serving her apprenticeship as a "housekeeper," resuming the same tasks every morning, at the same times, always in the same order, since nothing was rational that could not be returned to every day. A strangely different life from the one she had led on the Rue Saint-Florentin or at Valençay. "You will ask me perhaps if I am happy; I shall reply that for a long time now I have felt an inner poise; is that happiness? I have no idea; but at the age of thirty-four it is at all events a great deal, and if there is still something lacking, why, I can scarcely complain of that, since it is myself even more than others that I must take to task if the past has been so full of agitations that it still, even now, has the power to affect the future to some extent. . . ." There is still that same note of disillusioned honesty.

During August, however, Dorothée showed herself still true to Berry. Talleyrand, whom she had not seen for many months, was soon to be there after his summer visit to a spa, Louis would be spending his vacation there, and Alexandre too, if he had passed his final examination, would be staying there in September on his way from Angoulême to Brest.*

Though caught up once more in the complicated life at Valençay, Dorothée still did not lose her sense of the benefits to be derived from the peaceful life she lived at Rochecotte, and she wrote as much to Vitrolles on August 26 with satisfaction: "I have bid the world a very frank adieu; it was dictated by neither ill humor nor caprice but is the fruit of long reflections aided by many rather saddening experiences; in order to effect what I had come to realize was the only remedy, I had to have a place of my own; I have found it, and now a strange calm, a great absence of hostility, a complete indifference to everything that is not sincerely close to my heart, has entered my soul; the visits I make to M. de Talleyrand are easier for me, and my relations with the whole world seem to have changed for the better, all because I have a refuge of my very own; and I am quite willing to believe that others also find me easier to live with."

Talleyrand had followed the recent changes in his niece with perplexity and an indisputable feeling of sadness. Was the intimacy between them to be broken after more than twelve years? Since Dorothée had resolved once more to bury herself for the whole winter in Touraine, since she was avoiding the Rue Saint-Florentin and no longer came to Valençay for anything more than "visits," the old man, so skillful always in diplomacy and now inspired by love, decided that in the long run his niece would still come back to him as she had once before from Vienna, provided that she did not become accustomed to living away from him. Breaking with all his former habits therefore, he decided to spend the winter at Rochecotte, thereby consenting to and sanctioning by his presence any relationship that Dorothée might have with other men.

❖ ❖ ❖

* On October 24, Dorothée wrote to Vitrolles: "My sailor has done brilliantly in his examination and will be in Brest in two weeks. He's a perfect, but very funny, little devil."

166 • *Part Three*

Short, not physically well built, but with the traditional Talleyrand charm of manner, Louis de Périgord was placid, cautious and even-tempered. Though less brilliant than Alexandre, he was more stable, and his studies had progressed very well. In the summer of 1828 he was given his bachelor's degree, having studied philosophy and rhetoric concurrently. As a reward for this exemplary scholastic success, and also as a means of keeping him away from Paris, where they felt that his own idleness and his father's example would do him little good, Talleyrand and Dorothée decided that he should spend a year traveling in Italy. He was to be accompanied on the journey by Martin, for many years the tutor of all the Dino children, whom the Duchess, grateful for his devotion "despite the difficulties of his position" considered as a friend.

Vitrolles had just been appointed French Minister in Florence, and on October 24, 1828, Dorothée wrote asking his help on behalf of her son. "The longer he can remain under your wing the better it will be. Louis is too young to go to court, and in any case he has no uniform; but what I want for him is the best company in each town he visits; as to the rest, I hope he will not neglect to find out a little about the laws of the various countries and the moral and political effects they produce, for after all he will be a peer one day. I also hope he will not remain a stranger to agriculture, since he will have furrows of his own to plough eventually."

She also added, with visible regret: "Despite the very sincere pleasure I take in a retired life, I am having to make an extraordinary effort of mind not to accompany my son to Italy myself. But when I look at M. de Talleyrand and my daughter, then shake my purse, I know I really cannot think of it. . . ."

Louis de Périgord traveled first to Naples and Rome. He arrived in Florence during the second half of January 1829 and found a letter waiting there from his mother. It was an urgent summons recalling him to Paris, where he was to be married, at the age of eighteen, to Mlle de Montmorency, who was exactly the same age. "It is the match of the moment," Dorothée wrote rather sadly to Vitrolles on January 9, 1829, doubtless with her thoughts on the past, "and M. de Talleyrand was resolved to secure it for Louis, whom he has endowed magnificently. His generosity, the personal qualities and the advantages of the young lady, M. de Talleyrand's advanced age, the gentleness, the calm and poise of my son have combined to make me overcome the justifiable repugnance I felt to marrying my son at the age of eighteen."

While Dorothée was worrying about her child's happiness, Talleyrand for his part had resolved to assure his family, and more particularly this at long last chosen heir, of a new title. He asked Charles X for permission to present the young man to him under the new title of Marquis de Talleyrand. Charles X refused, but he created Louis Duke of Valençay.

The new Duke returned to Paris on February 21. Four days later the contract was signed, and on the 26th the marriage service itself was conducted by Mgr Quélen, whose address consisted mainly of a eulogy of the Cardinal de Périgord.

"In less than a week we have signed a contract making my son a wealthy man [Talleyrand had made the entire property of Valençay over to Louis] and tied his hands so that he can't dispose of a penny of it," Dorothée wrote to Vitrolles on March 3, 1829. "Valençay has been entailed to his children, which is as far into the future as the law will permit an entail to go; my daughter-in-law's dowry has been converted into a settlement trust under the marriage contract so that whatever happens it will remain quite safe; within a week of the marriage they were both presented, and everything in short has gone off in accordance with all the strictest and most time-honored observances of the best society; only the future can tell us if there is any place left for happiness in all this; but my son looks quite happy at the moment."

Dorothée then observed, with a certain bitterness, that if she had not already been aware of French society's real attitude toward her she might well have thought herself the best-liked woman in Paris. It was at this time too that Apponyi observed with amusement how, at a ball given by the Montmorencys, the Duke and Duchess of Dino remained at such a respectful distance from one another. The Austrian chronicler also adds

that the little Duke of Valençay lavished the most constant
and tender attentions upon his mother.

❖ ❖ ❖

While Talleyrand was away at Aix-la-Chapelle, Dorothée
returned joyfully to Rochecotte. The silence, the rest, the calm,
almost the monotony of her life there were becoming daily
more necessary to her. She returned also to the village school,
to the jelly broths made necessary by the scarcity and cost of
bread, to her dinners with the mayor who bought government
bonds and the parish priest who would not allow the peasant
girls to dance, and also, no doubt, to Piscatory.

In August, she went to Valençay to help Talleyrand receive
and entertain her new daughter-in-law's family. Her resulting
fatigue was then aggravated by a hurried visit to Brest, where
she kissed Alexandre good-bye before he left for Toulon and his
first two years at sea. His mother found the young sailor grown,
better-looking, and more mature in his manner. "After spending
a lot of time kissing him, then a lot more lecturing him, preach-
ing at him, encouraging him, advising him, and fitting him out,"
Dorothée wrote to Vitrolles on September 17, "I said good-bye
to him and saw him aboard the *Belle-Gabrielle*, which takes
all the young hopefuls down to Toulon. . . . I won't say anything about politics, since I have nothing to do with them any
more; all I know is that bread is too dear, the weather frightful,
and the mind of the onlooker tense, curious, but by no means
confident of the outcome."

Nothing to do with politics? When Piscatory had recently
brought his colleagues Thiers and Mignet to Rochecotte?
Nothing more to do with politics at a time when the whole
country was quivering on the brink of a great upheaval?

After the defeat of the projected electoral reforms on April
8, 1829, a defeat that had been brought about by a strange
cooperation between both left and right wing parties, the latter
opposing the reforms because they were too liberal and the
former because they were too moderate, Martignac had survived

in office for only a few more months. Had Charles X taken the opportunity offered him by those few months to think things over? One likes to think so, but the result of his reflections was somewhat surprising. The King could have recalled Villèle, refreshed after his eighteen months' absence from office, and that would have been a return to authoritarian rule. He could have picked his Prime Minister from one of the center-left leaders—Broglie, Sébastiani, Casimir Périer—and that would have been a slight advance further into liberalism, an intensification of the Martignac experiment. But Charles X did neither of these things: on August 9, 1829, he called Prince Jules de Polignac to office, and that meant a return to government by absolute whim. The country began to simmer.

Talleyrand felt his old passion for power reviving. He was very well acquainted with English history, in particular with the 1688 revolution, and had for a long time been weighing the possibilities of the Orléans branch.* But age had made him more cautious. Despite having once worked at Napoleon's overthrow almost in full view of his victim, he did not now dare to undertake the removal of the Bourbons except through intermediaries. He looked for his troops among the young Liberal journalists with whom his niece had surrounded him. After examining, measuring, judging, he picked out the most brilliant of them all, Adolphe Thiers, and decided to put him in command of the spearhead.

Late in October 1829, Talleyrand and Dorothée arrived to spend a few days in Paris. It was during this visit that Talleyrand declared that he had recalled the Bourbons in 1814 for the sake of peace, and that they would have to be got rid of in 1829 for the sake of everyone's peace of mind. It was then too that Vitrolles, back from Florence and visiting on the Rue Saint-Florentin one evening, reacted with such surprise to the sort of company the Duchess of Dino was playing hostess to. "I was greatly astonished to observe so many unknown faces there. I asked Pasquier to explain why this was, and he had

---

* "Take care, Monsieur de Vitrolles," he had said to the Count of Artois' friend early in the Restoration, "the Duke of Orléans is treading on their heels."

only to tell me their names for everything to become clear. I
recognized once more the wise man who is prepared for all
events. . . ."

Early in November, Dorothée traveled back to Rochecotte,
soon to be followed there by Talleyrand, who had recently suffered a terrible attack of quinsy. Dorothée was too intelligent
not to have been aware of Vitrolles' withdrawal and suspicions
during their single encounter in Paris—a withdrawal occasioned
by the changed political attitude he had observed in Talleyrand
and his niece, which was shocking to him as a sincere Royalist.
And he was also suspicious of a serious liaison with Piscatory,
a thing offensive to him both as a rejected lover and as an
aristocrat.

The letter written by Dorothée to Vitrolles on December
2, 1829, in the first in that long correspondence in which one
can detect a ring of insincerity. "I saw you only once during
the ten days I spent in Paris, and yet we had such a backlog
of conversation to make up. Not that it was either your fault
or mine, for you came and I had only gone out for a walk with
M. de Talleyrand, but that was always the moment you happened to choose. I meant to write and fix a time when we
could be sure to meet. But then M. de Talleyrand's morbid
worrying drove me out of Paris almost at a moment's notice.
And he has followed me with a swiftness that alarmed me. . . .

"We are living quite quietly here. . . . If you should chance
to have a few days free for which you can find no other use
and would like to come here and watch the Loire going by,
it would be a great kindness to your old friend."

When Dorothée sent this letter—the last but one she ever
wrote to Vitrolles *—she knew well enough that he would not

* The break between Vitrolles and Dorothée was total. How can this be
explained? The answer is that it cannot. We have merely two facts. First, a
break that occurred in January or February of 1830 could not have been moti-
vated solely by political reasons, since no really deep rift appeared between
the legitimists and the supporters of Louis-Philippe until July. Second,
Dorothée retained a particularly sour memory of this break, and in 1834 she
described Vitrolles acrimoniously as honey-tongued and subservient. And yet,
though so unfailingly prudent as a rule—she asked for all her letters back
from Royer-Collard and Mgr Dupanloup, went through them, and burned
most of them—she never dared to ask for the return of those written to
Vitrolles, which explains how they came to be preserved and published.

come. What would she have done with this Ultra at Rochecotte while Thiers, Mignet, and Carrel, having been offered Talleyrand's moral and financial support, were all there laying the foundations for their anti-dynastic newspaper *Le National,* of which the first number appeared on January 3, 1830?

❖ ❖ ❖

While Charles X's thoughtlessness was preparing the way for the 1830 revolution, Louis-Philippe's accession, and Talleyrand's return to political life, Edmond de Périgord's thoughtlessness was leading him into a dead end that finally forced him to leave the country, thus relieving Dorothée of the mortgage with which her husband's presence had been constantly encumbered her existence in the French capital.

The Duke of Dino was so entirely without talent, so incapable of filling a post of any importance, that the Restoration government, after making him a Commander of Saint-Louis and a Lieutenant-General at the time of the war in Spain, had put him on half pay. His only subsequent appointment was that of Inspector General of Cavalry in 1827 and 1828.

This quasi-idleness did not prove a good counselor, and Edmond had continued to run up debts, despite the pension of forty thousand francs a year he received from Dorothée. Both his father and his uncle had paid off his debts several times, but they might as well have offered to help the Danaïds fill their sieve, and Edmond's financial situation became steadily more critical. In the autumn of 1829, hounded by his creditors in Paris, he fled to England. In London, on the strength of his name, his connections, perhaps his appearance, he was able to raise a loan of three hundred thousand francs, which he hoped would enable him to straighten his affairs out again. But he almost immediately lost sixty thousand francs at gambling. His English creditors heard of this and insisted on complete repayment of the entire debt forthwith. Since he was of course sixty thousand francs short, they had him arrested and thrown into jail.

The French Ambassador at that time was the Duke of
Laval, a relative of the Monmorencys. He could, in fact, have
secured Edmond's release by claiming that he was attached to
the Embassy, and Lord Aberdeen, the Head of the Foreign
Office, was willing to sanction this move. Laval found such a
deceit repugnant however, and preferred to pay the money himself, even though his personal fortune was meager and he must
have had little hope of ever recovering his money.*

The scandal in England had also hardened the determination of the Duke of Dino's creditors at Rome. It was impossible
for Edmond to return to France since that would have meant
spending the rest of his life in Sainte-Pélagie prison. He moved
from London to Brussels, where his son the Duke of Valençay
went to visit him. Louis had a tender heart and a generous soul.
He would have been quite willing to strip himself of all his
wealth to help his father, but his hands were tied by the "pre-
servative" contract his mother had taken such pains over.

Talleyrand for his part thought that he had done enough
already. He had expressed his opinions on the matter to Mme
Vaudémont on December 18 when Edmond was still in his
English prison: "All the brains of all the business agents one
employs never produce anything but the same answer: 'Everything will be all right because M. de Talleyrand will pay up.'
But the unhappy fact is that M. de Talleyrand can't. He has
proved that if he could, then he would be only too happy to
do so; but there is a limit to everything. The fact is, when I did
have money there were the ones whose debts I had to pay off
(and considerable debts too), the ones I provided with pensions,
others for whom I had to find places to live, others who needed
marriage settlements, in fact Louis' marriage cleaned me out.
. . . All of which means that I can now do nothing, which is
very hard. Even my paintings have been pledged for a large
sum. . . ."

* Possoz, the mayor of Passy—one of Edmond's creditors who spent ten
years in litigation before he finally obtained repayment from Dorothée, in
October, 1838, of 12,000 francs he had loaned to Edmond on August 8, 1829
—asserts that the Duchess agreed to assign one half of the 40,000 franc yearly
payment to her husband to the English creditors until the debt had been
cleared.

Talleyrand therefore refused to guarantee his nephew's debts, and from that moment Edmond's fate was sealed. After spending a few days in Paris—doubtless under an assumed name —the Duke of Dino moved to Italy. During May of 1830 he arrived in Florence, and there, living on an annual allowance made to him first by his wife and later by his children, he remained for the next forty years.

Having thus created his final scandal, Edmond de Périgord faded from Dorothée's life for good as the new year dawned. 1830. After so many difficult years, was this disappearance perhaps an augury of happier times to come?

T HE DECREES signed by Charles X on July 25, 1830, were published in the *Moniteur* on the 26th. On the 27th, thanks to Thiers, the firebrand Talleyrand had been keeping in readiness for this moment so long, the explosion that the old diplomat had been expecting occurred. Lurking in ambush behind his windows on the Rue Saint-Florentin, Talleyrand followed the progress of the insurrection hour by hour. On the first day, he was doubtful; on the 28th, when he heard the tocsin proclaiming the crowd's entry into the Hotel de Ville, he hoped; on the 29th, when Marmont was forced to retreat with his troops and shield Saint-Cloud, he made his decision. Glancing at the clock standing on the mantelpiece he said calmly, "A few minutes from now, Charles X will no longer be King of France."

Talleyrand had no desire for a Republic. There was too much risk that it would lead to anarchy, and force France into war with a Europe immediately made belligerent by its apprehensions. He therefore intended to preserve the monarchic principle, and he had long since chosen his candidate for the throne: the Duke of Orléans. The Duke, a son of the Red Prince, was ambitious; his sister, Madame Adélaïde, was even more so.

During the afternoon of July 29, Talleyrand wrote an urgent note to the Princess at Neuilly: the Duke must come out of retirement and proceed to Paris. "Ah! that good Prince," Madame Adélaïde exclaimed upon reading this message, "I was quite certain he hadn't forgotten us." She then persuaded her brother to accede to Talleyrand's request. As Charles X, having abdicated, was making his journey into exile, the Duke of Orléans, after first being made Lieutenant-Général of the realm, then holding back for several days for the sake of form, agreed to accept the crown. On August 7, both chambers elected Louis-Phillipe King of the French.

Once the danger of a Republic had been avoided and a new government established, there remained the task of conciliating the rest of Europe and breaking up the coalition it was already in the process of forming. The German rulers were all waiting for the decision of the Tsar, who then announced that he would not recognize the new regime. The court of St. James alone had proffered a meager olive twig in the form of a curtly worded recognition of Louis-Philippe's accession. Who was there better equipped to seize this pledge and guarantee the nation peace than Talleyrand? At Vienna, he had won back France's place in the council of Europe; in London, perhaps he would be able to win acceptance for the new dynasty. Louis-Philippe decided to send the Prince to England.

❖ ❖ ❖

The Countess Edmond de Périgord was at Rosny when the Prince of Benevento overthrew the Empire; the Duchess of Dino was at Rochecotte when the Prince of Talleyrand invented the Orléans monarchy.

As soon as she heard of the insurrection in Paris, Dorothée's only wish was to be with her uncle and her daughter; but the Prefect of Tours, a rabid supporter of Charles X, refused her a travel permit: her political opinions were only too well-known; she must remain where she was. For three days, while the fires were breaking out, while the cannons thundered, while the horn * sounded perpetually to herald the arrival of visitors in quest of news, Dorothée stood watching for the arrival of the stagecoach. At last, draped with a revolutionary tricolor, it appeared.

Informed of all that had happened, reassured, delighted,† Dorothée became a woman of action once more. Talleyrand

---

* At Rochecotte, to conform with what she had been used to in her childhood at Löbikau, Dorothée had the bell which announced the arrival of visitors replaced by a horn.

† She wrote to Barante on August 8: "You know how much I liked the Palais-Royal and loathed the Tuileries."

had just given the country a new King: Dorothée gave her department a new Prefect. She dispatched d'Entraigues, a friend and neighbor whom she knew to be a good administrator, to Paris with a letter of recommendation to Guizot. The new Minister did not allow the opportunity to slip through his fingers: Indre-et-Loire was swiftly restored to peace and order.

Though attentive to local interests, Dorothée was no less so to her own chances for power in higher circles. On August 6, she wrote to Madame Adélaïde the first of many letters in a correspondence that, though entirely private, was in fact also entirely political since one of the ladies was the Egeria of the new King and the other that of the future Ambassador to England.

"Mademoiselle,* I hasten, with the whole of France, to salute you with the name of our good angel! Yes, Mademoiselle, that is what you showed yourself to be in the hour of danger and what you will always continue to be.

"To tell you, Mademoiselle, that the outcome of recent events now filling us with delighted wonder was ever the dearest wish of my heart would be superfluous. You have long known as much.

"How could one know you, and how could one be so closely attached to M. de Talleyrand without ardently desiring the triumph of your virtues and your cause, which is also that of the whole nation. . . ."

On September 1, Dorothée arrived back in Paris. Talleyrand's appointment was not yet absolutely settled. He was making the government beg for his services, and Molé, the new Minister for Foreign Affairs, slightly alarmed at the prospect of such an Ambassador, was begging without a great deal of conviction. Dorothée, on the other hand, made her decision immediately. Talleyrand must accept: after fifteen years of neglect, Fortune was offering him unexpected amends; he must seize that offer.

---

* With the flattery of a woman accustomed to court life and a recollection of the Ancien Régime, Dorothée addressed Madame Adélaïde, as Talleyrand later did, with the title reserved for the sister to the King: *Mademoiselle.*

Though Dorothée's first thought was for Talleyrand and his reputation, she was nevertheless concerned for her own personal future as well. If her uncle went to London she would accompany him, and this break with her present way of life was what she needed. Perhaps, as Mme de Boigne insinuates, she was tired of her quiet life at Rochecotte, and even more so of Piscatory, so that the possible departure for England presented itself to her as an excellent pretext for breaking off a liaison that in her heart of hearts she knew to be unworthy.

Besides, the lady of the château in Touraine had never really ousted the Princess of Courland, the great international aristocrat. Dorothée had never been truly accepted by Parisian high society and had never wanted to be, but she was too well born not to sense that she had been living below her rightful social level for the past few years; the rather mixed circles in which she had moved were not really the ones to which she properly belonged. Both on her own account and on that of her growing daughter, how could she have failed to prefer the idea of moving in the English society of that time, which was very severe about upbringing but tolerant with regard to morals, which, in short, had all the characteristics of an aristocratic society still untrammeled by the restraints imposed in France by the Revolution and the Congregation?

Above all, this intelligent and ambitious woman, whose mind had by now been even further developed by the difficulties of the past fifteen years, looked forward with satisfaction to making a re-entry onto the political scene. In Vienna she had been too young and too much distracted by the multiplicity of her interests; in London she would be able to demonstrate the full extent of her capabilities—and do justice to her partnership with the old magician who was now about to wield his magic wand once more.

On September 6, 1830, the *Moniteur* carried an announcement to the effect that M. le Prince de Talleyrand had been appointed Ambassador to England. This news earned Louis-Philippe his first diplomatic success: "Since M. de Talleyrand has associated himself with the new French government," the Tsar announced, "that government must necessarily have some chance of survival." And Nicolas I extended his recognition to the new French King.

❖　❖　❖

Talleyrand disembarked at Dover during the evening of September 24 and was received with unusual honors. Dorothée followed him on the 30th. It was a distressing journey for her since the nineteen-hour crossing made her appallingly seasick, despite the quantities of brandy and sherry lavished upon her by the sympathetic crew. Upon her arrival she found the Prince with an excellent color and in high good humor; the reception by the public was warm—the sight of the tricolor rosette drew bursts of cheering—and so was that of the cabinet—the Duke of Wellington had returned from the country for the express purpose of entertaining Talleyrand at dinner.

Though the Tories, generally speaking, felt regret at the downfall of the Bourbons, Polignac's efforts to secure an alliance with Russia and the Algiers expedition had both irritated them sufficiently to deprive this regret of any urgency. Moreover, Wellington, the Prime Minister, still felt for both Talleyrand and Dorothée the same firm feeling of friendship that had sprung up between them in Paris and Vienna during 1814 and 1815. Their occupancy of the French Embassy, then at No. 50, Portland Place, was therefore a personal pleasure to him. Furthermore, he looked upon it as a guarantee of peace and political stability. And lastly, he was counting on Talleyrand and himself, the one dominating the British cabinet with the incomparable prestige he had acquired at Waterloo, the other the French cabinet in Paris with his overwhelming personality, being able to resolve together a situation that the previous month's revolution in Belgium had made even more grave and complex.

On August 25, the Belgians had risen against King William of Holland, to whose rule they had been subjected by the treaties of 1815; on September 24, they set up a provisional government. On October 4, this government proclaimed Belgian independence; on October 10, it summoned a National Congress.

Could Europe—or rather, could the three Northern realms—accept this first and very serious derogation from the treaties they had signed in 1815? If Prussia were to go to the aid of Holland and help its king force the Belgians into submission once more, might the French not remember, delirious as they were with their own recovered liberty and the sight of the revolutionary flag, that they had once promised freedom to the whole world, and that the Flemish and Walloon territories now in question had been among the noblest conquests of their own Revolution? If so, then they would respond to the appeals being made to them by the Belgians, who were determined to accept annexation rather than to fall into the hands of the Dutch once more. Would England tolerate French aid to the Belgians? It was certain that it would not; thus the old coalitions would come into being again and all Europe would disappear perhaps in a fresh conflagration.

The Belgian question and the attempts at its solution dominated Talleyrand's mission in England. They were the principal themes upon which the whole symphony was based, from which it drew its intensity and its stature. And these were also the things that earned the Prince his best, his most indisputable title to fame. Behind that impassive face, behind those cold, heavy-lidded eyes, the flame of his intelligence burned clear and bright. Though now an old man of seventy-six, he still had an astonishing sense of the realities of any situation, just as he had retained that incomparable dexterity in unraveling the threads of even the most complicated problems. Whatever certain Belgians may have thought, whatever the suspicions that too long a tradition of profitable political bargaining may have brought to bear upon the Prince, the facts still speak for themselves. While peace was kept in London, across the Channel a new people was born, a people that has survived and prospered. The work that Talleyrand accomplished between 1830 and 1834 was lasting; it still endures today.

Dorothée, too, was intimately associated with this work and played her part, a large one, in its success. While Talleyrand was making his entrance into the political arena and establishing his pre-eminence there, Dorothée was making hers into English society and quickly becoming one of its leaders. "My niece, Mme la Duchesse de Dino, had agreed to accompany me to London," Talleyrand writes in his *Mémoires*, "and I was able to rely on all the resources of her capable and fascinating mind not only to supply me with valuable support but also to win for us both the good will of that English Society so well-known for its exclusiveness."

In these closing months of 1830, on the eve of the electoral reforms that gave rise in a few more years to the triumph of the middle classes and their subsequent blossoming in the Age of Victoria, political power was still in the hands of the landed aristocracy, whether Whig or Tory. There was no distinction between this political world and the world of Society. The members of both were identical, and they formed a closed circle in which everyone knew everyone else and all were linked by either family ties or friendship. It was a cultured circle, but one ruled by a taste for pleasure that was undeterred by a fear of scandal or extravagance. Though no British intruder was ever allowed inside its doors,* any foreigner of sufficient breeding was always assured of a warm welcome—provided he was amusing, intelligent, and well-mannered. Talleyrand made a good impression immediately with his aristocratic air, the Duchess with her beauty, and both with their wit and perfect breeding. Emboldened by a success of which she had forgotten the heady power during those fifteen years of hostility endured in France, Dorothée came into a second and maturer bloom in London. Her new self-assurance brought with it a new grace of manner, a new simplicity and charm, while her profound and unprejudiced intelligence opened itself with lively interest to this strange new country.

Before long, on October 5, she was given the opportunity

* "I am in no position," Dorothée said, "to be shocked by the excesses of the nobility here, or rather I am in a very good position; but on every side it is beyond what one could ever imagine. This country appears to me very far from any possibility of revolution, but if ever such a thing should occur, how many vanities there are piled up waiting for the moment of vengeance."

to try her mettle at a great diplomatic dinner given by the Duke of Wellington. She found herself once more in the world where she had been so happy in Vienna; she was immediately at ease there, she immediately began to sparkle. Questioned by Prince Paul Esterhazy, the Austrian Ambassador, with the "familiarity produced by their shared memories of Vienna," she told him everything about Paris that she wished him to repeat. Bülow, the Prussian representative in London, was the nephew of Alexander von Humboldt, whom she had known as a child, and this, too, helped to break the ice. Lord Burghersh asked Mme de Dino how her husband was. "I don't know anything about him," the Duchess replied in even tones—and Edmond's name was never mentioned in London again.

English society in fact accepted Talleyrand and his niece without hypocrisy and without equivocation. The ambiguous nature of her situation was considered no bar to Dorothée's assuming the function of Ambassadress since Wellington reminded the King that Countess Edmond de Périgord had always been treated as such in Vienna by the Emperor and Empress of Austria.

Dorothée's sexual morals were at that time the subject of much discussion, but none of the ladies of the English aristocracy allowed this to disturb them, whether they were themselves extremely free in their behavior or whether, on the contrary, they were extremely virtuous. Lady Grey, a woman of the highest moral principles where her own behavior was concerned and the mother of fifteen children, the wife of Wellington's successor as Prime Minister, declared quite simply: "I like Lady T. . . . the same with Madame de Dino and the Duchess of B.; they are always very good-humored and are very agreeable company; and as they never say anything to offend me I have nothing to do with all the different lovers they are said to have had. I take no credit to myself for being different from them: mine is a very lucky case."

Mme de Boigne—her father, the Marquis d'Osmond, had been the French Ambassador to London under the Restoration and therefore spoke with some knowledge of the subject—was obliged to confess with some annoyance that: "The position taken up by M. de Talleyrand in London had immediately placed the new throne very high on the diplomatic scale. All M. de Talleyrand's colleagues in England were acquainted with him from former times, and they still retained a habit of personal deference toward him that he was able to exploit in the interest of our government.

"He kept a very large house of which the Duchess of Dino did the honors perfectly; together, they had succeeded in placing themselves at the head of everything that was the fashion of the moment." *

At the same time, Charles Greville, the Secretary to the Council, and author of the *Journal of the Reign of Queen Victoria,* noted on November 15, 1830: ". . . In the evening I dined with Lord Sefton to meet Talleyrand and Mme de Dino. . . . People are easily delighted with whatever is in vogue."

❖   ❖   ❖

Though social successes—and in particular that of keeping, as in Vienna, the best table in town †—carried genuine weight in London, and though they facilitated a great many contacts, these social successes were not the only kind that Dorothée achieved during her stay in England. The Duchess of Dino's role in London was extraordinarily multi-faceted compared with that of Countess Edmond de Périgord in Vienna.

Not content with doing the honors of the French Embassy, Dorothée matured by her fifteen years of intimacy with Talleyrand, possessing the Prince's complete confidence and an all-

---

* The sour-tongued Countess added: "In this exclusive society, the Duchess of Dino had soaked herself once more in those aristocratic ideas that her life at Rochecotte may have allowed to become somewhat rusty."

† On October 27, Dorothée wrote to Barante: "Our dinners are earning us some success here and will probably go down as landmarks in the history of London's gastronomy, but they are ruinously costly and M. de Talleyrand is alarmed at the expense. . . . The cost of living here, and I mean of the basic necessities, not of luxury living, is quite beyond the means of most visitors from the continent. Indeed, even beyond those of Prince Esterhazy, who has managed somehow, despite his vast personal fortune and his large salary, to run up a million francs' worth of debts."

powerful influence over him, also followed with passionate interest his playing of the difficult hand that had once again been dealt him and that he was once again to win. During the whole period of her uncle's mission in London, Dorothée acted both as his private secretary and as his confidante, taking the place of Rouen, and to an even larger extent that previously occupied by La Besnardière in Vienna. She also acted as Talleyrand's secret agent as Dalberg had formerly done.

Talleyrand was not happy about the composition of his personnel. It had largely been forced upon him, and the Prince, uncertain both as to the reception he would be given in London and the the probable length of his mission,* had accepted it with good grace. But once he was firmly in the saddle and more assured of some permanence in his position, he set about surrounding himself with collaborators more suited to his needs. Bresson, whom Talleyrand did not like, was sent as an observer to Brussels and Adolphe de Bacourt, whom both he and Dorothée had come to know and appreciate during the last years of the Restoration, was sent for to fill the vacant post. But while waiting for these changes to be completed and for the newcomers to be trained, Talleyrand found that he could not cope single-handed; so Dorothée stepped in to replace the absent confidential secretary. Then, having grown accustomed to this situation, they both found that they enjoyed it too much not to have it continue.

This function was one that Dorothée found herself performing almost immediately upon her arrival. On October 6, Talleyrand presented his credentials to King William. The latter, a sailor with rather rough-and-ready manners and no intelligence who had scarcely been prepared for his eventual accession to the throne by sixty years of relative obscurity as the Duke of Clarence, had only recently succeeded George IV. He was still drunk with his unexpected good fortune, and this had done nothing to improve his natural lack of poise. How would this impulsive and rather unceremonious monarch receive

* During the whole of October, Talleyrand was contemplating returning to Paris. Partly because of the war scare over Belgium, partly because of his differences of opinion with Molé.

him? It was a question everyone was asking himself, and Talleyrand most of all.

The Ambassador was just finishing his toilette, and the
faithful Courtiade was about to begin pinning on his orders,
when Talleyrand, turning towards his niece, remarked that under
the Ancien Régime custom permitted one to make a little
speech to the sovereign on such occasions. Given the circumstances surrounding this particular occasion, he added, it would
be wise of him to take advantage of that fact.

"Now then, Madame de Dino, sit down and think up two
or three sentences for me. Then write them out in your very
biggest writing."

The Duchess did as she was bid, and Talleyrand then
revised the few lines she had scribbled out. While Courtiade
was completing his task, then handing the Prince his cane and
hat, Dorothée employed her delicate gift for penmanship to
produce an easily legible fair copy of the few short sentences
in which the ambassador of Louis-Philippe intended to convey
to "the descendant of the illustrious house of Brunswick" a
subtle reminder of the usurpation of 1688. . . . The audience
was a pleasant one, the allusion understood, accepted, approved.

An incomparable and delightful mistress of his house and
an efficient private secretary, Dorothée still found time, during
the whole of Talleyrand's mission in London, to act as his
secret agent and maintain communications with Madame Adélaïde and Thiers.

The correspondence between Dorothée and the new King of
France's sister began, it will be remembered, at the time of
Louis-Philippe's accession. It continued with occasional inter-
ruptions for several years. Whatever Talleyrand could not communicate officially to his Minister, and whatever he did not
wish to insinuate officially to the King, or even to his sister,
it was Dorothée's task to convey to Madame Adélaïde. But if
it was useful to brief, to enlighten, the Palais-Royal—a short
while later the Tuileries—it was even more important to remain
in close contact with Thiers, by then already one of the politicians most highly regarded by the new monarchy. The erstwhile
journalist of the *National* was soon to be a deputy and then a

minister, but Talleyrand and his niece, aware of his intelligence, though over-estimating his political maturity, saw him above all as one of the great future leaders.*

On October 1, twelve hours after her arrival in London, Dorothée sent Thiers a long letter describing the enthusiastic welcome that Talleyrand had received. Paris ought to know and recognize the importance of such an ambassador. The Minister for Foreign Affairs, since he was being honored by a representative of such distinction, should not only show great zeal in providing that representative with information but also allow him complete freedom of action. Molé nevertheless refused to understand, and Talleyrand became angry. On October 2, he complained to Madame Adélaïde of being kept insufficiently informed, and two days later Dorothée expressed regret in a letter to Thiers that they were not receiving "proper dispatches from Paris instead of mere visiting cards." By October 6, the tone had become more vehement. Dorothée wrote Thiers an account of the audience with the King, but then added: "I also wish to tell you something of which you may or may not make use as you yourself choose. You know that though what I tell you may be repeated, it is for the ears of God himself and not those of his saints. We are displeased with the tone of M. Molé's dispatches. He tells us nothing about the state of France or about that of its Foreign Affairs, and what is more, he insinuates in somewhat cavalier terms that he finds M. de Talleyrand's accounts of what is happening here insufficiently detailed."

This private dispute continued for a whole month, Molé trying to have the Belgian conference held in Paris, Talleyrand and Wellington preferring London. Since Madame Adélaïde

* Dorothée's correspondence with Thiers under the July monarchy is the equivalent of the one with Vitrolles under the Restoration. The letters have the same intimate tone, almost one of loving friendship, but the personal confidences of the earlier correspondence are in general replaced by political confidences. As with Vitrolles, the reasons for the sudden interruption of the correspondence are difficult to pin down. Political incompatibility. Social incompatibility aggravated by Thiers' marriage. Finally, Thiers' attitude at the time of Talleyrand's death—he complained of the dullness of the funeral sermon—transformed this lessening of their intimacy into a complete break.

and Thiers were on the side of the Ambassador, the scales were not equal however; they soon dipped in favor of the Prince, and on November 2, Lafitte, the new Premier, handed Foreign Affairs over to Sébastiani. The new incumbent proved more accommodating to Talleyrand's wishes, as he did also to Louis-Philippe's. He was to remain Minister for Foreign Affairs for almost two years, but eventually relinquished the post in October of 1832 when Broglie was asked to form a government.

November 1830 also brought the departure of Wellington from office. His power having already been threatened for several weeks by the supporters of the Reform Bill, Wellington finally found himself with a minority on November 15 and resigned next day. The Tories were replaced by the Whigs, Wellington by Lord Grey, and Lord Aberdeen, at the Foreign Office, by Lord Palmerston.

While all these changes in political office were taking place, and the newcomers settling themselves in, events had been developing rapidly, the Belgian question losing its latent dangers, thanks to a series of agreements that were also a series of personal successes for Talleyrand. A first protocol, on December 20, proclaimed Belgium's independence; a second, a month later, the new country's neutrality. But then, once the new kingdom had been constituted, it became necessary to find it a king and settle its frontiers. The negotiations were to prove long and delicate, and they would continue to require Talleyrand's presence in London, but from that time on Belgium ceased to be a tinder-box threatening to set all Europe aflame.

◇ ◇ ◇

Before Talleyrand and Dorothée had quite settled into the routine of their London life, they were visited during the early months of 1831 by several survivors from their distant as well as recent pasts.

First, there was Charles de Flahaut.

The Prince had for many years continued to show a very real affection for this amiable and creditable son of his, and during the first years of Dorothée's marriage she had often had occasion to meet this slender, blond boy with the handsome figure so usual among the Talleyrands. Possibly she became a little embittered towards him at that time because she was obliged to watch him becoming a General, then the Emperor's aide-de-camp, while Edmond was stagnating at the head of a regiment.

Father and son had later been separated by political events, and when Dorothée returned to Paris from Vienna in 1816 Charles de Flahaut was in exile in London. But in 1819 he had returned from his exile, unabashed and married to Margaret Elphinstone, an extremely rich and extremely well-born woman who, upon the death of her father, Lord Keith, in 1823 became an English peeress in her own right.

Despite Talleyrand's quarrel with Mme de Souza (the mother of Charles de Flahaut), the newly married couple had maintained a normal, if not particularly warm, relationship with the Prince and the Duchess of Dino. During the last years of the Restoration they had been brought somewhat closer together by their common opposition to the Bourbons. During 1828 the Flahauts had stayed for quite some time at Valençay, and it was at his son's house, it will be remembered, that Talleyrand had announced in the autumn of 1829 that the Bourbons would have to be got rid of for the sake of everyone's peace of mind.

The overthrow of Charles X and the accession of Louis-Philippe once more opened the possibility of a brilliant career to Napoleon's former aide-de-camp. This possibility inevitably created new exigencies for him, and it was not long, as early as late 1830 in fact, before they brought him into conflict with his father.

Full of ambition and passionately interested in politics, Mme de Flahaut had every intention of making her husband an ambassador. And where better than in England? He had lived there for ten years and formed a great many friendships amongst the Whigs. Talleyrand's present mission was an extraordinary one: once the Belgian question had been settled the Prince would soon tire of the routine Embassy life, and then he was very old. . . . Flahaut had no difficulty in bringing Sébastiani round to his point of view and the Minister sent him to London, in November 1830, with a plan for settling the Belgian question by means of a partition between France, Prussia, and Holland, but in fact so that he could prepare the way for his own succession to the ambassadorship.

Talleyrand had no difficulty in seeing through the plan and was angered by it. Dorothée even more so. She had little love for Flahaut because she was possessive and because this charming and half recognized son of Talleyrand had always rather irritated her. Possibly too he reminded her of Edmond—without the latter's shortcomings—and she found that unpleasant. Nor had she any greater fondness for Mme de Flahaut. Ambitious and with a love of intrigue herself, she was naturally apprehensive of these tendencies in the Scottish peeress, and possibly Lady Keith's rather outspoken virtue was also a thorn in her flesh. Lastly, it is probable that once relieved of competition from Talleyrand's legitimate family, by exile in Edmond's case and politics in that of the Esclignacs (Georgine de Péri- gord) and the Noailles, all legitimists living in retirement, she had no intention of allowing the illegitimate branch to fill the vacancy thus created and become her rivals, to however slight a degree, in the interest and affections of the Prince. It therefore suited her to further any estrangement between father and son, and it seems quite clear that instead of attempting to soften the effects of this diplomatic rivalry, which should not have been difficult, since Flahaut only wanted to "succeed" his father not to depose him, Dorothée went out of her way to make it more bitter.

Talleyrand rejected the Sébastiani plan, let Flahaut know that he was being importunate, and sent him back to Paris feeling rather hangdog about the whole business. Late in Jan- uary of 1831, however, when the Duke of Leuchtenberg's candi- dacy for the new Belgian throne suddenly threw Louis-Philippe into a panic, he reappeared on the London scene. This time, Talleyrand and Flahaut worked together in an attempt to appease the British cabinet, who had been alarmed in their turn by the possible choice of the Duke of Nemours, second son of the King of the French. Then, still working together, they laid the foundations for the accession of Leopold of Coburg. But this apparent understanding was still a fragile one: despite Flahaut's appointment to Berlin, where he only remained very few months in any case, Mme de Flahaut's intention to see her husband installed as French Ambassador in London was still as strong as ever.

The Three Glorious Days had reawakened the hopes of other oppressed peoples. After the Belgian uprising came another in Poland. Its leaders had counted on support from England and France, but those powers decided, since they were already occupied with the international threat produced by the Belgian question, that they could not intervene "between a monarch and his subjects." Both Paris and London were soon flooded with Polish refugees. Among these, one of the first to arrive in England was young Walewski, Napoleon's son, whom Adam Czartoryski, by then President of the Polish Committee, had sent to London to plead the insurgents' cause. Upon his arrival on March 24, Walewski was received by Palmerston, and then presented himself to Talleyrand. The old man wth the lumbering eyes may well have started at the sight of that face, so strangely did it bring back to life the features of the Emperor betrayed at Erfurt, exiled in Vienna. Talleyrand rarely spoke of Napoleon; it was as though the Corsican's great shadow never ceased to weigh on him. . . . "Without taking his eyes from his twisted foot as he swung it to and fro in time to his words," the former Prince of Benevento, now the Ambassador of Louis-Philippe, made the Emperor's son one or two vague promises.

Though Talleyrand was no more interested in Poland in 1831 than he had been in 1807 or 1814, Dorothée was disturbed at the thought of the martyrdom being inflicted on "a people to whom she half belonged." She received Walewski with interest and voiced her regret at being unable to express aloud in the Embassy drawing-rooms what her heart really felt for the Polish insurgents. Czartoryski's own arrival in London, shortly after the fall of Warsaw (September 8, 1831), increased her pity. The sight of the Polish Prince reawakened so many memories in Dorothée for a second time: memories of Piattoli and her long months of hope; memories of Mittau; memories of those anguished moments in 1809; memories too of the confidences made in Vienna, the disclosures that had perhaps decided her fate.

After Poland, Italy. Napoleon-Louis and Louis-Napoleon, the sons of Queen Hortense, went to fight in the Romagna. The first of them died there; from measles according to some, from a dagger wound according to others. The Queen hurried down from Arenenburg to save her only remaining son, took him to France, where they lived in hiding for a few days with the tacit consent of Louis-Philippe, then brought him over to England.

When Queen Hortense conveyed to him a desire that they should meet, Talleyrand judged it wiser to avoid so delicate an interview. He sent Montrond to see her first of all, then, after Dorothée's return from a short visit to Paris, his niece. Wrote Dorothée to Barante: "The Duchess of Saint-Leu has arrived to swell the motley crowd of visitors we have here just now, though she is only passing through, and I went to tell her myself on M. de Talleyrand's behalf that our government had authorized her to travel across France under the name of 'Mme d'Arenenburg' in order to return to her home on the shores of Lake Constance. She is exactly the same as when I knew her before. There are some people upon whose characters the greatest vicissitudes of fate are no more able to wreak any change than the passing years are to leave wrinkles on their faces."

But if these ghosts from the days of the Empire were a slight embarrassment to Talleyrand, the last flicker of a passion from her recent past was a very much greater one to Dorothée.

In February of 1831, she wrote to Madame Adélaïde: "My intention has been to come and spend a few weeks in France in order to attend to several pieces of personal business . . . but I hesitate to leave M. de Talleyrand without anyone *of his own* at a moment when he is so much preoccupied with complicated and serious affairs, and when he has recently been a prey to certain apprehensions and melancholy thoughts that Madame, having so kind a heart, will doubtless have shared with him! . . ."

Several weeks went by before she finally made the decision

to leave Talleyrand on his own. Then, early in May, Dorothée left for Paris. It was high time she did so. Since it was now evident that she must count on staying in England for some time, this meant that certain material changes in her personal affairs had become obligatory, and it meant above all that she must make the final break with Piscatory.

A malicious trick played on her by Montrond—Dorothée and he were carrying on a savage small-scale war with one another under her uncle's impartial eye—and a piece of clumsy and perhaps deliberate stupidity on the part of her provincial lover (a duel with Latouche, a journalist who had impugned Mme de Dino's virtue) *—had recently produced the unfortunate and ill-timed effect of recalling the public's attention to a liaison that Dorothée herself was now anxious to forget.

The break with Piscatory had to be unequivocal. It was desirable for the Duchess' social position in England, and it was indispensable for her intimate affections, which had now been directed towards another object. Piscatory must have recognized the inevitable and bowed before it. He disappeared from Dorothée's life. The last and longest of her love affairs under the Restoration faded into the shadows. . . .

* On May 15, 1831, Mérimée sent Stendhal a rather heavy-handedly satirical account of the episode: "Your friend Latouche was called out the other day by a valiant knight determined to defend the honor of damsels in distress. This is how it came about: M. de Colline-Ronde during a recent visit to England convinced Lord Palmerston's son that a young man like himself ought to have a woman like the Duchess of 10.no. [dix.no.], and that he should attack immediately. To the Duchess herself, on the other hand, he pointed out what an insult it would be to the honor of France, of which she is a representative there, should she permit herself to be climbed by a dandy, and urged her to employ all her skill in the use of those weapons with which nature had endowed her to repulse the audacious puppy attempting to board her. . . . He was duly scratched and repulsed with the loss of half his hair and lacerations of the nose. Much to the delight of Mephistophilis Ronde-Colline. Latouche gave an account of this affair in *Le Figaro*; to my mind a bad one, too obscure and unintelligible for provincial readers. These defects did not however prevent M. Piscatory from rushing to the virtuous lady's defense and firing a pistol shot at Latouche, who discharged his into the air. Happily, he did not succeed in killing his second. Whereupon the two enemies fell upon each other's necks and their seconds stood mopping their tears up with their handkerchiefs. Latouche has promised to say in the nicest possible way that Mme de 10.no is an honest woman and by no means a whore."

❖   ❖   ❖

"I am here surrounded by all the trials attendant upon moving to a new house. It had become impossible for me to stay in the one where I was, which in any case is up for sale," Talleyrand informed Madame Adélaïde in June of 1831.

The new house, No. 21, Hanover Square, close to Oxford Street and Regent Street, was a large town house built in the early eighteenth century. It was the property of the Duke of Devonshire and had been previously occupied by both the Greys and the Lievens. The drawing rooms were very fine, and Dorothée did justice to their specious proportions with magnificent furnishings. The only thing Dorothée disliked about the house was that it was haunted by the ghost of a man with a sad, pale face, and black eyes and hair. One night, carrying his candle, Lord Grey had been walking through the ground-floor dining room on the way to his personal apartments when he had suddenly noticed a stranger at the far end of the room, standing behind one of the pillars jutting out into it. He walked toward him, but the man disappeared. Next day, at breakfast, Lord Grey recounted the incident, and his daughter Georgiana then confessed that she had once been awakened during the night by someone breathing on her face. A dark, pale man had been leaning over her. She had closed her eyes, supposing it to be a dream. When she opened them again the man was still there. She screamed, and the ghostly visitor immediately vanished.

But it may have been necessary to be Scottish, or at least English, to see this ghost. None of the Lievens had ever seen it. Nor did Talleyrand or Dorothée ever receive a visit, and the gentle little Pauline occupied Georgiana Grey's former room without exhibiting the slightest fear. But the domestics shivered as they walked about the house in the evening, and the maids insisted on always doing so in pairs.

While the shape of Dorothée's life in England was thus being molded into its final form, so were certain aspects of her emotional life as well. The new intimacy she had just formed, later transformed into a profound and sincere friendship, was to last until her death.

1. The Duchess of Courland and her daughter Dorothée
from a painting by Grassi

2. Adam Czartoryski
(*Bibliothèque polonaise,*
Paris)

3. Alexander I
(*Photo Harlingue Viollet*)

4. Talleyrand by Prud'hon,
Chevrier Marcille Collection
(*Photo Bulloz*)

5. Caulaincourt by Gérard,
Gérard de Moustier Collection
(*Photo Bulloz*)

6. Countess Edmond de Périgord, the château of Valençay
(Photo Pétremand—Réalités)

ALEXANDRE EDMOND
DE TALLEYRAND-PERIGORD
DUC DE DINO, NÉ EN 1787

7. Edmond de Périgord, the château of Valençay
(*Photo Bonnefoy—Réalités*)

8. Rosny
(*Photo Josse-Lalance*)

9. The hôtel de Monaco (today the hôtel Matignon)
(*Photo René-Jacques*)

10. Talleyrand by Gérard, the château of Valençay
(Photo Pétremand—Réalités)

11. Countess Edmond de Périgord,
from a miniature by Agricole,
painted in Vienna in 1815.

12. Clam-Martinitz
(*Austrian National Library*)

13. The Congress of Vienna, from a painting by Isabey
(*Austrian National Library*)

14. Valençay
(Photo Jean Roubier)

15. The staircase of the hôtel Talleyrand,
rue Saint-Florentin, Paris
(Photo USIS)

16. The Duchess of Dino by Prud'hon, Castellane Collection
(Photo Bulloz)

17. The drawing room at Rochecotte with a portrait of Pauline
by Dubufe and a sketch of Talleyrand
(*Photo M. Nahmias—Réalités*)

18. Talleyrand at the end of his life, the château of Rochecotte
(*Photo Schnapp—Réalités*)

19. Adolphe de Bacourt, drawing by C. Wagner,
Michel Missoffe Collection
(Photo Schnapp—Réalités)

20. The King and Queen of Prussia
(Print collection,
Bibliothèque nationale, Paris)

21. The château of Sagan.
(*Photo Austrian National Library*)

22. Félix Lichnowsky
(*Photo Austrian National Library*)

23. The Duchess of Sagan in 1850

On February 26, 1831, the Austrian Neumann, who was supposed by many to be a son of the first Prince of Metternich, paid a visit to the Duchess of Dino. "She is a curious woman," he noted that evening, "full of charm. She has a powerful intelligence and a passionate heart. Also an indefinable air of mystery and inscrutability that adds still more to her powers of attraction."

Dorothée greeted Neumann with effusive pleasure, and complained at his not having spoken to her the previous evening at the Duchess of Cumberland's. "She told me that she was my friend and proved as much to me with her friendly and affectionate attitude. She expressed herself with such warmth that I might have been led to suspect something more than friendship had she not openly confessed to me what the present state of her affections was."

The present state of her affections? Both in Paris and in London there was but one name being linked with hers: that of Adolphe de Bacourt, the young Embassy secretary whom Talleyrand had so imperiously sent for in November of 1830— possibly at Dorothée's instigation.

Born in Nancy in 1801, Adolphe de Bacourt came from a very old family belonging to the lesser nobility of Lorraine. Having entered upon a diplomatic career at the age of twenty-one, he had been sent first to Sweden and then to Holland. Wherever he went, this slender and distinguished youth, well-endowed with good looks and extremely elegant, had won all hearts. Nervous, with delicate health, many-faceted and somewhat inconsistent, by turns slightly pompous and inordinately amusing, he possessed not only a sound and lively intelligence,* a robust Christian faith and an exacting conscience, but also a good and, above all, faithful heart.†

Himself the possessor of excellent manners, refined tastes and a clear, simple, judicious conversational gift, to quote Royer-Collard, Bacourt had no taste for any except the very best

---

* "I know of few people whose minds can be compared to M. de Bacourt's," Talleyrand declared, "and I have *never* met anyone who was more honest."

† Broglie said of him: "The most likable of all his traits was that once a sentiment had found its way into his heart it always remained there for the rest of his life."

society and always sought the company of those enjoying the privileges of high birth—and indeed of intelligence too. Somewhat ingenuous and rather snobbish, with more sensibility than true passion, how could he have failed to succumb—and for his lifetime—to this beautiful and intelligent woman whose maturity merely deepened her powers of attraction, and who was surrounded by the irresistible aura of her almost royal birth and her personal legend? *

❖   ❖   ❖

What were Dorothée's feelings towards Bacourt? We may be sure at all events that they were complex—as complex as the ardent nature of the woman herself, a being full of passion yet always prevented by her pride and uprightness of soul from ever deceiving herself about the implications of her wild emotional forays.

First, for a woman nearing forty, there was the physical attraction of this thirty-year-old man. Then the need to cheat an uneasy feeling that life was beginning to slip away from her, the need to know that she could still love and be loved. There was the fear of isolation that she sensed on the horizon. But above all, for this woman who longed to possess, there was the ecstasy of discovering, as she had sixteen years earlier in Vienna, a being "entirely one's own, without any mental reservations, without secrets, without divergent interests," a being to whom she could entrust the contents of her heart and mind with utter openness.

That sense of security, that profound feeling of trust that had been in such large measure responsible for Dorothée's attachment to Talleyrand was now, by some strange cyclic trick of destiny, being offered to her again. In a minor key, it is true, with certain reserves, with forbidden areas on the Duchess's

---

* Talleyrand once observed of the Countess of Brionne: "A woman's beauty, her noble pride mingling with the prestige of an illustrious ancestry . . . imbue with a particular charm the feelings she inspires. . . ." It is as though he were defining, in advance, the irresistible attraction that the Duchess of Dino exerted upon Bacourt.

side. On the other hand, this new security was being offered, not by an old man forty years her senior but by a man younger than she, who could accompany her, help her through the difficulties of life, and take up the magic wand that would soon slip from the Prince's emaciated fingers. We should also add that this perfect gentleman—what in the age of Louis XIV was termed an "honnête homme"—though he did not have the makings of greatness, did nevertheless have a great deal of attractiveness and charm. And above all he had appeared at exactly the right moment. While satisfying Dorothée's fundamental need for love, he also extended that love into a plane of intellectual exchange and genuine affection that her liaison with Piscatory had never attained.

Talleyrand had received Bacourt favorably upon his arrival and swiftly made him his chosen collaborator. He was not slow to sense what Dorothée and the young diplomat were feeling for one another, but he did not allow it to disturb him, any more than he had allowed himself to be disturbed by his niece's affairs under the Restoration. The pleasures of the flesh had almost ceased to have any further meaning for this infirm and very old man, but he was too experienced not to know that a woman of Dorothée's temperament would not yet be similarly disinterested. Any price he was called upon to pay was a cheap one to him apparently, provided he was allowed to keep her near him, provided he was still the ruler of her head and heart.

Thanks to the Prince, Bacourt's advancement proved rapid. Before long he was First Secretary, and in 1833 he became chargé d'affaires. Nevertheless, during that same year the relations between him and Talleyrand deteriorated somewhat. The liaison between Bacourt and Dorothée was still going on, and it was beginning to encroach on areas that Talleyrand considered exclusively his. He became jealous, and he showed it.

On November 10, 1833, Bacourt wrote to Dorothée at Valençay, where she was in residence at the time. After recounting a little London gossip, including an account of a recent evening party at the Princess Lieven's, Bacourt suddenly changes his tone and tackles rather more intimate topics.

"I must admit that the idea of bending once more beneath

the yoke of M. de Talleyrand's ill humor is one that fills me with real repugnance. Nor does your description of him as having become as gentle as a lamb do anything to lessen that feeling. And besides, there is now a rift between us that can never be mended. I can of course forgive him the ill treatment I have received at his hands by putting it down to his age, his ill-health and the pressure of affairs, but I have nonetheless firmly resolved to keep our relationship here strictly on the footing of employer and employee, and never to try to be to him again what I once was. Once free of the proximity imposed on us by our work and both safely established on neutral ground the situation will change, and we shall find it easy to live in peace with one another. And I hope, my dear friend, that you will not accuse me of trying to create an insurmountable obstacle to our meeting again. No, I shall never be away from you in heart—nor in fact, when the fact is dependent on my will. . . .

"That is a very fine passage in your letter, my angel, in which you condemn the kind of treacherous women who snatch away others' lovers or who whisper corrosive confidences distilled from their own spleen and jealousy; I share your opinions in this respect. That is why I am convinced that the fewer confidants there are associated with any intimate connection the better. And I am even more abundantly of your opinion that people who love one another must eschew society and seek out some well-hidden little corner all their own. . . ." *

During the course of their retirement to Valençay in the autumn of 1833, while Talleyrand was hesitating for so long as to whether or not he should return to London, did some

---

* Whenever they were apart, Dorothée and Bacourt used to write letters to one another almost daily. This continued for thirty years, with the exception of one long break between 1844 and 1847. The letters written by the Duchess, after being somewhat watered down, were used as the basis of her *Chroniques.* As for Bacourt, his *Souvenirs d'un Diplomate,* published in 1882 by his niece, Mme Mirabeau, are in fact made up of the letters he wrote to Dorothée from America between 1840 and 1842. The letters were severely cut—only one was ever published *in extenso,* the one written on November 10, 1833. Like the one written by Dorothée to Talleyrand on June 4, 1816, it must have been mislaid. And like that letter, too, its evidence is as indisputable as it is enlightening.

sort of confrontation take place between uncle and niece? We may be allowed to presume so. The Prince's love was a true one, and no doubt he succeeded in stifling his selfish jealousy. Perhaps he already felt what he later wrote to his niece on February 6, 1837, that during his last moments, those moments that he could no longer doubt were imminent, his only cause for concern would be her future and her happiness. The clouds were dispelled, and from that time onward Talleyrand treated Bacourt with a constant and trusting cordiality.

❖ ❖ ❖

During the whole of 1831, the Belgian problem had continued to make bumpy but fairly consistent progress, thanks to the constant efforts of Talleyrand, assisted, for the most part, by Palmerston. Having been elected King of the Belgians on June 4, Leopold of Coburg had accepted the crown on the 26th. Then, on July 9, the Belgian Congress resigned itself to accepting the Treaty of the Eighteen Articles, a document drawn up by the conference in London that was in fact the new state's birth certificate. At this point, the King of Holland took it into his head to interrupt the proceedings by committing a singular piece of folly. On August 1, he denounced the armistice and marched into Belgium. On August 9, the French army moved in to help the Belgians, and the Dutch king was immediately forced to withdraw in panic.

This fresh incident convinced the conference that the sooner the whole business could be settled the better. During the autumn of 1831, the Treaty of the Twenty-Four Articles, accepted by the Belgian Parliament on November 15, settled the frontiers of the new state. The only thing that then remained was to obtain the already certain ratification of France and England, the probable ratification of Austria and Prussia, the rather more doubtful ratification of Russia, and the extremely unlikely ratification of Holland, whose king was still occupying Antwerp.

Since the matter was now practically concluded, the Belgian

question no longer required Talleyrand's presence in London. Not having left his post in almost two years, and feeling the need for a rest, he resolved to go and spend a few months in France, despite the regret expressed at this decision by the English cabinet, by the Duke of Wellington on behalf of the opposition, and by William IV. Dashing Charles de Flahaut's hopes yet again, the Prince sent for Durant and Mareuil to fulfill his functions while he was away.

The death of Casimir Périer on May 16 almost made this absence permanent, and Talleyrand Premier of France. The disappearance of the energetic man who had for a year held the tiller of the French state with so firm a hand left the cabinet weak and disunited, and the political parties divided among themselves. Another Bourbon in love with power, Louis-Philippe himself may well have been in no hurry to give himself a new master, but the politicians did not share his feelings; as soon as Périer was buried, the "Juste Milieu" (Royer-Collard, Guizot, Broglie, Bertin de Vaux, Sébastiani) dispatched Charles de Rémusat to London with instructions to persuade Talleyrand to accept the Premiership.

Like Vitrolles on a former occasion, Rémusat decided that the best way to persuade the Prince was by first convincing Mme de Dino. A difficult task.

To begin with, the messenger had been badly chosen. "He has a good mind," Dorothée noted on May 24, 1832, "but it is a mind too much given to disdain and denigration and too much encumbered with dogma and prejudice; even at the time when I was seeing the most of his kind of people I always found him in particular singularly disagreeable, and I find it highly unlikely that he will make any different an impression on me now."

Secondly, the Duchess had no desire whatever for Talleyrand to leave London and move to Paris—principally for his own sake. She believed that such a task was not suited to him —the experiment in 1815 had proved as much, and the situation in this instance was an even more difficult one. She also felt, and with some reason, that this old man of seventy-eight, who by an astonishing and kindly caprice of fortune had just succeeded in writing one of the decisive pages in European history, ought not to risk the loss of that genuine triumph by meddling with these dubious domestic quarrels.

Nor for her own sake did Dorothée want Talleyrand in Paris. She was enjoying herself in London, and she was being appreciated: there were five or six houses where she could take her work in the evenings and know that she had only to ask in order to have a place at table set for her. And apart from that, where else—while still moving in the very best society—could she find such freedom to live her own life, such tolerance toward her own and everyone's behavior and eccentricities? And lastly, Dorothée still retained a bitter memory of Paris and its cruelty towards her. With Talleyrand as Premier, she would be living in a house of glass. . . .

Rémusat therefore had very little chance of convincing the Duchess, and though he spent two long hours on May 25 attempting to "apprise her of Paris," it was in vain. Though useless from the political point of view, this visit did inspire the doctrinaire Rémusat to draw an astonishing and cruelly etched portrait of hs hostess.

"Dorothée of Courland was then thirty-nine and still in possession of almost all the glory of her beauty, which had never owed anything to the freshness of youth. She was of middle height, but elegant, and her carriage and bearing had a graceful dignity that made her seem rather taller than in fact she was. . . . What lit up her rather small and sharp-chinned face, below a wide brow bordered by jet black wings of hair, were the incomparable gray-blue eyes, set between long lashes and surrounded by dark circles that enhanced her ardent, caressing, and infinitely expressive gaze. She normally kept them rather narrowed, since her eyesight was poor, and this increased their gentleness; yet so full of life were they that on seeing her again after some period of time, one would have sworn that she had huge, dark eyes as black as coal. The seduction exerted by her mouth and eyes was extreme, and without any other defect than that of seeming rather too much like a seduction. . . .

"I therefore went to lunch with her.* The meal was served

---

* Talleyrand did not rise until very late and was never present at lunch. Dorothée was therefore always alone and free at this meal. During the Restoration she had often invited Vitrolles to share it with her.

in her sitting room. 'I loathe servants,' she said, and dismissed her footman. So there we were left to chat with one another, and with exactly the air of two characters who have decided to play the scene of a political discussion disguised as a social visit. I felt as though I were acting in some high-society comedy. For a moment I even wondered whether I ought not to fulfill all the conditions of that genre by mingling a little love-making with our business. She was beautiful, and her beauty at that hour was by no means unadorned; the brilliance of her gaze owed something to make-up, and her coiffure had been arranged with a visible art that the insufficient beauty of her hair made indispensable. I had so often heard that it was obligatory in the high society of earlier days always to make a tête-à-tête into a tryst, and the Duchess herself was generally thought to have preserved the principles of the Ancien Régime so well in this respect, that it flashed through my mind that I should perhaps do well to tell her she was beautiful. Happily, however, I was blinded neither by genuine temptation nor by vanity; I was saved from making myself ridiculous and contented myself with eating my eggs and cutlets while mustering all the native wit at my command. We discussed more or less every subject one can think of; but the purpose of the conversation was to convey the following answer to me: 'You wish to make M. de Talleyrand Prime Minister; spare yourself the trouble of persisting in this attempt, since the post would not suit him, he has no desire for it, and even if he had, I would prevent him accepting.' When this last sentence, or its equivalent, had been spoken: 'The decree has been issued then, madame,' I replied, 'and I submit to it.' Her personal repugnance in the matter made it quite clear that she was alarmed on her own account at the thought of playing a leading part as the *Curé's Niece*, and at the idea of the responsibility that would attend her genuine or supposed influence at the heart of a government operating in broad daylight and exposed to all the rumors resulting from such publicity. From that moment I resolved to press M. de Talleyrand himself no more than was necessary in order not to seem insufficiently persevering, and I let General Sébastiani know of this decision."

◇ ◇ ◇

After spending the summer in France, Talleyrand, swiftly followed by Dorothée, left for England on October 10, before the Broglie government had finally assumed power.

On October 22, French troops were authorized by an international agreement to besiege Antwerp, which the Dutch king was still refusing to evacuate. Yet another success for the French Ambassador. But the fact remains that the last two years of his appointment were very different from the first two. The social position of both the Prince and the Duchess remained as brilliant as ever; but the Ambassador's political standing, in London as well as in Paris, was no longer the same.

The weak and mediocre Sébastiani had been replaced by Broglie at the Ministry for Foreign Affairs. Austere and incorruptible, an iron-clad, invulnerable doctrinaire, entirely imbued with abstract principles, the Duke meant to be undisputed head of his own department. He wished to be informed, heeded, and obeyed by his ambassadors. Not wishing to precipitate a head-on conflict with Talleyrand, he decided, as Molé had done, to deal with as many English affairs as possible in Paris itself. Wellington had thwarted Molé's attempts to achieve this end earlier; but Palmerston was only too ready to comply, for he disliked Talleyrand, who had already thwarted him, and whose political and social prestige was a thorn in the Englishman's flesh—as was that of Prince Lieven, the Russian Ambassador.

Meanwhile, perhaps influenced by his daughter, the new Queen of the Belgians, who was accusing Talleyrand of having sold himself to the Dutch, Louis-Philippe began to waver in his support of the Prince, and Lord Grey too, doubtless affected by the exasperated murmurs of Mme de Flahaut, was now veering towards an attitude of semi-hostility.

The acuteness of her perceptions and her experience of the world immediately made Dorothée aware of this change in the atmosphere, and she began to think that the Prince's age and health would serve, should the need arise, as an elegant pretext for his retirement. The surrender of Antwerp, on December 23, meant that the Belgian question was finally settled once and for all. To leave at that moment appeared not only easy but also desirable since it would mean leaving at the height of the Prince's success. On February 19, 1833, Thomas Raikes noted in his diary: "Talleyrand is going to leave us; his health begins to break, though his intellect remains unimpaired. Mme de Dino is anxious to go; and she will gain her point. They talk at present of going to Rochecotte. . . ."

The Duke of Orléans' visit to England in May 1833 obliged Talleyrand to postpone his decision, however, and at the same time involved him in fresh complications.

Louis-Philippe wanted his heir apparent to travel. But where could he be sent? The Duke of Orléans would have received a very cold welcome from any of the German rulers. Only the Court of St. James could be counted on to receive him. And even then, if the reception was to be genuinely eager, the presence of the old Ambassador and the Duchess of Dino was a necessity, for who else was in a position to smooth away certain difficulties or had the personal prestige to guarantee the success of the visit?

Though initially put out by the arrival of the Duke, whose friendship with the Flahauts was a source of irritation to them, Talleyrand and Dorothée resigned themselves to it and did everything necessary to make his stay a success. They were wholly successful in attaining this end, and the Duke was cordially received by Lord Grey on behalf of the cabinet, by the Duke of Wellington on behalf of the opposition, and by the Queen and the Duchess of Cumberland on behalf of the court itself. Both the Queen and the Duchess, though fundamentally hostile to the July monarchy, were won over by the handsome appearance of the French heir apparent.

The Duke of Orléans and the French Ambassador observed the strictest reserve in their relations with one another; the former told the latter nothing about affairs in France; the latter told the former nothing about affairs in England. Yet the Duke of Orléans, more naturally a prince than he ever permitted himself to appear in France, was aware how much the July monarchy, sometimes rather middle-class in Paris, owed the grandeur of its prestige in London to Talleyrand and the Duchess. This was a source of pleasure and gratification to him. He communicated his impressions on this score to Paris, and on May 25 Louis-Philippe sent his thanks to Talleyrand, associating Mme de Dino "most particularly" with his expressions of gratitude.

This further success would probably have encouraged Talleyrand to settle down for a longer stay in London, despite the lukewarm attitude of Broglie and the enmity of Palmerston, had not the Flahaut affair almost led Lord Grey into an open declaration of hostility. The Duke of Orléans had expressed a wish that Charles de Flahaut should accompany him. Talleyrand, having passed the stage of mere irritation, had by now developed toward his son, possibly with help from Dorothée, a feeling of "pronounced hatred" (the phrase is Castellane's). The idea of Flahaut's coming to England in the royal Duke's retinue was odious to him, and he saw to it that his name was struck off the list sent to the King and Queen of England for their approval. He was thereby killing two birds with one stone: Flahaut was prevented from accompanying the Duke, and all hopes of a future ambassadorial appointment were destroyed. But it was also a Pyrrhic victory, since Mme de Flahaut's cries of protest now rose to such a pitch that they finally influenced Lady Grey, who was no longer attempting to disguise her antipathy for Talleyrand, and soon Lord Grey as well.

On September 24, 1833, Talleyrand and Dorothée left London after dining the previous evening at Princess Lieven's. Having regarded Talleyrand's arrival in London with a suspicious eye, and fearing at first that the Duchess would prove a rival, the wife of the Russian Ambassador had been completely won over by the Prince ("he amuses me," she wrote to Lord Grey), and they had become very close friends. The Princess noted, and took care to pass her observation on to the Prime Minister, that Talleyrand and his niece both seemed to think they were leaving for good. Lord Grey replied without warmth: "I thought him greatly changed and enfeebled, and at eighty a man does not easily recover. There are those who think that Mme de Dino, seeing this, would not wish him to return. . . ."

The Prince and the Duchess, first at Rochecotte then at Valençay, hesitated through the entire autumn as to what decision they ought to make. Talleyrand found it difficult to contemplate giving up that last remnant of power, that high position, that pleasant life in an aristocratic world that he could never duplicate in France. Dorothée, on the other hand, though she enjoyed her life in England enormously, thought that the moment had come to cast off those already fraying bonds themselves, "to retreat to safety." She observed that Broglie never wrote to the Prince, that Madame Adélaïde's letters, though still friendly, were nevertheless becoming less explicit, and that she sensed the existence of a tacit agreement between Palmerston and Granville,* to which Lord Grey was secretly an accomplice, to exclude Talleyrand altogether. Yet she still did not dare to throw the whole weight of her influence into the scale as she was to do a year later. There were sincere and well-informed friends, such as Royer-Collard, who did not share her apprehensions, and she began to doubt the validity of what was in fact nothing but an instinct and not a certainty.

On November 3, she wrote to Bacourt and confessed to him that she did not know what advice to give. "He is terrified, and I am terrified for him, of the isolation, the boredom, the languor of life in the provinces or the country, but he is also convinced of the impossibility of Paris, where he would be carrying a political responsibility in the eyes of the public without deriving any benefit from it himself and without having any real power. Nor does he attempt to conceal the complexity and gravity of the affairs that he would find upon his return to London,† which would be made even more difficult by the nature of the individuals with whom he would be forced to deal on both sides of the Channel. Lastly, he has an admirable perception of the ease with which he may now lose on a single card everything that he has so miraculously gained during the past three years."

Several days later, Broglie asked Talleyrand to confer with him in Paris. The Prince promised to be there on December 4 and agreed, in principle, to consider returning to London for

---

* The British Ambassador in Paris.
† The Spanish and Portuguese imbroglios, to say nothing of the Eastern question, which had flared up again a few months earlier.

a few more months. In fact, he had still not really made up his mind to do so, and Dorothée was even less persuaded, when a letter arrived from Lord Grey addressed to Talleyrand himself —it had been obtained through the intermediary of Lord Sefton, a common friend of the Prince and the English Prime Minister —which precipitated his decision: the Prince set out once more for England.

◇   ◇   ◇

Though both Louis-Philippe and Lord Grey did genuinely desire Talleyrand's return, Broglie and Palmerston on the other hand had been forced into accepting it against their wills, and they let the Prince feel this. "On his return," Princess Lieven recounts, "he promptly discovered that ministers would not deal with him, that all business matters were being carried on between M. de Broglie and the British Ambassador in Paris; that however pleasant Lord Palmerston might appear, he would tell him nothing; that although they might write flattering letters from the Tuileries, yet his cabinet left him in total ignorance of their intentions. For a man of his known ability and talent such a rôle was scarcely flattering, and he is quite dumbfounded. Mme de Dino weeps—and he does not laugh. . . ." Princess Lieven was not painting an exaggerated picture from unconscious jealousy; she spoke the plain truth.

"Although they never stop telling us here that they could never reach any sort of understanding with anybody but us, and that with anyone else here Europe would already be in flames, I nevertheless continue to wish with all my heart that M. de Talleyrand had stayed at Valençay, for I can see nothing but trouble and strife ahead of him here," the Duchess confessed sadly to Thiers on February 5, 1834. And from that moment on, once she had weighed the situation to her satisfaction, Dorothée, realistic and wholehearted in her decision as always, set about persuading Talleyrand to leave for good.

Palmerston soon ceased to be "charming." And his arrogance and discourtesy did not take long to wound the Prince. Not

content with making the latter wait for two hours in his antechamber before granting him an audience, the head of the
Foreign Office systematically refused all invitations to dine at the
French Embassy, and these refusals, by the time they had continued throughout a whole season, eventually became insulting.*
Yet Talleyrand still resisted his niece's pressure. The resignation of Broglie on March 28, 1834, his replacement by Admiral
de Rigny, the steady disintegration of the Grey cabinet, and
the growing hope of a new Tory government all offered some
grounds for hesitation to the old man still so susceptible to
"the gnawing of a still lively ambition."

Dorothée however, now completely decided, was watching
with affectionate vigilance for the most favorable moment to
impose her will. "I realized," she noted on July 13, apropos of
Lord Grey's departure from office, "that in a public career it is
especially necessary to concentrate on selecting a good line of
retreat, then to use it without hesitation at the right moment,
thus quitting the political scene with apparent nonchalance
and with good grace, which is necessary if one is to draw the
spectators' plaudits and escape being hissed."

For a whole month Dorothée bided her time without allowing her vigilance to relax. "Last year, the King of England said
to M. de Talleyrand as he left for the continent: 'When will
you come back?' The year before he had said: 'I have instructed
my Ambassador in Paris to tell your government that I set great
store by keeping you.' This year he is saying 'When do you
leave?' "

Several days later, she added: "Lady Holland and Lady
Cowper are doing everything within their powers to see that
M. de Talleyrand and Lord Palmerston part on good terms. . . .
They will succeed, I am sure, in seeing that the parting is a
courteous one, without harsh words, without an outright break;
but it is impossible for a leaven that has been fermenting for

---

* Palmerston was at the same time provoking the departure of Prince
Lieven. In 1833, the head of the Foreign Office had appointed Stratford Can-
ning British Ambassador in St. Petersburg, even though he knew that it was
an appointment displeasing to the Tsar. Nicholas I refused to receive Canning.
Palmerston stubbornly refused to go back on his unfortunate choice, and in
May 1834 the Tsar recalled his own ambassador.

so long not to leave behind a seed of unease, of embarrassment, of rancor. . . . In spite of all the very pleasant and satisfying memories that still make me so attached to England, I confess that where M. de Talleyrand is concerned I shall feel the most genuine relief at seeing him free of public affairs."

On August 18—Talleyrand was leaving the next day for Paris and the Duchess was due to follow him four days later—Dorothée handed the Prince a long letter in which she set out, tenderly but very firmly, all her thoughts on this matter.

"I have the greatest duties to fulfill towards you, and I am never more deeply aware of this fact than when your reputation seems to me in danger. I sometimes vex you a little when I talk, and at those times I cease to speak, before having said everything I think, before having spoken the whole truth. Permit me therefore to write it to you, and be good enough to pass over whatever in these words you may find unpleasant in recognition of the conscientious devotion that has dictated them. Besides, without pretending to lay claim to a very great degree of understanding I cannot think that understanding limited when it is applied to yourself, whom I know so well and whose difficulties and problems I am so well placed to judge and appreciate. It is not lightly, therefore, that I urge you to quit public life. . . . You know how apprehensive I was last year, when I saw you returning again to England. I sensed in advance all the unpleasantness that the performance of your task was bound to bring you with the instruments provided; you must admit that my predictions have for the most part been realized. During the past year, the problem has been aggravated even further by any number of distressing incidents. . . . When you came, four years ago, it was not to make your fortune, to establish your reputation, to make a career; all that had been accomplished many years before; nor did you come out of affection for the individuals who govern us, for whom you have little esteem or love; you came only, at a time of earthquake, to render a great service to your country! A perilous enterprise at your age! To reappear after fifteen years of retirement, to face the rising storm and then to quell it, this was a daring venture. You have accomplished what you intended, let that suffice; henceforward you could do nothing that would not weaken the prestige of what you have already done. . . . In youth, any moment is a good one to enter the fray; in age, there is nothing left but a careful choice of the moment to leave it. . . . When, like you, one belongs to history, one should not think of any other future than the one being prepared for you in its pages. And, as you know, it judges the end of a life more harshly than its beginning. If, as I am proud enough to believe, you place some value on my judgment as well as on my affection, you will be as honest with yourself as I am permitting myself to be at this moment; you will renounce all voluntary illusions, all specious quibbles, all the subtle temptations of vanity, and you will bring to an end a situation that would soon lower you from your present position as much in the eyes of others as in my own. Do not haggle with the public. Dictate its verdict, do not have it forced upon you; say that you are old so that others shall not say that you are aging; say nobly, simply, for all the world to hear: the time has come!"

❖   ❖   ❖

Talleyrand understood and recognized the truth of Dorothée's letter. And yet he hesitated still. All his life he had come to his decisions slowly, with a kind of nonchalance.

The Duchess and he rested all through September at Valençay. In October, they entertained a houseful of guests: the family, including the Valençays and the Duchess of Montmorency; some English friends, including Lady Clanricarde, Canning's daughter, and Henry Greville, the writer's brother. Their days began with a buffet lunch, quite informal, at half past eleven. After entertaining themselves in the drawing room until about two, the afternoon was taken up with a walk. At half past five dinner was served, a sumptuous meal with many courses.* The evening was a long one—according to Greville, interminable—even though Talleyrand interrupted it at nine

---

* The Englishman Motteux managed to consume portions of sixteen of them on one and the same evening.

to go for a drive in his carriage. From ten until eleven, the Prince played whist while waiting for the post from Paris.

On October 26, the Duke of Orléans arrived at Valençay. He stayed for three days, made much of, extremely courteous. His visit helped to ripen Talleyrand's decision. The Duke let it be understood that since Palmerston was remaining in office, perhaps the Prince's place was no longer in London, and Talleyrand recognized the truth of this.

Meanwhile, Royer-Collard had rallied completely to Dorothée's way of thinking, and he would have liked to see the step he so approved of already taken. "His last master stroke will be to end his career in time, even, I am tempted to say, to break at one and the same moment with both England and France as they have become during the past year." The news of an ephemeral government under Bassano—it lasted forty-eight hours—including Bresson, the Prince's subordinate in London, as Minister for Foreign Affairs, finally put an end to Talleyrand's irresolution: on November 13, 1834, he handed in his resignation.

For the Prince, this was the end of his political life, his farewell to power. As for the Duchess, she noted on December 31, 1834: "These four years . . . have given a new shape to my life, provided me with a fresh point of departure, set me off on a new line of thought; they have modified the world's opinion of me. What I owe to England will never leave me again, I hope, and will go with me, wherever I go, for the rest of my life."

O N AUGUST 18, 1834, Dorothée had written to Talleyrand: "History judges the end of a life more harshly than its
beginning." Now, with all her will and because of her deep
attachment to him, Dorothée desired that Talleyrand should
live through this "end of his life" with dignity and in a spirit
of order. With dignity by renouncing temporal power without
any lingering regret. In a spirit of order by reconciling himself
without equivocation to the Church.

Helping Talleyrand to live his old age was for Dorothée an
essential task, though there were others awaiting her too, ones
of which she was aware, and which she appraised with a lucid
eye: to create a stable existence for herself now that the years
in England had stripped her life of the tares sown under the
Restoration; to take advantage of the support that Talleyrand
was still in a position to give her in preparing a future for
Pauline.

Neither Louis-Philippe nor Madame Adélaïde, more particularly the latter, were anxious that the July monarchy should
be deprived of Talleyrand's services. They appreciated those
the Prince had already rendered to it at their true value; they
also remembered the Empire and the Restoration and in consequence feared quite probably that retirement in his case was
only another word for opposition.

Talleyrand had announced his intention of resigning to
Madame Adélaïde on November 12. By return post, the King's
sister asked the Prince to postpone his decision. She added,
"If you don't wish to go back to London, what is to prevent
you from going to Vienna, where you would be so useful?"

A tempting offer for the still ambitious veteran: Metternich
would be glad to see him. Nevertheless, on November 17 Talleyrand rejected the offer. "England is out of the question for me;
Vienna would please me in many ways and would also suit

Mme de Dino whose total devotion to me consoles her only with difficulty for having to leave London where she was so appreciated. But at my age one no longer goes looking for tasks so far from home . . . a permanent appointment would no longer suit me, above all in Vienna, where I was once, these twenty years ago, the man of the Restoration. . . ."

Such scruples were something new to Talleyrand, who had not hesitated to go to Vienna in order to help dismember the still warm body of Napoleon's Empire. There can be little risk of error if we attribute this new attitude to the influence of Dorothée and her prudence.* Both were exerted two days later when the news that Melbourne's government had fallen seemed about to reopen the question of the Prince's resignation.

Suddenly, Palmerston was no longer an obstacle to Talleyrand's return to London. Indeed, Wellington was now requesting his presence there. Would the Prince allow himself to be persuaded, seduced, by Mme Adélaïde, Louise-Philippe and the Duke of Orléans? "You *alone* were able to achieve it [an entente between France and England]," Madame Adélaïde wrote on November 18, "and you *alone* can preserve it in the present circumstances; this is something of which the King is deeply persuaded. . . . My nephew has formed the same hopes in regard to your decision; he has written to Mme de Dino; she will be his interpreter to you in this matter; there could be no better one. . . ." † In a separate letter written on the same day, Louis-Philippe repeated and confirmed all that his sister had said.

---

* On December 24, Metternich wrote to Apponyi: "Mme de Dino wrote a few days ago to Esterhazy informing him of M. de Talleyrand's decision to withdraw entirely from public life. She says that the post of French Ambassador in Vienna was offered him on two separate occasions, but that he refused it on account of his age and infirmities."

† On November 16, in a letter to Madame Adélaïde, Talleyrand had read the heir to the throne a lesson: "While staying in this very house, Mgr le Duc d'Orléans made it clear in front of the English people also of the party that in his opinion I could no longer be of any use to the King in London. The absolute silence that the Royal Prince has maintained in regard to us since his departure from Valençay could then only confirm me further in this thought. . . ." The lesson had evidently been understood, at the Tuileries as well as at the Pavillon de Marsan.

Dispatched by special courier, these letters arrived at Valençay on the morning of the 19th. "Coaxing, supplications, there's nothing they haven't tried," Dorothée wrote to Bacourt that evening, "even my name, constantly repeated, has been called upon for help . . . it's all extremely kind, but in no way conclusive."

Then four days of suspense of which no account has survived. Finally, on November 23, Talleyrand wrote to the King and his sister confirming his resignation. One sentence in a letter written to Bacourt on the 24th reveals to us what the Duchess had thought, desired, resolved, insisted upon; * "M. de Talleyrand, fortunately, is persisting in his resignation."

Early in December, Talleyrand and his niece arrived in Paris. This return to the capital was to mark a new phase in their existence. How would the Prince accommodate himself to the "complete and sincere retirement," to the "simple and peaceful private life" that he had announced the beginning of to Mme Adélaïde? How would the Duchess fare in attempting to renew the bonds that had been broken under the Restoration? In London, she had received a taste for the world of international high society to which in fact she belonged. And now she meant to make her way back into the equivalent social stratum in Paris, in other words to win acceptance in the Faubourg Saint-Germain, which was for the most part Carlist, and to be reconciled with the Talleyrand family, which had been ignoring her more or less openly since 1822. Such connections had become necessary in order to assure the future of Pauline, now growing into a woman, ingenuous and pious,

* The Duchess of Dino refused to deceive herself about the Prince's physical decline. She was also apprehensive of the difficulties he would be likely to meet in Paris in the event of Broglie's possible return to public life—a return that did occur during March, 1835—or in London if the Tories were unable to maintain themselves in power and Melbourne, with Palmerston at the F.O., were to be made Prime Minister again—in fact, Melbourne's second cabinet was formed late in April, 1835. She was therefore obliged to use every ounce of power she possessed to force Talleyrand into this decision that he found so difficult to accept. The Prince's irritability was remarked upon in Paris during December of 1834, and on February 22, 1836, the Duchess was still talking of a "fresh outburst of rage against Paris, against his age, against his position, and a new sharpness in his regret at having given up London."

between a Talleyrand all tender astonishment and a mother whose attitude was almost one of respect. Dorothée was determined that this child she loved so much should attain happiness, "that honest and regular happiness" that she herself had never known and had so much yearned for. Her daughter's happiness was to be her true revenge on fortune.

One fact immediately became apparent; Talleyrand's years in London had restored to him the prestige that the disgrace inflicted on him by Louis XVIII and the long period of retirement that followed it had so badly damaged. The mezzanine on the Rue Saint-Florentin was besieged by visitors, both French and foreign.

Then a second fact became equally apparent: the role played by the Duchess of Dino in London at the side of the French Ambassador had placed her in the forefront of Parisian society. She was to find herself surrounded by all those who courted success, and many who had dropped her under the Restoration now returned.

The day following her return, the Duchess received a visit from Royer-Collard. The friendship between Dorothée and this "rather gentle Jansenist" was a sincere one, somewhat passionate on his side and very trusting on hers." * Royer-Collard had come as an intermediary. Talleyrand and Molé had quarreled during the autumn of 1830 and were still at odds. Aware that the wind was changing, Napoleon's former Grand Judge was now anxious to renew his connection with the Rue Saint-Florentin and, as a first step, expressed a desire to see Dorothée alone.

Royer-Collard had scarcely left when the Duke of Orléans arrived. This first visit was to be followed by many others and to prove the foundations of a genuine friendship between the heir to the throne, already a close friend of Louis de Valençay, and the Duchess of Dino. Although still under the influence of the Flahauts, the Duke had appreciated the prestige for the

* Dorothée made more than one confession during her correspondence with Royer-Collard. She came to feel later that these were dangerous. As we have already noted, she asked the philosopher to return her letters and then had them burned.

Orléans dynasty that was won by Talleyrand's aristocratic mode of life in London. Though he had decided that Palmerston's hostility made it impossible for the old ambassador to continue at his post, the heir apparent was nevertheless still anxious that Talleyrand should continue to be publicly connected with the July monarchy.

But the Duke had above all appreciated the subtle intelligence of Talleyrand's niece, and it had occurred to him that this great lady, adopted by London society, with the highest connections both in Vienna and Berlin, could advise him better than anyone else on certain points of European politics, as well as giving him a few pointers on the subject of his marriage, a question that was by then beginning to be one of steadily increasing concern at the Tuileries. After his visit on the 6th, the Duke came back again on the 7th to tell Dorothée about a visit made by the brother of Robert Peel, the future Prime Minister of England.

On Monday the 8th, at four in the afternoon, Dorothée received Molé. "Everything went off as though we'd seen each other only the day before, with him telling me, as he always used to do, about himself, his affections, his intimate relations, his present attitudes of mind, all with that charm that he alone possesses. He told me that I was much more amiable than I had been four years ago, and he stayed for nearly an hour. I have always found that there is no one else with whom one can converse so perfectly, so rapidly, so agreeably as with him; he has such very good taste in an age when no one else has any at all. . . . A great many names, a great many facts and things came back to us both during that hour . . . in short, everything turned out for the best. . . ."

This reconciliation with Molé was the herald of another: with Mme de Castellane. It took place during Thiers' reception into the Académie Française on December 13. Dorothée had gone to the Institut with Lady Clanricarde, and Thiers, with a sensitivity to her feelings that pleased the Duchess, had taken care to have them seated at a distance from her family and near to Mme de Boigne, the Maréchal Gérard, Molé and Mme de Castellane. "The latter has thickened out, become fatter and heavier, but she still has an agreeable physiognomy and pretty tricks of expression in the lower half of her face. She seemed so delighted, so moved, so touched at seeing me again that her emotion affected me too; we shook hands. She said to me: 'Will you allow me to come and see you again?' To which I replied: 'With all my heart.'"

◇　◇　◇

These reconciliations with Molé and Mme de Castellane, whose opinions had led them to swear allegiance to the Juste Milieu but who both, by birth and through their connections, belonged to the very best society, brought Dorothée an initial reassurance. Nevertheless, if she was to achieve the position in Paris society that she had determined upon, there were still two difficulties to be overcome.

She wished to remain friendly with the royal court and yet to actually appear there as little as possible. In December of 1833, during the several days she had spent in Paris at that time, she had observed that Faubourg Saint-Germain was still stubbornly ignoring the Tuileries. "The fact is," Dorothée had added, "that unless one is actually obliged to go there the court is too mixed to be attractive. I am distressed at it for the sake of the Queen, whom I love and honor. . . ."

Marie-Amélie, who lent her support to a usurpation that she thought reprehensible only because of her love for her husband, was more or less without illusions as to the company her borrowed royalty was obliging her to keep. Perhaps that was one of the reasons for the exclusively family atmosphere that she maintained within the Tuileries. Since she possessed great delicacy of mind, the Queen did not wish to impose on people what they had no desire for, and since she herself was much preoccupied with her difficulties in marrying her own daughters she was able to sympathize with Mme de Dino's anxiety over Pauline. In short, the two women seem to have reached a tacit understanding.

On December 11, Talleyrand and his niece dined at the Tuileries with the Molliens, the Valençays, and the Baron de

Montmorency. Not a single guest who might have caused them embarrassment. To express her gratitude, Dorothée attended a court function on the evening of January 2. "They were very gracious to me, and I think attached some value to the fact that I went there on the occasion of a large reception that one might call *public*. There was a fear that I might wish to limit myself only to private audiences. That, it seems to me, would have been bad taste; it is possible that I might not wish to go at all, but when one is prepared to see people in private it does not do to behave as though one is hiding the fact and to renounce them in public. As soon as I had been seen, the Queen herself told me to leave; the little door was opened for me (the one into the private apartments) and I escaped, delighted at being done with such an unpleasant duty."

Not to make one's presence too obvious at the Tuileries was one preliminary condition for winning the acceptance of the Faubourg Saint-Germain. Once that had been fulfilled, there remained the task of finding a mediator. On that same day, January 2, Dorothée found one. Before leaving for the Tuileries she had received a visit from the Duke of Noailles. They had been brought together by an event of great sadness for them both, the death, on December 29, of the young Princess of Chalais, who had been the Duke of Noailles's niece, distantly related to the Duchess of Dino through the Périgords, and dearly loved by them both. They wept together over this shared grief, then fell to talking of politics and society. "He stayed a very long while, apparently completely at ease and enjoying himself greatly. He expressed a desire to see me often and to get to know us better. . . . He is extremely ugly and looks old without in fact being so; he is scholarly, distinguished and very well-bred." Though broad-minded, and not at all opposed to a reconciliation in practice, the Duke of Noailles was nevertheless strictly Carlist. His friendship was to open much wider the doors of the Faubourg Saint-Germain to Dorothée.*

---

* On April 26, Lady Granville wrote to her sister: "Mme de **Dino** is always with Mme de Lieven. It is supposed that she, Dino, has been making a violent and successful attack on the heart of the Duke of Noailles, and that his family are doubly frantic at the infidelity and the chance of her persuading him to attach himself to the present court."

Though Dorothée had every reason to be satisfied with these preliminary contacts with Paris society, she still did not deceive herself about the fundamental facts of the matter. "You don't know what Paris is like, my dear Count," she confided to Rodolphe Apponyi on January 17, 1835. "Take my own case, for example. I have been in France now for more than twenty years, in a position that one would have supposed made me immune to prejudices; well, I still haven't overcome them, I am still considered a foreigner, and if ever I have begun to think that I was at last at home here, then I have very quickly been shown how wrong I was. To the whole of society, even to the members of the family into which I married, I am a foreigner. . . ."

Sad and bitter words. They explain, and foreshadow, Dorothée's return to Germany after Talleyrand's death.

❖ ❖ ❖

Although on the day of Thiers's reception into the Académie the entire assembly in the Institut had risen to its feet as a gesture of greeting and homage at Talleyrand's entrance, although every evening after dinner the house on the Rue Saint-Florentin was packed with a "deafening procession of visitors," nevertheless the Prince, nervous and melancholic, was once more seized by the need for continual movement that had already helped him to fend off the black threat of boredom under the Restoration. By late December 1834 he was already anxious to go to Rochecotte. Dorothée resisted for a while, then gave in.

They spent four months in Touraine, during all of which Talleyrand remained in a rather despondent and irritable mood, something not at all characteristic of him. Faced with the relative solitude of Rochecotte—La Besnardière, the Countess of Balbi, Alexis de Saint-Priest and Bacourt had come down to prevent its being absolute—the Prince, according to his niece, was constantly trying to pick quarrels with his guests in order to give vent to his emotional unrest so that he spent his time perpetually up in arms in the midst of an otherwise totally pacific atmosphere. Nevertheless, Talleyrand once again enjoyed being in that great, light-filled house so beautifully situated on its hill above the river. On April 20, he wrote to his friend Gagern, the German diplomat: "You don't know Rochecotte, otherwise you could not ask: 'Why Rochecotte?'. Even as I write this I am looking down on a real garden two leagues wide and four leagues long. . . . Besides, there's another thing that makes me prefer Rochecotte to every other place, which is that not only am I with Mme de Dino here, I am also in her home, which is for me an added pleasure."

The dissatisfaction which she sensed was gnawing at her uncle disturbed Dorothée unutterably. She had wanted the Prince to go into retirement because she believed it necessary and prudent, but now she was worried that his boredom and unassuaged ambition might impel him to revoke his former decision. Throughout the spring of 1835, encouraged to trust him by their recent reconciliation, Dorothée wrote to Molé with great freedom. On April 24, while also expressing her uneasiness on his score, she made a very curious evaluation of Talleyrand: "There are some minds that can only be content in the midst of dangers. In the prime of life, they will sacrifice the very highest interests for the sake of risk; in old age, they seek the unexpected even in the least important material details of their lives. By remaining thus always in suspense they keep others in suspense too; they reached their term without being prepared for it but not without regrets. It is sometimes a curious study, and usually a sad one, for the constant and fond spectator who wishes to see a career that has been in all respects remarkable and without any loss of dignity or happiness. When I perceive so clearly that one of these is always on the point of being sacrificed to the other I am filled with an inexpressible anxiety. . . ." *

* In a postscript, Dorothée urgently requested Molé to burn this letter: "I should be very distressed if I were obliged to stop writing to you informally like this, and yet if you cannot honestly promise to burn everything I send I shall have to stop doing so; for even more than the next woman I pay for such pleasures with my fear of all the fatal possibilities inherent in the written word." Still the same allusions, the same confessions.

In June, 1835, the Prince and the Duchess returned to Paris for Pauline's confirmation, then moved to Pont-de-Sains.* Early in July, while Talleyrand went with his great-niece to Bourbonne, Dorothée traveled to Baden. She met Princess Lieven again while there, and the two talked about the happy times they had shared in the past—in England. Bacourt also came to the spa.

Dorothée's liaison with Bacourt had always been discreet—and it remained so. Yet this intimacy, this lasting marriage of two hearts was still a very close one, and in September of 1834 Dorothée thought nothing of confessing it openly to Thiers with all the immodesty of the great lady.

"Now you must render me the most *personal* of services. Lend M. de Bacourt your support in the Council, with the King, and with M. de Rigny. His position in London is presently most difficult and delicate. . . . That is what I had to tell you, because it is my own affair, and because there is scarcely another in the world more capable of affecting me. You are the only person to whom I speak in this way: I know that I may do so without fear of impropriety. Please take it as the best possible proof of my esteem, my affection and my confidence, and do not mistake it. I can do nothing for you, and in this matter you can do a great deal for me. . . . Please write your answer in two separate parts. As you see, this letter has been composed thus."

London without Talleyrand, Hanover Place without Dorothée, no longer suited Bacourt, and on December 8, 1834, by which time the Prince's resignation was in no further doubt, the young diplomat asked to be transferred from England on the pretext that his ill health was being aggravated by the British climate. He was hoping to be offered a legation: Munich if he was lucky, Karlsruhe at the very least. The bitter feelings that

* Dorothée confessed to Barante that she found these perpetual changes of residence absurd. She resigned herself to them, however, because of her affection for her uncle. While always prepared to offer the very strongest resistance to any suggested resumption of public life "because she always placed dignity before happiness" (the very same words she had used when writing to Molé), to make up for this she avoided even the slightest show of resistance in matters where dignity was not involved. "It would merely be introducing a note of bitterness between us to no real purpose."

had arisen between the Ambassador and his secretary in 1833 had by this time died down for good, and Talleyrand regarded his former subordinate as a relative by adoption.* He did everything in his power to secure this promotion. "I think, my dear Bacourt," he wrote on December 23, 1834, "that your affairs have now been arranged more or less as you want them. . . ." Next day, Talleyrand added: "When you come to Paris you must stay with me. I am keeping d'Alava's apartments for you." †

Bacourt's new appointment was compromised, however, by Broglie's return to power in March of 1835. A Doctrinaire, and as ill-disposed towards Talleyrand and his friends as ever, the new Premier revoked the promise made by his predecessor; Talleyrand was obliged to make a personal overture to Louis-Philippe, and the Duchess of Dino another to the Duke of Orléans, before the matter was at last satisfactorily concluded in September of 1835. Bacourt was to remain four years in Karlsruhe, though the stay was interrupted by frequent visits to Paris, where he stayed as a guest on the Rue Saint-Florentin, and by seasons in Baden.‡

* In the codicil added to his will on January 17, 1838, Talleyrand made Bacourt a legacy of 50,000 francs and charged him with the task, should Mme de Dino be unable to fulfill it, of publishing his memoirs thirty years after the Prince's death.

† General d'Alava, a Spanish politician with whom Talleyrand was very friendly. He also stayed frequently at Valençay and Rochecotte.

‡ Dorothée was still displaying the same interest in Bacourt's career in 1837 as she had in 1834; we have a letter of hers written in that year to Molé, then Premier and Minister for Foreign Affairs, which is a curious counterpart of the one addressed to Thiers three years earlier: "It is as a friend that I am writing to you. There are few things outside my home that interest me, very few by which I can be touched or wounded, but there are some, and I am in fact faced with one at present." After asking Molé to appoint Bacourt to a post at the Hague, she goes on: "You know that I have been discreet ever since you became Premier; *personally* I have asked nothing of you; now I am asking for something, and asking for it with the *utmost urgency*, and as one of the things by which you can give me proof that I have good cause to count on your friendship. Remember that it is only very rarely that there is an opportunity to oblige a person with such independence of position, heart, and mind as myself. Such an opportunity has now presented itself. Will you let it slip by? I cannot think that you will.

"I am dining with you, but I wanted to tell you, before I saw you, that it is within your power to do me a very personal kindness, and one that I should find it bitter to be deprived of."

◇   ◇   ◇

The Duchess of Dino was more than a woman of high society anxious to maintain her station, more than an ambitious intriguer greedy for power and influence. She was also a woman with an enlightened conscience, an intelligent woman aware of the spiritual problems in life. The aridity of her marriage had prevented her conversion in 1811 from bearing fruit. Then had come the storms that ravaged her early womanhood. But their very violence had helped to crush the pride in her soul, to plow and harrow it, leaving it fertile and ready to receive the seed that was one day to be planted there. After this difficult period ("Heaven does not answer when I question it," she had written to Vitrolles at that time), her stay in England, despite the social and political activity it involved, had been a time of mental repose during which she had begun to revise her sense of values. Finally, Bacourt's appearance in her life, though blameworthy from the point of view of strict morality, had nevertheless paved the way for Dorothée's return to those realms of the soul from which she had seemed to be so far removed. This inner development had made her more aware of the necessity for reconciling Talleyrand with the Church.

Mgr Quélen too, undeterred by his failure ten years earlier, his anxiety now increased by the great age of the Prince, was still resolved to secure this indispensable submission.

After a separation of five years, Dorothée and the Archbishop of Paris had been provided with an opportunity to renew their acquaintance on the occasion of Pauline de Périgord's confirmation in June of 1835.* The prelate confided to the Duchess that having been struck by the tone of Talleyrand's letter of resignation, a tone that semed to indicate a return

---

* Mgr. de Quélen was a confirmed Carlist and had viewed the formation of the July monarchy without pleasure. He had paid for this attitude by the sack of the Archbishop's palace on February 14, 1831, as a result of the anti-clerical riots in Saint-Germain-l'Auxerrois. He never appeared at the Tuileries, and Notre-Dame was closed to the King. The Archbishop did not reopen the doors of his cathedral to Louis-Philippe until after the assassination attempt by Fieschi. The failure of this attempt was celebrated by a *Te Deum* on August 6, 1835.

to a more serious view of things,* he had begun to entertain a gratifying suspicion that the time to act had perhaps arrived. He had written off to Rome, and the Pope had granted him powers of absolution and reconciliation, together with permission to delegate these powers to the Archbishops of Bourges and Tours whose areas of jurisdiction included Valençay and Rochecotte respectively.

Dorothée's reply took some time coming. She contented herself with the observation that any direct approach would probably produce exactly the opposite effect from the one desired. "As for myself," she added, "I shall be forced to confine myself to a purely passive role."

The caution of this reply is surprising, coming as it does from a woman usually so intrepid, but it can be explained by the respect, almost the fear, that she felt toward Talleyrand,† as well as by the still indecisive nature of her own faith.

Nevertheless, this conversation had made its mark, and Dorothée made a careful note of it, adding, as though to excuse herself: "I can hold myself equally aloof from any action contrary to the desired goal of the Church, and from any action that might disturb the peace of mind that I am responsible for, without producing the desired result. If that result can ever be achieved, it is for a voice far higher and more powerfully persuasive than any human voice to obtain it."

The human voices did not remain silent, however. In October of 1835, Talleyrand and Dorothée returned to Paris. Several weeks later, on November 23, Dorothée received a letter signed "Sister Thérèse de Jésus." This was a distant cousin, Louisa de

---

* At the end of this letter, the Prince wrote: "My great age, the infirmities that are its natural consequence, the repose that it requires, the thoughts that it suggests. . . ." Though it was the Duchess who had composed the rough draft of this letter, it was Royer-Collard who had replaced the words "warnings that it brings" by "thoughts that it suggests."

† These terms may perhaps cause surprise in view of the profound influence that Dorothée exerted over Talleyrand. Yet they are accurate. She could "lead" the Prince, but only at the price of infinite precautions and constant apprehensions. Since she was defenseless against Talleyrand's disdainful irony when he was angry, she often did not dare to express her thoughts verbally, and when the matter was of moment she sometimes wrote them to him, as she did on August 18, 1834, and as she was to do in April, 1838.

Chabannes, who, after an unhappy girlhood had made her into a thin, colorless, nervous, and taciturn woman, had entered a Carmelite convent seven years previously and taken the name Sister Thérèse de Jésus.

Sister Thérèse wrote to Dorothée that she had obtained permission from her superiors to see her; she begged her to come immediately because this was one of the rare days on which visitors were allowed. In order to prevent any possible alarm on Dorothée's part, her cousin also added that she would receive her alone and with her face uncovered.

At about two in the afternoon on a cold autumn day, Dorothée set out for the Rue d'Enfer. Her carriage drew up in front of a large gate with a cross on the top of it. The nun in attendance showed the visitor into the icy and deserted nave of the chapel; at the far end, behind the great brown curtain, Vespers were still in progress.

When the service was over, Dorothée was led into a little unheated visiting-room. Trembling with the cold, she sat down in a cane armchair standing beside an iron grille. The grille had vertical wooden reinforcements, and behind it stretched another expanse of dark woolen curtain.

After a few moments, there was a noise of footsteps; then a clear voice said: "*Deo gratias.*" Not knowing what to reply, Dorothée said nothing. "*Deo gratias,*" the same voice repeated. "I wasn't told what I ought to reply," the visitor decided to confess. Then a tiny burst of laughter: "Good day, cousin, it was only to make sure you were there."

"The curtain was drawn aside and I found myself confronted with a round, fresh face, two sparkling blue eyes and a smiling mouth. The voice, far from being dead and toneless, as I had expected, was both vibrant and animated, swift in its expression of the kindest and most gentle thoughts, together with assurances of a well-being and contentment that were fully confirmed by the most consoling visual impression it would be possible to receive of a nun belonging to so strictly closed an order. She is now forty-eight but looks no more than thirty-six. She thanked me a great deal for having come and handed me a little medal with a figure of the Holy Virgin on it, begging me to see that M. de Talleyrand wore it about his person, without his knowing it. 'This medal,' she told me, 'can restore their faith even to those who have wandered furthest from it.' I did not refuse to accept it, nor did I refuse to use it in the way she desired, for that would have been obviously cruel. Besides, there is something contagious in a faith as lively and as sincere as that! I said that I would watch for a favorable opportunity to fulfill those holy intentions.

"I left the convent very much touched, very much taken up with my own thoughts," Dorothée confessed to Bacourt.

❖   ❖   ❖

The years in England had created a gap between Dorothée and her sons. In Louis's case this gap was measurable in miles alone, but Alexandre was a young man of difficult character and clear-cut opinions, and with him the break had been much more serious.

At the time of the July Revolution, he had been campaigning on the coast of South America. When he returned to France for a month in August of 1830, although a legitimist at heart he did not give up his naval career, and on September 18 left once more for the South Seas. For another eighteen months he continued his life afloat, showing courage,* intelligence, but also "a burning imagination, with more attachment to his own pleasures than to the Navy."

Upon his return to Brest in May 1832, the young officer was given three months' leave. He came to Paris, but saw little of his mother, who was in London until early June and then went to take a cure for her liver at Baden in July. Were there disagreements at that time between Alexandre and Dorothée, between Alexandre and Talleyrand? One is inclined to believe so, judging from the young officer's behavior the following year. Having been promoted to Lieutenant on January 1, 1833,

---

* In May of 1831, in the course of a terrible storm, he rushed to the rescue of a man who had fallen overboard; Alexandre himself almost perished.

Alexandre de Périgord served successively on the brig *Dragon*, the frigate *Iphigénie*, and the transport vessel *Durance*. On May 7, he joined a Sardinian merchant vessel, the *Notre-Dame-del-Carmine*, which brought him back, on June 9, to Marseilles. This date was to mark the end of the young officer's naval career.* He went to stay with his father in Florence—which was rather a slap in the face for Dorothée and Talleyrand but doubtless a necessity in the face of dunning creditors—and wrote from Italy, on July 8, asking for six months' leave. Leave of absence was granted, then renewed on the pretext of eye trouble. Finally, on August 1, 1835, again from Florence, Alexandre de Périgord sent in his resignation.

A month later, the young man decided to return to France, where his mother was settled once more. Possibly he had had his fill of Italy, possibly his mother had cleared his debts. On November 19, without having received any reply to his first letter of resignation, and despite his mother's protests, Alexandre de Périgord sent in his resignation a second time. On December 10, 1835, it was officially accepted.

For this now idle, quick-tempered son, apparently as spendthrift as his father, Dorothée could see no solution other than a good, rich and, if possible, happy marriage. She had already selected a candidate, but there remained the task of finding a go-between to facilitate the task. The young lady she had set her sights on was Mlle Fougères.

On November 23, therefore, after leaving the Carmelite convent where she had visited her cousin, Dorothée drove to the convent of the Dames-de-Saint-Michel on the Rue Saint-Jacques, where Mgr de Quélen had taken refuge. The Duke of Noailles was an excellent go-between with regard to her own social position, but where a marriage was concerned the Archbishop, almost a haloed martyr in the eyes of the Faubourg Saint-Ger-

---

* His record was excellent. In March of 1833, Rear Admiral de Freycinet, Commanding Officer of Toulon, wrote the following report of him: "Good education, good appearance, enthusiasm, natural aptitude." Yet one is forced to wonder whether it was not at this time that a certain rumored incident occurred. Alexandre was said to have picked a quarrel with a superior officer, an Orleanist, and insulted him. This led to a duel. But there is nothing in the Admiralty archives to confirm the rumor.

main because of his ill-treatment by the new regime, was an even better one.

The prelate and his visitor talked first about Talleyrand. Mgr de Quélen told the Duchess yet again how much he counted on her aiding the work of divine grace and pity upon the Prince. This time, Dorothée did not evade the problem. She urged the Archbishop to pay occasional morning visits on Talleyrand, as he had been in the habit of doing previously. Then she spoke of her problems with regard to the marriages of her children, especially that of Alexandre. Mgr de Quélen displayed great understanding in the matter, and declared himself ready to help her in every way within his power.* In other words, a tacit agreement had been reached. Dorothée knew what was now expected of her, and she was too honest not to do her best to fulfill those expectations.

❖   ❖   ❖

Dorothée had often questioned Talleyrand about his strange marriage. "To be honest with you," the Prince had nonchalantly replied, "I can give you no sufficient explanation; it happened at a time of general disorder. In those days one did not attach a great deal of importance to anything, either to oneself or to others. Family, society, both had vanished: wars were being fought, empires collapsing, and one simply did things without caring a rap one way or the other. You have no idea how far men can stray from the path of reason during times of great social upheaval."

These words seemed to indicate a complete objectivity in the matter. And yet, when Dorothée learned from Charlotte, early in October of 1835, that Mme de Talleyrand was dying, she did not know how to pass the news on to the Prince. He seemed sad and morose at the time, in poor health, and deeply affected by the disappearance of many of his contemporaries, in

---

* Though the Fougères marriage continued to hang fire for a long time.

particular by that of Bourdois, his doctor. It was not, she confessed to Bacourt, that she was afraid of causing him any distress of heart, since that was in no way involved in the matter; but she did think that the death of a person more or less his own age, one with whom he had lived, whom he had once loved or at least considered sufficiently to give her his name, would affect the old man very deeply.

Dorothée approached the subject with an anxious heart. Talleyrand heard her out in silence. Then he did not refer to the matter until the following day, when he seemed mainly interested in its material consequences: the funeral and the announcement cards, the income he would no longer have to pay, the properties he would recover. For the remainder of that day, the Prince displayed a serenity and liveliness of manner that had not been seen in him for a very long time. He even began to hum. Somewhat taken aback, the Duchess could not prevent herself from asking him "if it was the prospect of becoming a widower that was making him so excited." Talleyrand's only answer was to pull a face, like a mischievous child. Dorothée supposed that he was relieved, without liking to admit it, at seeing the dissolution of "a bond that had been the greatest scandal of his life, because it had been the only irremediable one."

On December 10, early in the morning, the Duchess was informed that Mme de Talleyrand had died. Dorothée was still hesitant about telling the Prince; he had been suffering for some while from palpitations that gave some reason to fear the possibility of a sudden death. She first of all made some reference to the Princess being on her deathbed, then later on revealed the truth. Talleyrand was no more disturbed by the news than he had been six weeks earlier when told of his wife's danger. He remained quite calm, and simply murmured, "This simplifies my position a great deal."

The lucid verdict of an honest mind concerned only with facts. Although this death did create somewhat of a commotion before this simplification of Talleyrand's position was finally achieved.

"M. de Talleyrand and Mme de Dino have just been

through a very difficult week," Molé wrote to Barante on December 15. "*La France,* a Carlist newspaper, printed the most scandalous article à propos of Mme de Talleyrand's funeral. Then someone was contemptible enough to send a copy of it under plain cover to the old Prince, who, as you know, is himself suffering from an advanced heart condition. The two young nephews [Louis and Alexandre] went to see the editor and gave him a choice between being called out and a retraction: he chose the latter. But the fight between M. de Talleyrand and Mme d'Esclignac over the two caskets left by Mme de Talleyrand is still going on. Mme de Dino is behaving with great nobility, Mme de Poix [Countess Just de Noailles] and even her husband have all been to see Mme d'Esclignac hoping to persuade her to a compromise, but in vain." *

At the beginning of 1836 despite the painful incidents of the previous December, Talleyrand's health had improved, no doubt as a result of his deliverance from a wife "whom Bonaparte had nailed to her husband like a derisive warning." † "M. de Talleyrand is once more in relatively good health, but my own peace of mind is beyond recall," Dorothée confided to Barante on January 5, 1836. "The warning has been too serious, and besides, the infirmities that attend upon so advanced an age, though long postponed, have now established their rights, and I can hope for no improvement! He stays indoors more, and his thoughts are often overcast and full of discouragement; but as soon as there is company his spirit revives, his conversation becomes lively again, and his strength of both mind and soul astonishes all who come to see him. . . ."

Meanwhile, Princess Lieven was writing to Lord Grey: "M. de Talleyrand is quite well again now. I see him constantly, and in society he is, as ever, charming. We have little dinners at his house that are perfectly delightful—he and Mme de Dino, with M. Thiers, M. Guizot or M. Molé alternatively. Never

---

* On the strength of the 8th clause of his marriage contract, Talleyrand had claimed ownership of two locked caskets that Mme de Talleyrand had supposedly given to Georgine d'Esclignac. Mgr de Quélen brought them back when the seals were affixed.

† This savage phrase is Chateaubriand's.

more than six in all. The conversation is of the pleasantest. . . ."

With this return to health, Talleyrand's ambition, never quite dead, flared up again for the last time. In August 1834, at the time of his leaving London, there had once more been question of appointing him to the Premiership. But there had not been much foundation for the scheme, and a word from Thiers on the inevitable opposition of Mme de Dino had swiftly quashed it. Then, in September of 1835, exasperated by his difficulties with Broglie, and sensing that the government was about to topple, Louis-Philippe had confided to the Duchess of Dino that the Premiership itself was the root of the trouble, because it brought out the vanity in everyone. The King had conceived a desire to abolish the post altogether and, with this end in view, he proposed to entrust it for a short while to someone not in the ordinary running, someone who would exclude all possibility of competitors and, above all, of a successor, in short, to Talleyrand. Airy talk or a way of sounding out the Duchess' possible attitude? Dorothée had listened to all the monarch had to say without venturing any comment.

Early in February of 1836, the government formed in 1832, which had maintained itself doggedly in power ever since, despite frequent refittings, collapsed after Broglie, Premier and Minister for Foreign Affairs since March 1835, had stirred up a violent outburst of resentment in the Chamber by his clumsily arrogant attitude.

For a brief moment, Talleyrand thought of becoming Premier without portfolio. Dorothée did not dare to dissuade him from his dream, to deprive him of such a hope. But Royer-Collard intervened, and with his usual brutal honesty reminded her of the duty she owed her uncle: "Can you think of it, Madame? Can it be that you wish to bring dishonor upon M. de Talleyrand's last moments? Are you not aware that he can scarcely now keep up a conversation? Make him the head of the French government in such a condition? It would be nothing but the cruelest of jokes!"

The Premiership was not mentioned again.

Since he could no longer hold power himself, however, Talleyrand at least wished to secure himself one last political triumph by imposing on the nation a man of his own choice, a man who had been under his wing now for nearly ten years. While malicious tongues were predicting a Ladies' Government in which Mme de Dino would be in charge of Foreign Affairs, Talleyrand and Dorothée were using every ounce of influence they could muster—and at the Tuileries that was still a great deal—to have the Premiership conferred on Thiers, who was in any case considered to be an inevitable choice by many other people as well. On February 22, 1836, Thiers formed his first cabinet.*

❖ ❖ ❖

Regretfully, with his hesitant and limping step, Talleyrand was making his exit from the world's stage. At the same moment, Pauline de Périgord, who was perhaps the child of the Prince's old age and without any doubt at all his greatest favorite, was making her entrance on to it.

Dorothée had always been determined that her daughter should not have an abnormal and unhappy childhood such as her own had been. Pauline had led an ordinary little girl's life as a child, surrounded by friends of her own age, and in particular by her Talleyrand cousins—the children of Charlotte. When she was more grown, her mother and uncle had entrusted her to the charge of a carefully chosen governess, Mlle Henriette Larcher. Being not only an intelligent and broad-minded woman but also a profoundly religious one, Mlle Larcher had brought the little girl up with a gentle faith in God.

In both France and England, Pauline had lived in her mother's shadow, and even more so in that of Talleyrand's. Even in the bitterest of English winter weather, the French Ambassador had not hesitated to go out into the country to bring the child back from his friends the Cowpers after she had spent Christmas with them. And in summer, while the Duchess

---

* It was only to last a few months. Until August 1836, to be exact.

disappeared on her travels, Pauline would go with Talleyrand to Bourbonne or, more often still, to Valençay, and if Mlle Larcher was indisposed, then the Prince would give up his usual visit to Royer-Collard in order to look after Pauline himself.

In 1834, just before they were to leave England, while Pauline was still living in her nursery, Dorothée apparently considered the possibility of a marriage for her daughter with the son of the Austrian Ambassador, Prince Esterhazy. The match would have been a brilliant one, since Princess Esterhazy was born Tour and Taxis, a niece of Queen Louise of Prussia, and its international character seemed not only natural but desirable to a mother born Princess of Courland. However, this scheme never came to anything.

Having assured her daughter of a happy childhood, Dorothée now wanted to make sure that Pauline's entry into the world should be pleasant and free from shocks, that she should arrive peacefully at the haven of marriage, and that she should find happiness once she was there. And so, while she was laying the foundations for this happiness from a social point of view, as she had already done from a moral one, Dorothée removed her daughter gently from the schoolroom and launched her into the ballroom.

In December, 1834, the young girl was present for the first time at one of the great dinners on the Rue Saint-Florentin. "There is no harm in her learning how to listen to serious conversation without becoming bored; she carries herself well in society, and I think people find her open expression and courtesy of manner attractive."

The next summer, after leaving Baden, Dorothée took Pauline with her to visit Switzerland, as she had taken Louis eleven years earlier. Pink cheeked, her blue eyes sparkling with light, Pauline was delighted with everything, and especially at having all to herself the mother so often taken from her by the demands of society. On their return, they went on a tour of the châteaux. Talleyrand, a little sad to be left thus alone, stayed at Valençay and followed the two travelers in thought. On September 12, he announced contentedly to Bacourt: "I am expecting Pauline back tomorrow. According to the letters I have received, the mountains have made her taller. It was a thing I had very much hoped for, and the only thing left for me to wish her."

Pauline made her official debut early in 1836, before Lent. The date originally planned for this event was abandoned because of the death in February of the little two year old Yolande de Valençay,* and it was not until April 10, 1836, that the Duchess finally took her daughter to a lottery being held for charity at the home of the Duchess of Montmorency: "It was packed: the whole of the Faubourg Saint-Germain was there. . . . Pauline enjoyed herself in the way one does enjoy oneself at fifteen. . . . She was looking particularly beautiful, hair done very simply, but by the great Edouard after all, sky-blue dress,† fresh as a rose, carrying herself very prettily, quite calmly, quite naturally . . . at any rate, she was a success and very well approved of."

Three weeks later, on April 30, Dorothée gave a very successful ball: "Not a great crush, a great many lights, very gay and pretty young ladies, polite young gentlemen to lead the young misses onto the floor; impeccable taste, perfect style, guests hand-picked from the best society; no obvious attempt at exclusion, but the Faubourg Saint-Germain definitely predominating. . . .‡ I was very satisfied with our little success and with Pauline's delight at it."

---

* According to Bacourt, the Duchess of Dino had the "soul of a nursing sister." She did in fact nurse her grandchild with devoted care, and closed the little girl's eyes with her own hands. It will be remembered that she had been kept away from her own little daughter's deathbed many years before and had been unable to do anything for the child, that other two year old of whom she never spoke.

† Talleyrand had shown some concern about the modesty of Pauline's attire. "When what one displays is a delight to the eye, then it is immodest; when what one displays is ugly, then it is very ugly indeed," he had commented.

‡ Always tending to be half in jest, half in earnest, where the Duchess of Dino was concerned, Molé wrote to Barante on June 13, 1836: "Mme de Dino has devoted her winter to coaxing the solemn Faubourg set; she invited them all to dance to the exclusion of everyone else; she has quite thrown aside the cabinet she plotted for so persistently and cleverly; in short, she has spared no pains to achieve her reconciliation with the society in which she apparently intends to pass the rest of her life. And that is where she will find her daughter a husband. . . ."

But though her young daughter may have been amusing herself without apparently giving a thought to marriage as yet, the Duchess was thinking about just that with a kind of desperate anxiety. For it must be remembered that she very much wanted to see her childrens' futures fixed while Talleyrand was still there to help her.

Made bold by the success of her ball, confident in the friendship of the Duke of Noailles, possibly aware that Pauline was not without a certain inclination towards the young man in question, Dorothée now began to think on her daughter's behalf of the young girl's cousin, Antonin de Noailles,* the second son of her sister-in-law Mélanie. The connection was obviously excellent, but the boy was a younger son with no personal fortune. For him, the match would have been an extremely advantageous one; yet when the offer was made to him, in July, 1836, he refused it, saying that he did not find Pauline attractive. Probably he had been influenced by his mother who loathed Dorothée.†

❖ ❖ ❖

During the spring of 1836, Dorothée was also preparing Louis's political future. Under the Restoration, farsighted mother that she was, Dorothée had seen to it that her elder son became first the playmate, then the companion of the Duke of Chartres. Yielding to the influence of his mother and uncle, the Duke of Valençay had given his support to the July monarchy, even though the majority of the Montmorency family

* Lady Holland—who knew something about such matters—said that Antonin de Noailles was quite the handsomest man in Paris.

† Rodolphe Apponyi has left an account of a meeting he had with Mélanie do Noailles during August, 1829: "She spoke to us at length about her sister-in-law and the misfortune it was to have someone of that character in one's family.

" 'It is a thing that severs the holiest ties,' she said. 'As soon as intrigue takes root in a family all the charm of family life disappears, and one can truly say that nothing is left of it but the name. Can you believe it, I see my sister-in-law no more than once or twice a year, and all the other members of the family likewise? . . .' "

were Carlists. But this support was merely on a social level; it meant that the Valençays appeared at the Tuileries,* but did nothing toward making the young Duke modify the frivolous and idle way of life that was already disturbing Dorothée and angering Talleyrand.†

One of the principal concerns of the new monarchy was still, as we have seen, the marriage of the royal heir. One projected match, with Princess Sophie of Wurtemburg, had already come to nothing in 1835. Louis-Philippe and his son had both been affected by this rebuff and had blamed Broglie for it since the Premier was heartily detested by the entire diplomatic corps of Europe, with the one exception of the British Ambassador— who had no princess to offer.

Having been very well received by all the European representatives in Paris—a development that many considered Talleyrand's masterpiece—Thiers now believed that he was going to be the one to produce the longed for princess. He revived and urged on the Tuileries the idea, first conceived by his predecessor, of a state visit to Germany by Louis-Philippe's two eldest sons.

Having often been questioned by the Duke of Orléans about her opinions of the matches that had been offered to him, or those that might be desirable,‡ Dorothée had been informed of

* Though on the Duchess of Valençay's part this support also had a sentimental motive. Jean-Pons Viennet, a French Peer and Academician now thoroughly forgotten, noted on November 24, 1836, that she had been one of the Duke of Orléans' mistresses.

† On October 3, 1836, Talleyrand told Bacourt that he had just handed in his resignation as a member of the General Council for the department of the Indre, and that he was hoping to have himself replaced by Louis de Valençay. It would be a first step towards making him a peer. It would start Louis on a career and remove him from "the ranks of all those little gentlemen who think that their complete nullity and the utter idleness of their existence constitute some sort of homage to the last monarchy."

‡ Dorothée's influence in this quarter was a source of irritation to the Queen of the Belgians. On August 2, 1836, she wrote: "The Old Man's [Talleyrand's] plan of finding a match for Chartres as a means of getting his hooks into him will in fact only result in estranging him from them [Talleyrand and Dorothée]. Leopold says that the Danish branch of the Hesse family is quite well thought of and generally considered to be less treacherous than the other.

"For my part, if we must have a Protestant princess I would prefer the fair Helen, and I prefer anything at all to a scheme cooked up by the Old Man and Dorothée."

this idea at the time of its original conception; she had written to her sister Sagan about it and the latter had tested the ground by mentioning it to Metternich: apparently the ground was by no means solid.*

Once the German visit had been decided upon, the date of departure appointed—May 4—and the itinerary fixed—Berlin, Vienna, Turin—Dorothée persuaded the Duke of Orléans to take Valençay with him. But being proud and not forgetting that she was a Courland, being prudent and not wishing to jeopardize Louis's future in Germany,† the Duchess refused all title and functions for her son. "I had no wish for them, since my son has no need of such things in order to be well received anywhere," she wrote to Bacourt.

This act of sending Louis to Germany was the prelude to a new page in Dorothée's life on which the name of Talleyrand would no longer appear. Never properly acclimatized to France, she had found herself much more at home in England. But there she could never have lived on the scale she desired, and her thoughts were perhaps already turning to Prussia. Louis was a herald; the reception he was given, the contacts he might renew would tell his mother what she needed to know.

"Yesterday I had a letter from my son Valençay from Berlin," Dorothée wrote to Bacourt on May 22. "He is enchanted, and he has reason to be, since apart from the generally satisfactory nature of the visit he is being treated everywhere with a particular kindness that touches him and goes straight to my heart because it is being shown on my behalf. The Prince Royal told him that he had always looked upon me as

* "The Duke of Orléans' proposed visit is an extremely risky enterprise and certainly very ill-timed," Metternich wrote to Apponyi on February 3, 1836. "He will of course be received everywhere, and particularly in Vienna, with all the courtesy due to the son of a King of the French with whom one is at peace. But to expect more than that would be self-deception, and to believe in any possibility of a marriage for him here would be an even greater one. The experiments we have already made in that line have been far too unfortunate for the memory of them to be so quickly erased, and I know of no Archduchess who would be prepared to make a third. . . ."

† Neither the Duchess of Sagan nor the Duchess of Acerenza had any legitimate children. The Princess Hohenzollern's son, married since 1826 to Princess Eugénie of Leuchtenburg, had none either. It was therefore possible that Sagan might one day revert to the Dino children, to say nothing of the great properties that Dorothée had always owned in her own right in Silesia.

a sister, that he would treat Louis as a nephew, that my letter was charming, but that he could have wished it to have a stronger flavor of *Die Kinderstube* [the nursery]." *

From Berlin, where they had made a good impression, the Duke of Orléans and the Duke of Nemours continued on to Vienna; Thiers was hoping that once there the French heir would win the affections of Archduchess Theresa, daughter of Archduke Charles. The young lady did in fact find the elegant, blond and handsome young horseman charming; she had not yet given her reply however, when the d'Alibaud incident on June 25, 1836, as Dorothée puts it, killed the Princess Royal.†

In Vienna, Louis de Valençay had been received very amiably not only by his aunt Sagan,‡ which was only natural, but also by Archduchess Sophie, who still remembered Mme de Dino and had shown her son particular regard, and by Archduke Charles, who had spoken to him of Talleyrand.

* The future Frederick-Wilhelm IV's reply, in French, was at one time in the Sagan archives: "The childhood memories that you wish to reawaken have never in fact faded from my mind, and even before knowing that the Duke, your son, had been charged with a letter for me I had the impertinence to tell him that, since you and I had been like a brother and sister during our childhood, I should take the liberty of treating him a little as though he were my nephew. I can still see you now, your hair done in its girlish curls, wearing your plum colored dress, between the two Misses Hoffmann, the brunette and the blonde—and it was always a red letter day for my brother Wilhelm and myself when we dared to go and spend an evening with you: *um Mores zu lernen* (to learn our manners), for although you were so much cried up to us as such a very good little girl, which you were, that never prevented us from having a delightful time, in all the ways one does have a delightful time at eight or ten years old."

A sincere letter, but also a well-calculated one. There had been a day when Frederick II was only too pleased to have the old Duke of Courland settle in Prussia. Perhaps the court of Berlin was now hopeful of attracting Dorothée into Silesia in the same way. Whatever the truth of the matter, the Duchess could not but be affected by such kindness or by the certainty of a reception in Berlin that would place her in the first rank after the royal family itself.

† On June 25, 1836, as he was coming out of the Tuileries, Louis-Philippe just missed being killed by an assassin named Alibaud. Metternich, who was not in favor of the proposed marriage of the Duke of Orléans and Archduchess Theresa, took advantage of the incident to frighten the young girl and her parents with the result that the marriage plans fell through. That is why Dorothée said, "I am afraid that shot has killed our Princess Royal."

‡ Dorothée noted, without further comment, that her son also met Count Clam at the Duchess of Sagan's.

Louis's visit had thus brought Dorothée the most gratifying assurances possible of an amicable reception in Germany should she ever decide to settle there once more.* As for her son's future when the Duke of Orléans should have come to the throne, the two months spent in such close companionship with the royal heir had been beneficial too in this respect. After his return to France, the latter expressed to Dorothée the extent of his regard for her son: "I was able to convince myself of the complete reliability of his excellent character, as of the unostentatious attachment that he has for myself and my family. Those are all rare qualities, even though the whole world lays claim to them; I retain a vivid appreciation of them, and I can assure you that he has in me a friend who is no less devoted for not being demonstrative."

⟥ ⟥ ⟥

Talleyrand and Dorothée had taken up residence at Valençay in the latter half of May. Their stay there was disturbed by a fall sustained by the Prince and by a visit from Princess Lieven, whose changing moods and the boredom she was unable to conceal proved a trial to her hosts.

Having recovered from the accident that, at his age and in his present state of health, could have been serious, and once more a prey to his need for change, Talleyrand came back to Paris late in July for a few days in order to pay his respects to the King following the Alibaud incident. He was joined in the capital shortly afterwards by his niece.

Mme de Gonneville, Bacourt's sister, was at that time passing through Paris with her husband and her daughter, a child of about ten who was to become the Countess of Mirabeau. Dorothée went to visit Mme de Gonneville at the Richepanse

---

* Dorothée immediately began to think of making a journey beyond the Rhine herself. In October, 1836, she noted: "Were it not for the uneasiness of mind I should suffer at leaving M. de Talleyrand and my daughter, a visit to Prussia would be a perfect balm to my heart."

house on the day of the official military parade, July 28. "Mme de Dino, who in 1836 was forty-three years old, was still very beautiful," Mme de Mirabeau was to write many years later. "She wore a dress of embroidered tulle lined with sky-blue taffeta, and on her rice straw hat there were gently waving clouds of marabou feathers. Her black eyes, the circles around them rather too dark, seemed quite improbably huge. . . . She often closed them for the space of a few seconds as she talked. Her features were mobile and expressive, she had that immediate, exuberant, and affectionate amiability of manner that was not generally fashionable until twenty years later, under the Second Empire, but which, in her, failed to detract in any way from the air of supreme distinction."

Dorothée talked to the little girl. Amused by her enthusiasm, she invited the Gonnevilles round to the Rue Saint-Florentin to watch the fireworks. When they arrived, at each window of the great drawing rooms looking out onto the Rue de Rivoli there was a half-circle of people conversing with one another and waiting for the first rockets to go up.

"My uncle is very unwell this evening," the Duchess told M. de Gonneville, "and is not seeing anyone; but he would like to see your daughter. . . ."

The little girl was somewhat alarmed when confronted with Talleyrand sitting very straight in an immense armchair with a square back; "one leg stretched out and resting on a stool so that one could not miss his short, rounded foot, a real club foot. He was swathed in a quilted wrap of white silk with a Chinese pattern on it. . . ."

After a while, the child regained her confidence and went nearer to him; as he talked to her, the old man began to toy with the big pink satin sash she was wearing.

Before long, Talleyrand was seized by a violent fit of coughing, and Dorothée offered him a cup of beef tea.

"When your uncle is old like me, you must take care of him the way my niece takes care of me," Talleyrand murmured to the little girl when he had caught his breath again.

❖ ❖ ❖

The Duchess of Dino still read Bossuet, just as she had done when she was the Countess Edmond de Périgord. She displayed a particular predilection for the Princess Palatin's funeral oration. Perhaps she was attracted by a similarity between Anne of Gonzaga's destiny and her own? Perhaps, as she left the Carmelite monastery after seeing her cousin, moved and much taken up with her own thoughts, she remembered the passage in which Bossuet paraphrases a passage from Isaiah: "I have led thee back from the furthest ends of the earth, from the most distant places, from the winding ways where thou wert lost, given over to thine own senses. . . . Even as thou wast saying in thy rebellious heart: 'I cannot give myself up into captivity,' I laid the power of my hand upon thee, and I said: 'Thou shalt be my handmaid, I have chosen thee from all Eternity and I have not refused thy proud and haughty spirit.' "

Proud and haughty spirit? Those words were true for Dorothée as well.

For the Princess Palatine, a dream had been the first sign of "Providence's hidden and pitiful regard." Dorothée too, while in England, had been struck "by the innumerable favors that heaven had granted her," and she had "wondered at God's patience with regard to her." In April, 1835, talking to Molé about her life, which did not have the merit of being Christian but was simply "practical," she added that possibly her concern to fulfill her task on earth would eventually bring her into contact with "a realm of higher and imperishable thoughts. I have never been antagonistic to them, I now have a desire for them, but it is no more than a tendency as yet. . . ."

From then on the signs became ever more numerous. The death of little Yolande de Valençay had been one of the most noticeable on the emotional plane, while on the intellectual plane there were her conversations with Royer-Collard, who at that time was attempting with his characteristic robustness of mind and uprightness of heart "to divest himself of all philosophic doubt."

Early in March of 1836, Dorothée was with Pauline one day in the latter's apartment when she happened to open the *Imitation of Christ*. She was struck immediately by the first lines, then read on with growing admiration. The work begun by the solid magnificence of Bossuet was completed within the next few months by the implacable gentleness of the monk.

Not that Dorothée achieved a complete abandonment of self to the will of Providence, any more than she completely submitted, completely bowed to a discipline that wounded her pride—the marrow of her being—and stirred up rebellion in her still active senses. Nevertheless, in June of 1836 she was aware of her own weakness and her need of a guide. "I have sought and I have found; I have knocked and it has been opened unto me; I have asked and it has been given," she wrote to Barante on June 21. "All very incompletely still, however, because when one is so little prepared and walking alone as I am, it is not possible to avoid taking wrong paths sometimes and stumbling at every step. . . . When I ask myself for an account of my progress, I am humiliated when I see how little it amounts to. . . . There is nothing so difficult, nothing that takes so much time, effort, and perseverance as putting one's conscience in order."

She added lastly, thinking to make quite clear in this way the limits of an adherence that she wished to remain in the background of her life: "My behavior has no great appearance of piety as yet, and I may say that I am much further advanced in regard to the matter than in regard to the form; I am even doubtful whether I shall ever change greatly with respect to the latter."

But it is difficult to circumscribe God's role in things. Though she never adopted any great outward show of piety, Dorothée's allegiance to the Roman Catholic religion was too sincere, despite all her attempted reservations, not to influence her behavior almost in spite of herself—and particularly in regard to Talleyrand.

On August 28, 1836, a terrible thunderstorm broke over Valençay. While the sky was filled with the flashes of lightning and the rolling of thunder, suddenly the keep chimneys collapsed. When the noise at last died down, Talleyrand asked his niece what she had thought of when the storm was at its height. Dorothée replied without hesitation:

"If there had been a priest in the room I should have confessed to him; I have a fear of sudden deaths. The idea of dying unprepared, of having to take such a heavy burden as my sins away with me fills me with terror; and no matter how carefully one studies to lead a blameless life, there is still the need for reconciliation and forgiveness."

The Prince offered no comment on this speech and went on with his piquet.

Next day, Dorothée wrote Bacourt an account of the incident: "Whenever the opportunity arises, I make my beliefs quite clear, and in that way I am hoping to reawaken his; but there is always the risk of provoking him. One has to have such a light touch in matters of this nature!"

Fifteen months earlier, Dorothée had been rather evasive in her manner when Mgr Quélen first began making his overtures to her, and had said, it will be remembered, that she could play nothing more than a passive role in this matter. Both her faith and her courage had increased in strength to a startling degree since then.

❖   ❖   ❖

The year 1836 had witnessed Talleyrand's farewell to political life. At the same time, Dorothée's spiritual development was leading her to become increasingly and more directly concerned with achieving a reconcilation between the Prince and the Catholic Church, a reconciliation which was also, and we must emphasize this, a social necessity for Talleyrand, and even more so for his niece. Nevertheless, more than a year was to go by before there were any visible effects. In the course of these months, Talleyrand made one last visit to the court, on the occasion of the Duke of Orléans' marriage, in May 1837, at Fontainebleau. Meanwhile Dorothée's religious convictions were taking even stronger root, though without succeeding in piercing the Prince's shell of indifference.

One day, after Talleyrand and his niece had been to hear Mass celebrated with great pomp on a court occasion, as she stepped up into their carriage she ventured to ask him:

"Doesn't it have a very strange effect on you, hearing a priest say Mass?"

"No, why?"

"Oh I don't know, it just seemed to me . . ." and she began to stumble over her words with embarrassment. "It just seemed to me that it couldn't possibly be the same for you as for other people."

"But why should you expect it to be at all odd for me to hear Mass? I listen to it the way you do, the way everyone does; you always forget that I was secularized, which makes my position quite simple."

How was she to destroy this illusion, whether feigned or sincere, without reminding the old man too brutally of his approaching death?

The Prince and Dorothée spent the summer of 1837 together at Valençay. Early in November they moved to Rochecotte where the Duchess of Sagan and Alexandre de Périgord arrived on a visit during the first days of December. Shortly after this Dorothée, who had been rather unwell for several weeks, suddenly became gravely ill. At one point, it looked as though she might not recover and she sent for the village priest to administer the Last Sacraments. Was this in fact an indirect warning intended for the Prince? It seems likely.

Dorothée's danger had disturbed Talleyrand. When his niece was a little better, the Prince said to her with agonized astonishment. "So you can die. I might have outlived you. It would not have been for long." The silent disdain with which he had dismissed every insinuation until that moment was laid aside. He seemed to have heeded the warning and now expressed an interest in Dorothée's new faith.

"So that's how things are with you. But how did it happen?" he asked Dorothée shortly afterward.

His niece answered him quite frankly, and the Prince listened with visible interest. When she added finally that amongst the very many other serious motives affecting her decision she had not failed to consider the question of giving a good example, Talleyrand broke in abruptly with the words:

"Yes indeed, there is nothing less aristocratic than unbelief."

Two days later the old man returned to the subject, asking her to repeat the same details again.

"So you believe then?" he said finally.

"Yes, monsieur, firmly."

❖   ❖   ❖

On January 6, 1838, Talleyrand arrived in Paris with Pauline. Several days later, Dorothée left Rochecotte in her turn, accompanied by Alexandre and the Duchess of Sagan. The Prince had already resumed his usual existence on the Rue Saint-Florentin, but just when it seemed that he was going to postpone his reckoning for one more winter he suffered another fall while at the British Embassy one evening and was condemned to several weeks in bed. During the day, he was surrounded by people from ten in the morning until past midnight; but when they finally left him alone in the darkness, lying there worn out, unable to sleep, he began to think of "a terrible number of things."

Although the Abbé Dupanloup, formerly vicar of the Madeleine, by then Superior of the little seminary of Saint-Nicolas du Chardonnet, had been Pauline de Périgord's spiritual director since she first began to learn her catechism, and although Dorothée knew her daughter's confessor very well, Talleyrand himself had never met the Abbé when, early in February of 1838, he expressed a desire to make his acquaintance.

An opportunity to do so immediately presented itself: his niece's saint's day fell on February 6, and Talleyrand instructed Dorothée to invite the Abbé for dinner that evening. By some amazing aberration, the Superior of Saint-Nicolas, unable to overcome the instinctive repugnance that Talleyrand inspired in him, refused the invitation—to the Duchess's consternation. "He has less sense than I thought," Talleyrand commented with contemptuous surprise; "he should have been anxious to come, both for his own sake and for mine."

Once this fit of ill humor had passed, having been assured

by Dorothée that Mgr de Quélen had deplored Abbé Dupanloup's refusal and done his utmost to make sure that it was not repeated, Talleyrand sent a second invitation, this time written in his own hand, and it was agreed that the Abbé should visit him on February 18.

"I like your Abbé; he's very well-bred," Talleyrand remarked to Dorothée and Pauline later that same evening. He had just chosen the mediator who, when the day and the hour came, was to reconcile him with God.

When the day and the hour came, Talleyrand had no desire to be hurried or to hurry. He had always conducted his negotiations without haste. Even with God he had no intention of changing his methods. Besides, before finally taking the path of submission he wished to say farewell to a world whose pleasures had so completely occupied his spirit for so long.

On March 3, 1838, he attended a session of the Académie des Sciences Morales et Politiques in order to deliver the eulogy of Reinhard, an obscure Minister for Foreign Affairs, an occasion that provided Talleyrand, the illustrious diplomat, with an opportunity to give his definition of a diplomat.

Dorothée had helped her uncle in the composition of this political testament. She knew the great importance he attached to it, but since women were not allowed into this particular Académie she was unable to accompany him except with anxious thoughts. She was not afraid of his failing, but she was very apprehensive of what effect such a tremendous effort was going to have on a man whose health, though there was nothing definite, nothing serious as yet, had been worrying her for several weeks.

Talleyrand's success was dazzling but dearly bought: the Prince returned home "crushed, unable even to fight back against his fatigue." On March 4, Apponyi went to visit on the Rue Saint-Florentin: "There were very few people there: the Duchess of Dino, who never leaves his side, Mlle de Périgord, the Duke of Noailles and the Sardinian Ambassadress, and MM. de Montrand and de Valençay, all of whom may be considered as members of the household; they were all much occupied by Marshal Soult, whose presence seemed to be tiring the Prince.

The drawing room was very badly lit. M. de Talleyrand was frequently taken with very bad fits of coughing which seemed to cause Mme de Dino an extraordinary degree of concern; she was so worried that she was unable to follow the conversation for more than a few moments at a time."

Yet after a few days Talleyrand was considerably improved again. On March 9, Abbé Dupanloup came to thank the Prince for sending him a copy of his speech. Pauline took him in to see Talleyrand and the two men spoke for a long time together, as they had done already on February 18. There was nothing out in the open as yet. As the Abbé was about to withdraw, the Prince asked:

"How did you find Mme de Dino, Monsieur l'Abbé?"

"Extremely unwell, Prince, but more concerned with you than with herself."

"That is true."

"I found both Mme de Dino and her daughter very profoundly, very seriously occupied with thoughts of you," the Abbé insisted, and was assured in reply that Talleyrand had taken his meaning.

When he had said good-bye to the Prince, Abbé Dupanloup went up to see the Duchess and offered her some hope. "All this is to the good," Dorothée wrote next day to Bacourt, "just as long as we're in time! For though he is no longer sick, I can perceive a great exhaustion there, as well as a visible alteration in his features, and there is simply no way of hurrying a mind like his! My God, what a task!"

On March 13, Dorothée went to Conflans to see Mgr de Quélen. The Archbishop asked her to give him some indication of how, in her opinion, the reparation or retraction they had to obtain from the Prince ought to be framed.* Three days later, Dorothée drove to Saint-Nicolas du Chardonnet and showed Abbé Dupanloup the letter she had drafted. It was approved. Finally, on the 24th, the Duchess went to Conflans again. "We are gradually coming closer to an agreement on

* This retraction bore on three separate points: the oath of the clergy to the civil constitution; the consecration of constitutional bishops; the scandal of Talleyrand's marriage.

the terms of the letter, and I hope that something good will come of it; but we need time, and we need to be helped by outside circumstances, which is something beyond our control, something we have to ask for from a greater power than ours."

Now that the ground had been cleared and the Duchess thoroughly acquainted with what the Catholic Church wanted, it was time for Abbé Dupanloup to renew contact with the Prince. He sent Talleyrand a book he had written, together with a long letter in which he talked about Saint-Sulpice, and also about Cardinal du Périgord.

When Dorothée went into Talleyrand's room that day— March 27—she found him very preoccupied. The Prince gave her Abbé Dupanloup's letter to read, then said very abruptly:

"If I were to fall seriously ill, I should ask for a priest. Do you think Abbé Dupanloup would be happy to come?"

"I'm sure he would, but in order for him to be of any use to you, it would first be necessary for you to return to that normal order of things from which you have unhappily departed."

"Yes, yes," Talleyrand replied, "there is that matter to be settled with Rome of course. I've been thinking of getting it over with for quite some time, as a matter of fact."

"Really, and since when?"

"Since the Archbishop of Bourges' last visit to Valençay,* and even more so since Abbé Taury's visit.† I wondered at the time why the Archbishop, who is even more directly my pastor down there, didn't urge me to it. And why that good Abbé Taury didn't mention the matter to me."

"Alas, Monsieur! They wouldn't have dared."

"And yet I should have been glad to hear them talk of it."

The Duchess took the Prince's hands in hers. With tears in her eyes, she asked:

"But why wait for them to urge you to it? Why not perform spontaneously, freely, generously an action that would bring

---

* In June, 1837.

† The Abbé Taury, a Sulpicien, Superior General of the Sisters of Saint-André established by the Prince at Valençay, had dined at the château during the summer of 1837.

so much honor upon yourself and so much consolation to the Catholic Church and all decent people? You would find Rome well disposed toward you I know, and Mgr the Archbishop of Paris is very much attached to you. Try . . ."

Dorothée then seized this opportunity to go more deeply into the problems involved. As she was finishing her explanations, Talleyrand and she were interrupted.

Going back up to her apartments, she immediately wrote to Abbé Dupanloup: "I do not wish to lose a moment in telling you, Monsieur l'Abbé, that your admirable letter has at last provoked the *great conversation* we were so anxiously awaiting. . . . I hope it will produce good results, and I know this letter will bring joy to your good heart. I am still so moved and exhausted that my hand is shaking."

Next day, Dorothée sent off the news of this event to Bacourt, whom she kept constantly informed of her fears as to Talleyrand's health and of her hopes as to the possibility of his submission to Rome. "Yesterday I had the most important of all conversations with M. de Talleyrand, and I discovered new ways opened into his heart that seem to me miraculous. I hope that the path ahead of me is now assured, and though the goal may still be a long way off, I also hope that no precipice will come between him and my efforts."

Several days later, on April 12, following what was an habitual procedure with her when she wished to discuss some particularly serious matter with her uncle, Dorothée handed Talleyrand a letter containing a résumé of all the demands specified to her by Mgr de Quélen. "There was no storm of protest at the time," she wrote next day to Bacourt. "I imagine that he read it through again thoroughly last evening, and that I shall see today whether one has blown up or not overnight." On the 4th, with great relief, she announced: "My little essay has met with complete success."

❖　❖　❖

Several days after Easter (April 15), Abbé Dupanloup paid a third visit at Talleyrand's request. They had a serious conversation about Holy Week, about the services on Maundy Thursday, about the new religious movement, and about Pauline's devotion to her religion. It was a step in the right direction. But a step was not enough, and there was reason to wonder whether Talleyrand would decide to make the necessary gesture or not.

At the same time the Prince's health began to improve, and he began to make plans for the summer, for the autumn, for the next winter. But then, on April 28, the Duke of Talleyrand, Archambauld de Périgord, the Prince's brother, died.

When he heard the news, Talleyrand put his hand over his eyes and said to Dorothée:

"Another warning, my dear child. Do you know if my brother recovered his memory before he died?"

"No, monsieur, unhappily he didn't."

He went on then, with great sadness:

"Do you realize how frightful it is to slip like that from the most worldly of lives back into childhood and then from childhood into death?"

Abbé Dupanloup came a fourth time to the house on the Rue Saint-Florentin, this time to present his condolences.

Early in May, without mentioning it to Dorothée, the Prince drafted a retraction. Then, one day when his niece was about to leave on a visit to Conflans, he opened a drawer in his desk and took out a sheet of paper. It was covered with writing on both sides, and in places there were sentences scratched out.

"Here, this will make you very welcome where you are going. You can tell me what the Archbishop has to say about it."

Though very long—too long—this retraction was, nevertheless not sufficiently explicit. Mgr de Quélen was moved by it, but he instructed the Duchess to reply that the sentiments expressed in it should be presented in more strictly formal terms. He would send round an ecclesiastical formulation of them in a few days.

Talleyrand was surprised by this lack of enthusiasm but confined himself to remarking: "Whatever I sign will have to be dated the same week as my speech to the Académie; I don't want anyone to be able to say that I was in my second childhood."

Suddenly, however, as though the patience of providence had been exhausted, events began to move more precipitately. On Saturday, May 12, after dinner, Talleyrand was shaken by a long trembling fit, which in turn was followed by a fever and serious attacks of discomfort. He was rather better during the daylight hours of the 13th, but in the evening his fever returned, and Cruveilhier, his doctor, diagnosed an anthrax in the lumbar region. It was decided to operate on it next day, the 14th.

On the morning of the 14th, before the Prince's operation, Dorothée wrote to Abbé Dupanloup: "I have received a letter from Rome that I should like you to know the contents of. But above all I need to talk to you . . . about the anxiety I have been feeling for the past thirty-six hours in regard to M. de Talleyrand's health. He has had an attack that at first seemed to be no more than an ordinary fever, but since yesterday evening there has been a new symptom that seems to me to be serious. He has no idea of it, and I may be exaggerating; but I do believe that it is more essential than ever to reach an agreement and to hold ourselves in readiness for any emergency."

Talleyrand bore the operation with fortitude, and it appeared to have proved successful. Bacourt, who by that time had been in Paris for several weeks, came in to visit the Prince later in the day. He found him much altered in face and suffering from a violent fever, but "his mind was clear and under control, his conversation as agreeable as ever, even if slightly less coherent; there were seven or eight persons with him. He insisted that tea be served as usual."

Having been summoned to the Rue Saint-Florentin most urgently on the morning of the 15th, Abbé Dupanloup hurried round with the text of the retraction formulated by Mgr de Quélen. Talleyrand read it slowly and meticulously. "Monsieur d'Abbé, I am extremely pleased with this," he said. But then added: "Would you mind leaving this paper with me? I should like to read it through once again."

For another two days Talleyrand continued to evade the

entreaties of his niece and Pauline.* Not until May 17, 1838, at six o'clock in the morning—he died at four the next afternoon—did there gather in his room Dorothée and the five witnesses appointed by the Archbishop of Paris: the Duke of Poix, Sainte-Aulaire, Barante, Royer-Collard, and Molé. In their presence the Duchess of Dino, in a slow voice and clearly enunciating each word,† read out the retraction to him one last time, and the former Bishop of Autun set his great official signature—Charles-Maurice, Prince de Talleyrand—to a final treaty—this time with God.

And of all those who worked to bring about that treaty, none had striven harder or more effectively than Dorothée.

---

* The moving role played by this girl of eighteen, upheld by her affection for the man whom she referred to always as her "good uncle," is well known. Pauline approached Talleyrand three times in an effort to obtain his signature to the retraction. On the 16th, with her mother and Abbé Dupanloup; on the evening of the same day with Abbé Dupanloup; then later that same evening at about 11 o'clock, alone this time, and at the request of Bacourt, who was sitting up with the Prince and had become very uneasy. It was in fact Pauline who twice—at 8 in the evening then at 11 in the evening of the 16th—obtained the Prince's promise that he would sign the retraction at six o'clock on the morning of the 17th.

† "I found the strength to read it slowly and gravely," she wrote to Abbé Dupanloup on May 10, 1839, "because it was both my wish and my duty to make sure that there was no circumstance that would detract from the merit of that act. It was essential that he should be entirely and perfectly aware of the deed he was about to perform. And his faculties, God be thanked, were still so far from being impaired, his attention still so far from wandering, that he would never have been satisfied with an indistinct or hurried reading. It was also my duty to justify his touching trust in asking that it should be *I* who performed that very important task. And my only means of doing so was by the firmness and clarity of my speech. For in that way I was leaving him, until the very last moment, not only an exact awareness of the deed to be accomplished but also all *his free will.*"

Part Four

FRANCE

OR

PRUSSIA? (1838-1843)

❖

ESPITE THE storms that had occasionally swept through her life, the Duchess of Dino had never attempted to reconsider the choice she made in Vienna in February 1816. Nor does she ever seem to have regretted it. Over a period of twenty-two years, the devotion that Talleyrand and Dorothée had felt for one another, the unfailing intimacy of their hearts and minds, the years themselves, had slowly purged all dross from their relationship. And it was the remaining gold that had afforded Talleyrand the serenity and calm of his last moments.

Such an end was what Dorothée, more than anyone, had most desired for her uncle, for that friend whom she loved, admired profoundly, and almost feared. And she, again more than anyone, had done her best to secure it for him. The Duchess of Dino never for a moment flagged beneath the burden that Countess Edmond de Périgord, a little blindly perhaps, had taken so many years before upon her youthful shoulders. At the right moment, she had steered Talleyrand into retirement. After three years of continued efforts, of cautious preparation, impelled by the sincerity of her own faith and a deeply-rooted sense of order, she also guided him at last, with the aid of her daughter Pauline, the child who was without any doubt the most precious of the links between them, toward the reconcilation with the Roman Church that was an example he owed it to himself, his birth and his country to provide.

No matter how one interprets these facts, Talleyrand himself, in the will he signed in London on January 10, 1834, has stilled all malice in advance: "I beg Mme de Dino to accept at this time my most heartfelt thanks for the happiness that I have enjoyed, and that I acknowledge to have been entirely due to her, for the past twenty-five years; I hope she will accept my tenderest farewells." Montrond too, for so long the Prince's constant companion and confidant, when Mme de Castellane remarked that Talleyrand owed it to his family to return into the Church, replied: "To his family? But out of all that family, no one, except for Mme de Dino, ever did anything at all for the Prince. . . ."

"I still have you, stay with me still," Talleyrand said to Dorothée once, and Dorothée was still there at the end. Now that task had been accomplished. What was she to do with her life?

The new Duchess of Talleyrand—all the important changes in Dorothée's life brought with them a transformation in her name as well, as though the better to mark off its separate phases—had for a long time been living, sometimes with an effort, though never with rebellion, in subjection to Talleyrand's tender tyranny. Twenty-two years of obedience had made submissiveness an ingrained quality of her soul, and she had loved the constraint upon her for the feeling of security, of belonging, that it brought. "When I am no longer here, Madame de Dino, you will miss me terribly," the Prince had often murmured as he discussed and arranged the details of Dorothée's existence with anxious and farsighted affection. He knew that this woman, so intelligent, so virile in mind, was nevertheless very much a woman as well. He was aware that she needed a man's arm to lean on, and that he would be leaving her alone, with no other supports but Louis, gentle and insignificant, and Bacourt, who was by nature a follower.

"Charting one's course through the storms of life is so very difficult, and I no longer feel myself at all fitted for the task," Dorothée wrote in 1841. "I no longer have a pilot, and now I'm on my own I don't know how to steer my ship; I am in constant fear of sinking it on one reef or another. All my many past experiences have done nothing to make me a better navigator, they have merely made me mistrust my own skill, and that is not enough to ensure one a safe voyage."

The next five years of the Duchess of Talleyrand's voyage were spent tacking continually between France and Germany, until the day when, caught up in one last violent eddy of emotion, reclaimed by the land of her birth, she became entirely

Prussian once again. Without forgetting Talleyrand, for his memory would never leave her, she nevertheless abandoned France, the country to which he had summoned her, but where even he had never been able to make her take root.

On May 18, the day after Talleyrand's death, Maître Chatelain presented the Prince's will to the President of the Lower Court of the department of the Seine. Louis de Périgord's marriage contract, made in 1829, had assured him of Valençay plus a capital sum of 2,100,000 francs to compensate for the three mortgages of 800,000 francs, 500,000 francs and 800,000 francs taken out on behalf of Charlotte de Talleyrand, Georgine d'Esclignac and Alexandre de Périgord respectively. The will ratified these arangements. Edmond received 300,000, the remainder of the entail on his peerage. It was swallowed up forthwith by his creditors. Pont-de-Sains, which brought in a yearly income of 80,000 livres, was left to Pauline, together with the Prince's gold watch which had a miniature of Dorothée in its lid.

Everything else went to the Duchess of Talleyrand, the residuary legatee, together with the responsibility for settling all debts, providing innumerable pensions for old retainers, and paying out several minor bequests. The amount of Talleyrand's fortune has never been discovered, but one fact is certain: his income had diminished considerably during the course of his last few years. It therefore seems very likely that Dorothée's inheritance consisted of no more than the house on the Rue Saint-Florentin and its contents.

Four days later, on May 22, Talleyrand's funeral service was celebrated with great pomp in the Chapelle de l'Assomption. The Duchess of Talleyrand, in compliance with French custom, did not attend.

Since she was financially a prudent woman, and also because new surroundings would make it easier to find her balance in her new life, Dorothée had never envisaged keeping the house on the Rue Saint-Florentin. In 1836, she had expressed a wish to buy the hôtel Carnvalet, then on the market at an asking price of 140,000 francs; after the Prince's death, while Pauline was still in bed sick with grief, she very quickly, almost without thinking, rented a large apartment in the hôtel de Galliffet, which was situated on the Rue de Grenelle, in the very heart of the Faubourg Saint-Germain. She moved in on June 21.

"Yesterday was a bad day," she wrote on June 22 to Barante, who was on his way back to his post as French Ambassador in St. Petersburg. "I left our house—perhaps never to return— the house in which twenty-three years of my life have been spent, and what years! The years that constitute my life, properly speaking. I am writing to you within an hour of waking up. This place seems less strange now because I have filled it with things that remind me of the past though they also have the effect of sharpening the contrast. You see, I can't tell yet what consoles me and what hurts me, and I can feel that it will take me a long time to get on an even keel again. It won't be long before I leave. . . ."

Three days later she wrote, still to Barante: "You will have received my leter of the 22nd. I wrote it only very few hours after a separation that, despite its being entirely a material one, nonetheless broke my heart! Ever since I left the Rue Saint-Florentin I have been feeling strangely drained of all strength; my grief sharper and the power to bear it less. Though my new establishment here is really quite acceptable; that's something. I know I should hate it if it weren't; but all the same, how unimportant the external things in one's life are, and how far the void is from being filled in that way. If you had been in Paris, I would have asked you to help me move in. . . ."

A strange sentence that last one, if one remembers that Bacourt was there in Paris at the time. And one that cannot be dismissed as mere politeness, since the Duchess then added, à propos of certain difficulties she had encountered having to do with Talleyrand's personal papers: "There is not one of the people generally accepted to be my friends who inspires me with sufficient confidence for me to place absolute trust in his advice. I would have done what you told me though, for you are the only person in whom I have unlimited confidence."

On June 27, 1838, Dorothée and Pauline left for Baden.

Several days later, the Talleyrand town house was sold by auction. It was bought by James de Rothschild for 1,181,000 francs.* Lastly, on July 9, having been divided into four hundred and twelve lots containing works of every kind, the Prince's library was broken up.

On September 2, while the Duchess of Talleyrand and her daughter were still lingering in Heidelberg with the Duchess of Sagan (they did not return to Paris until September 4), Talleyrand's funeral cortege set out for Valençay, where he was buried on the 5th. Several days later, by way of Bonnétable, the country house of Mme de Laval's niece the Duchess Mathieu de Montmorency, Dorothée and Pauline reached Rochecotte. It was in Touraine that the Duchess wanted to set up her real home, and she began by building herself a library and a chapel there.

She did not stay long at Rochecotte however; she had to go back to Paris, to move back into the apartment, to settle Pauline's future. Not only that, the stay at Rochcotte had been painful; it had filled her with a terrified awareness of how empty her life had become. And she was afraid that this feeling was going to be intensified still further at Valençay, which she wanted to visit also on her way back to Paris. "There is something inside me driving me toward that last refuge of the man who took up so large a part of my life. I shall do no more than hear Mass there, say one prayer, then drive on again," she wrote to Barante on September 25.

◇ ◇ ◇

Despite thirty years in France, despite so many months in Paris, so many months spent in the heart of the countryside,

---

* On July 15, the Duchess told Barante: "My house fetched a rather poor price; it was bought by the Paris Rothschild. So at least I found a very solvent purchaser, and one who can practically pay cash down, which is a consideration."

Dorothée had remained instinctively German in her reactions. Astute and self-assured in cosmopolitan circles, when faced with Parisian society she was still unsure of herself, always veering between arrogance and discomfiture. Before, Talleyrand had always been there to protect her, to shore up her uncertainty with his infallible savoir-faire; now, confronted by a cloaked but indubitable hostility, the Duchess was beginning to lose her footing.

"Are you going to become one of those great Faubourg Saint-Germain ladies?" Montrond asked her shortly after her return to the capital. Completely taken aback by this question, Dorothée answered stumblingly with a string of meaningless platitudes. She was what she was, a woman of independent means, a princess who need defer to no one in regard to either her opinions or her position. In memory of Talleyrand she meant to maintain her cordial relations with the Tuileries. Because she preferred to be with people of breeding she wished to live with her family, surrounded by people of her own kind. It was a difficult position to defend in the society of that time, still split into opposite camps by the July monarchy.

This feeling of uneasiness did not escape the notice of the sharp-tongued Princess Lieven, by then, much to Dorothée's chagrin, occupying the mezzanine of the former Talleyrand house. She noted with satisfaction: "The Duchess of Talleyrand appears to me hardly to have settled down into her new position. She wished to be on good terms with all the world, but with this object in view she flatters people rather too much and indiscriminately both to right and to left. Her attentions thereby lose much of their value, and she sometimes makes such a mess of things that it must require the greatest cleverness on her part to get out of the imbroglio. But then, she is very clever."

Though he writes of her admiringly, Sosthène de la Rochefoucald, the Duchess Mathieu de Montmorency's son-in-law, had observed the same behavior: "Since she is very anxious to be on good terms with everyone, she closes her eyes and ears so as not to see or hear anything of which she would be obliged to disapprove, and even those who criticize her extreme condescension when she is not there are completely disarmed in her presence.

"Besides, she is a model of elegance and distinction, a woman superior in every way. I have no idea how far her indulgence is calculated; but no one has ever quoted a malicious remark from her lips, and I am inclined to believe that her discretion springs much more from real goodness than from prudence; for her character is as noble as it is generous."

This new humility, this deliberate and universal good will was in fact the product, in a woman now all on her own with no hope of support either from her own family or from the Talleyrands, of her anxious determination to achieve a good and happy marriage for Pauline. Faced with this delicate task, one in which the Prince would have been indispensable had he been alive, she could not rely on either Mgr de Quélen or Abbé Dupanloup, for though they were both good priests the first was too intelligent and the second too low-born for the Duchess to count on their possessing all the discernment and experience desirable in such a matter.

While still in the fresh bloom of her eighteenth year, "sweeter and more amiable than ever" (the phrase is Apponyi's), Pauline de Périgord had now been transformed by Talleyrand's death into a wealthy heiress, and many suitors had appeared to ask for her hand. Jules de Clermont-Tonnerre looked common; the Duke of Saulx-Tavannes not only came from a family that was half mad but also had the physical appearance of an elephant; the Duke of Guiche was penniless; the Marquis de Biron, though very rich and well-behaved, was unbelievably stupid and even more Carlist; Elie de Gontaut had no ambition. There had also been some talk before Talleyrand's death of a Mérode match that the Prince had thought highly of; but the idea had since been abandoned.

Henri de Castellane seemed to be the candidate most worthy of serious consideration. His mother was practically laying physical siege to the Duchess, and Madame Adélaïde was very favorable to the match because it wouldn't prevent Pauline going to the Tuileries. The young man, who had been brought up by his grandparents, a very cultivated couple, himself possessed a

naturally distinguished mind which had been brought into perfect flower by the refined and intellectual environment in which
he had grown up. A close friend of the upright Falloux, reserved
and somewhat mysterious, he was always held up as a model
to the other young men of the Faubourg Saint-Germain.

On October 30, Dorothée went to ask the advice of Mgr
de Quélen and Abbé Dupanloup. Both were of the opinion that
Henri de Castellane was the candidate whose personal merits
seemed to offer most chance of "a happy home life," for Pauline.
Both also added that Pauline herself ought to make the choice,
after proper consideration.

That same evening, following Abbé Dupanloup's advice,
Dorothée informed her daughter of the various suitors who
had presented themselves. Pauline dismissed them all without
hesitation—except for Castellane. She had seen him twice and
liked him very much, but she wanted to know him better, to
assure herself of his principles and his attitude towards religion
before committing herself further.

Dorothée still remembered the haste with which she had
been forced into her own marriage. She begged her daughter
on no account to hurry her decision: Pauline could wait, and
she for her part did not wish any marriage at all to take place
before her affairs were all in order, the financial matters arising
from her uncle's will settled, and their year's mourning elapsed.

Next day, Dorothée wrote a report of this conversation to
Bacourt, whom she knew to be very fond of Pauline; "Here I
am in a new phase of my life, one in which I find myself obliged
to invite a young man into my home so that I can decide what
he's worth. I have known M. de Castellane personally for a
great many years, but unfortunately I haven't seen him at all
recently; though it's not I who am to marry him anyway, it's
Pauline. He has a good mind and a well-filled one, I know him
to be diligent and I believe he is ambitious. He is steady and
very well-mannered, lives a quiet life, but when he goes into
society it is always of the very best. He is a good son and a
good brother; he has a great name, even a very great one, but
he has no title or any expectation of one; few close relatives,
but would like to live in Paris (with a separate household) in

the same house as myself; wants a religious wife though not a practising Catholic himself; an income of twenty thousand livres settled on him at marriage, thirty thousand more when his grandmother and his mother . . ." The Duchess then concluded by saying once again that her daughter must make the choice.

In fact, one is more or less forced to conclude that Pauline had already made her choice, or at least that she had already begun to feel the violent inclination for Henri de Castellane that marriage was quickly to transform into a blind passion. This explains the furious haste with which matters were pushed forward and the way in which Dorothée's cautiously planned timetable was brushed aside.

"The day after tomorrow I shall be in my apartment (Rue de Grenelle-Saint-Germain, 87)," Dorothée wrote hurriedly to Barante on April 5, 1839. "On the 8th, we shall sign my daughter's marriage contract there; on the 9th, we shall have the civil marriage, on the 10th, the ceremony at Saint-Thomas-d'Aquin.

"Ever since I was obliged to start making the actual preparations for Pauline's marriage I have been on the brink of tears every moment of every day. To see her young girl's life ending, about to make way for such a new, such a different, such a serious phase of existence—it fills me with an inexpressible anguish. And after that we shall soon be reaching the saddest anniversary of my life! . . ."

❖ ❖ ❖

Several weeks before Dorothée had become the wife of Edmond de Périgord, Adélaïde-Josèphe Bourlon de Chavanges had been married, on February 23, 1809, to Maréchal Augereau, Duke of Castiglione. The two newlyweds seemed to be unsuited to each other in every way. To begin with, in age: the wife was less than twenty, the husband over fifty. Then their opinions: the Bourlon de Chavanges family, lesser nobility from

Champagne with more honor than money, were all out-and-out Royalists; Augereau, a child of the Revolution, was still a republican at heart. However, his duke's title, the endowments that had accompanied it, and the "tidy profits" he had earned on his campaigns had combined to bridge the gulf.

Extremely beautiful and very intelligent, the young wife soon achieved a considerable influence over a husband who was, after all, nothing but a simple soldier. In 1814, she urged Augereau into a very prompt offer of support to the Bourbons. She had never given any cause for gossip about herself, and although appointed lady-in-waiting to the Empress Marie-Louise in September of 1810, along with so many others, she had scarcely ever appeared at the Imperial court because she always accompanied her husband on his campaigns.

Having been a virtuous wife to a husband she did not love, Adélaïde de Chavanges made no attempt to play the inconsolable widow when Augereau died in 1816. She quickly married again, this time Count Camille de Sainte-Aldegonde, aide-de-camp to the Duke of Orléans. She had several children by him, one of them a girl, Valentine, born in 1820.

Under the Restoration, the Duchess of Dino and the Duchess of Castiglione had rather lost sight of each other. Then the July monarchy had brought them together again, and quite friendly relations were established between Valençay and Beauregard, Mme de Sainte-Aldegonde's château outside Blois.

She had been separated from her second husband, who had gone off to pursue his military career in Russia and eventually become the Tsar's aide-de-camp and Chief of Staff. Mme de Sainte-Aldegonde held one of the highest ranks in the Queen's household and was a "great friend" of the Baron de Montmorency who had just missed becoming Madame Adélaïde's Lauzun. The Countess of Sainte-Aldegonde was one of the women most highly thought of by the Juste Milieu. Her friendship with Montmorency also assured her of a place on the fringes of the Faubourg Saint-Germain. "She is somewhat loud-voiced and dictatorial." Dorothée noted in October 1834, "and although courteous and reasonably well-bred she lacks that natural ease and obligingness of manner that can only be acquired by an acquaintance with true elegance very early in life: a person may be acceptable when born without such things, but never distinguished. But still, taken all in all, she will do."

A rather grudging approval.

It may be supposed without much risk or error that Dorothée was just as grudging in her approval of the marriage that was arranged, during the summer of 1839, between Valentine de Sainte-Aldegonde and Alexandre de Périgord, now Duke of Dino. The connection was not a very good one. Louis had married a Montmorency, Pauline a Castellane, and the Saint-Aldegondes were certainly not in the same class. The young lady in question was beautiful and intelligent like her mother; unfortunately she also took after her mother in being ambitious and greedy, and what is more, she had not repulsed the unseasonable and pressing attentions of the strange Anatol Demidoff.

But since that day in November 1835, when Dorothée had told Mgr de Quélen about her hopes and fears for her younger son, Alexandre's situation had by no means improved. Idleness, as for his father before him, had not proved a good counselor, his debts had mounted, his creditors had become more and more pressing, and it had taken almost a full year of negotiations and lawsuits before Louis and the Duchess had finally dared, in June of 1839, to make over to Alexandre the sum he had inherited from Talleyrand with any degree of assurance that it would not immediately be attached.

There seemed a good reason to take advantage of this respite, this brief period during which the young man's affairs were for the time being in good order, to marry him off. Dorothée must have considered so at all events, and she must also have considered how very few families would not be alarmed at the thought of her son's spendthrift ways, how Talleyrand was no longer there to overcome all these difficulties, and, in short, that her best course was to resign herself to the Sainte-Aldegonde marriage in the hope that the beautiful, and so very forward, Valentine would achieve an ascendancy over her young husband and use it to guide him wisely.

Alexandre de Dino married Valentine de Sainte-Aldegonde

on October 8, 1839. "At the marriage service of the young Duke of Dino, which was held in a château in an attempt to copy the old feudal traditions, Anatol [Demidoff] joined with the beautiful young bride in becoming godfather to a new church bell," Fortunée Hamelin wrote several days later to Montrond. "Two wagonloads of bonbons then arrived crammed with the entire contents of the Rue des Lombards and the Palais-Royal. The bridegroom presented gold vases to the church, dowries to six young girls, six thousand francs to the poor, and then, while all the neighboring villagers were filing through to look at the banquet, his grooms handed out all manner of shawls and laces and aprons to the peasant women; the whole thing topped by a diamond and ruby tiara for Mlle de Sainte-Aldegonde that has been estimated at thirty thousand francs. I confess that in her mother's place I should not have allowed her to accept it."

❖   ❖   ❖

Whenever Talleyrand had thought of his niece's future, of what her life would be like when he himself was gone and Alexandre and Pauline married, he had always predicted that Dorothée would leave the world of society and live mainly in the country. What he almost certainly did not predict was that the Duchess of Talleyrand would also leave France and return to Germany. But during the autumn of 1839, without Dorothée herself being aware of it perhaps, a series of events took place that began to loosen her bonds with a country not hers by birth.

Edmond was becoming bored in Florence, despite the ties that he had formed with Mrs. Hugh MacDonnel. The three hundred thousand francs from the entail on his peerage, and possibly a few scraps left him by his father, who died, it will be remembered, only two weeks before Talleyrand, had at last appeased his creditors. If he was also willing to sacrifice a large portion of the income allowed to him by Dorothée it was now possible for him to return to France. The question of his doing so arose during the autumn of 1839, and Dorothée must have been aware of it. Paris without Talleyrand was already scarcely bearable. Paris without Talleyrand and with Edmond was totally unthinkable.

In November of 1839, Bacourt was appointed to Washington This "exile" * angered the Duchess and made her entertain even more seriously the prospect of spending the spring of 1840, after Bacourt's departure, making her long visit to Prussia that she had been considering for several years. She knew that she would be welcomed in Berlin. In a letter written on May 3, 1839, the heir to the Prussian throne, the future Frederick-Wilhelm IV, after congratulating her on Pauline's marriage had added: "I must confess to you, madame, that the propect of seeing you here, you and your family, on the occasion of your projected visit to Silesia, was what most enchanted me in the contents of your letter. I entreat you, madame! do not cheat us of this hope, and remember that you owe us vast damages for the destroyed hopes that we have entertained in vain for so many years. . . ."

The death of the Duchess of Sagan in Vienna, on November 29, 1839, then crystallized Dorothée's intentions even further. Though the Duchess her sister had left most of her personal fortune and the freehold lands attached to Sagan to her sister the Princess Hohenzollern, the fief itself was entailed to Louis and Alexandre should their Hohenzollern cousin continue to remain without issue. This meant more business to be settled, more financial problems to be hammered out.

Another loss, the death of Mgr de Quélen late in December of 1839, then came to sever one of the few emotional ties still keeping the Duchess of Talleyrand in Paris, And besides, Talleyrand's death and Dorothée's own semi-retirement had still not disarmed the malice of French society towards her. In January of 1840, Lady Holland, taking it upon herself to spread the latest Paris rumors, rumors that Dorothée herself could

---

* She wrote to Bacourt on August 7, 1840: "If poor dear M. de Talleyrand had been alive, I doubt whether he would have allowed you to exile yourself so far away from us."

not have been in ignorance of, wrote to her son: "Scandal says the Duchess Dino proposes making a long séjour in Germany but in reality to conceal what others display. The favorite is a very young, handsome employé; his name I have forgotten."

❖　　❖　　❖

With Pauline safely and happily delivered of a daughter Marie-Dorothée, born on February 19, 1840, and Bacourt on the brink of his departure for London and then America, Dorothée and her son Louis de Valençay set out from Paris on May 14 or 15, 1840, in the direction of Prussia.

They traveled by short stages. Amiens, Lille, Liège, then Bergheim. In the latter, their first stop in Prussia itself, they found the inn clean but the beds very strange and the cold bone-chilling. Worse, it was impossible without risk of suffocation to light the cast iron stoves. Then came Cologne, followed by several less well-known towns. Finally, on May 25, in beating rain, after making her way across the breadth of a country she had been astonished to find so ugly, Dorothée drove once more into the city of her birth and took up residence at the hôtel de Russie, opposite the castle.

Though fascinated at this rediscovery of the country where she had spent her childhood, Dorothée nevertheless failed to be moved by it. She found, to her amazement almost, that the "patriotic partiality" she had felt toward Germany for so long no longer existed. An absolute stranger to both places and people, she was assailed by a sensation of rootlessness and even found herself stumbling over the language. In short, she was "for the most part ill at ease in Germany, and ashamed of being so."

Despite the then grave concern over Frederick-Wilhelm III's health—he died on June 7—the Duchess was given an affectionate welcome by the heir-apparent and his brother Wilhelm. She was also presented to the future Queen Elisabeth, who was cordial enough to her, and to Princess Wilhelm—shortly to become the Princess Royal of Prussia—who was eager to show her every kindness.

After attending the ex-king's funeral on June 10, Dorothée left for Silesia. On June 13, she arrived at Günthersdorf, "in her own domains," a few leagues from Sagan.

The reception she had received from the court and society of Berlin had satisfied the Duchess's pride. The countryside and forests of Silesia touched her heart; while the sight of all the towns and villages that were her property reawakened in her soul the feudal instincts that thirty years in France, the land of equality, had merely lulled to sleep.

Günthersdorf was simply a large house painted orange-yellow, which supported the weight of an enormous roof. On the ground floor, to the right, there were a vaulted vestibule, the drawing rooms, and the dining room; to the left, the Duchess's own apartments. On the floor above there were four master bedrooms with appropriate accommodations opening off them; only one of these suites was furnished, and even that very meagerly. The garden was pleasant and well tended, the woods very fine.

Next day was a Sunday; leaving Günthersdorf, which was entirely Protestant, the Duchess and Louis drove over to hear Mass four leagues away at Wartenberg, a little town that was Dorothée's property and all of whose householders paid her ground rent. The priest greeted them on the outskirts with holy water and a fine speech of welcome. The Duchess and Louis took their places in a special pew strewn with flowers.

After luncheon, M. de Wurmb, the manager of her estates, * asked Dorothée's permission to present to her all those employed in the management of her estates. It was a long ceremony, for they were presented individually, and the administration of the Duchess's properties required a staff of huge proportions, all ultimately dependent on appointment by Dorothée hereslf: an architect, a doctor, two bailiffs, two chief tax-collectors, a

---

* A former officer in the Prussian army, Wurmb was the husband of Mlle de Goeckingk, daughter of Dorothée's former guardian and her own childhood playmate. "People of good family in Germany are not afraid to help manage the affairs of those whom they look upon as the great of the land," Dorothée commented when speaking of him.

head steward, a head warden, four Catholic priests, three Protestant pastors, and lastly the mayor. They all seemed to Dorothée to be "real gentlemen and very well brought up."

During the next few days, the Duchess and Louis continued their visits of inspection around Dorothée's estates: farms, schools, churches, villages, all were owned directly by the lord of the estate. They also made visits to several neighbors, all of whom made them very welcome, and Dorothée began to think that this country, despite the harshness of its climate, might prove a very acceptable refuge from her troubled life in the west of Europe.

The Princess Hohenzollern and her son were not interested in Sagan for its own sake, but they were nevertheless trying to extract as much profit from it as possible: they had even had things removed and sold that were properly part of the fief. Herr von Wolff, Dorothée's business agent in Berlin, had written to advise her of this fact, adding that he was now on his way to Sagan in order to lodge a protest; he suggested that she also should try to be there at the same time, bringing Louis de Valençay with her since he too was an interested party.

"I have taken rooms at the inn," Dorothée wrote to Bacourt on June 21, 1840. "With things as they are I decided it would not be proper to stay at the château itself. But what a strange feeling it does give me! Here, where my father and my sister lived, where I spent so much of my own childhood, to be staying at the inn!

"After an hour's discussion with M. de Wolff, we went on up to the château. Everything looked the same as ever, except for all the things that they have been in rather too much of a hurry to remove and which may well have to be brought back."

In one of the outhouses, Dorothée came across a gilded carriage upholstered in red velvet. It reminded her of the one left behind by the royal Spanish captives at Valençay. It was the carriage in which Duke Pierre had left Courland. The Princess Hohenzollern's business agent had put it up for sale. The Duchess went to the auction and bought it—for thirty-five crowns.

Before leaving Sagan, Dorothée had a long business conference. The question of the fief was a complicated one, and it seemed likely to go on being so for some time. Wolff and Wurmb both advised the Duchess to offer her sister her (Dorothée's) share in the family's Bohemian estate, Nachod, in exchange for the freehold woods attached to Sagan. Nachod would revert to her sons one day in any case. Dorothée did not reject the idea although the woods in question were magnificent and she loved them. She wanted to think the matter over. Both men also pressed her to spend the whole year in Germany, but the Duchess was too much alarmed—at that time —by the prospect of spending the winter in so harsh a climate. She would come back again in the spring.

Shortly before she left Silesia, Dorothée summed up her impressions in a letter to Bacourt: "The position of the great landowner is very different here from what it is in France." She added: "It has quite gone to my son's head." But was she quite sure that it had not gone to hers as well?

❖ ❖ ❖

The Duchess's journey into Germany had given her the opportunity to renew old links not only with the Prussian court but also with her remaining sisters, Princess Hohenzollern and the Duchess of Acerenza, whom she had not seen since her visit in 1824, sixteen years earlier. Thanks to this renewal of personal contacts, Dorothée now had the knowledge that she could always make a new life for herself in Germany if ever she felt too much cut off in France.

At first glance, however, there seemed no reason why such a choice should be necessary. It is true that the Duchess scarcely spent any time in her new Paris home, 73, Rue de Lille,* a secluded house, tucked away between a courtyard and a garden, that she recently acquired; but there was nevertheless a great

* She did not dispose of it until 1862.

deal of quiet pleasure for her in the autumn and winter spent
at Rochecotte with her younger children: Pauline and her husband and child, Alexandre with his wife. They were six months
of peaceful, unbroken family life during which Dorothée's uneasy heart was able to regain its calm.

If the Duchess had not set out once more to visit Germany
in the spring of 1841, she might have gone on living for the
rest of her life in Touraine. But her business agents were in-
sisting on her presence in Silesia, and Frederick-Wilhelm IV had
invited her to visit him at Sans-Souci. The invitation was
couched in the most affectionate of terms; but Dorothée, her
thoughts on the future of Sagan decided to take it as an order.

The Duchess arrived in Berlin on May 16, 1841. Her stay
there was a repetition of the previous year's visit: the same warm
welcome at the court; the same eagerness to please on the part
of Berlin society; the same monotony too—mornings spent
closeted with her business agents, long dinners monopolized
by the innumerable royal princes. . . .

The year before, Dorothée had promised her sisters to visit
them in Vienna. She had not been back to the Austrian capital
since February 1816, and it was not without emotion that she
drove back into it on June 18, 1841. "It was here that I first
began to devote my life to M. de Talleyrand, that I formed
the singular, unique association that could be broken only by
death, and when I say broken, that is a mistake; I ought to say
suspended, for I feel a thousand times a year that we shall meet
again elsewhere." And she added: "I am not at all sure I shall
sleep tonight; I am very much disturbed by all the phantoms
that this place evokes, and all of them speaking to me of the
selfsame thing, the utter vanity of all worldly things."

Metternich, and Viennese society, could not have given the
Duchess of Talleyrand a more enthusiastic reception. And yet
Dorothée enjoyed herself less in Vienna than she had in Berlin.
If it ever became necessary for her to take up city life again,
she had already decided which city she would choose. "In Vienna
they are richer and much more aristocratic in their manner,
very natural, too natural. . . . Their way of life is extremely
free and easy; they all do what they please and it doesn't

seem at all eccentric; but even though they never express astonishment about other people's behavior, that doesn't stop them
speaking a great deal of ill of their neighbors, and I am tempted
to say that there is a *false bonhomie* prevalent here that is very
dangerous. . . ."

Above all, Dorothée had disliked the familiarity in Vienna.
"There were twenty people who addressed me or referred to
me as Dorothée; those less familiar said Duchess Dorothée; the
very formal ones, dear Duchess; not one of them ever said
Madame, or Madame la Duchesse; and as for my hands, I'm
surprised I have any left; and my cheeks took a terrible hammering too, for I tried to substitute them for my lips whenever
possible. Viennese women are obviously very free in the matter
of love affairs and make no attempt to conceal them, though this
does not prevent all the churches from being full or the con-
fessionals from being perpetually besieged. . . ."

From Vienna, Dorothée continued on into nearby Silesia
in order to meet her business agents and continue her attempts
to settle the vexed question of the Sagan estate. She found herself pleased to be back at Günthersdorf, the big orange-yellow
house with the ugly roof. She spent three very quiet months
there, despite a visit from the King and Queen of Prussia on
August 31. Two days after that, the Duchess left on her way
back to France. But before leaving she gave orders for enlarging
the garden and altering the roof. She really liked being in Silesia
very much, and she meant to return. Imperceptibly, the scales
were tipping in favor of Prussia, where Dorothée was slowly,
almost regretfully, picking up the threads of the past.

❖   ❖   ❖

Back in Paris, the Duchess found some letters waiting from
Pauline that gave her cause for some concern. Her daughter,
always somewhat delicate, had experienced great difficulty in
recovering from a bad sore throat the previous spring. A visit

to Geneva, then a summer spent in the Auvergne, at Aubijoux,* had left her drained of all energy. She and her husband were contemplating spending the winter in the South of France, or in Rome if the Duchess didn't want to join them in Nice.

Dorothée hesitated slightly. She felt a need for genuine rest, for "settling herself down" at Rochecotte for a good length of time. But she also felt a keen longing to see Pauline again, to be with the ailing daughter who had appealed to her so tenderly. She finally decided to go to Nice in December and to stay there for three full months.

The Duchess took over the second floor of a house on the "Terrasse," facing the sea. On rainy days, the great gray stretch of water that melted indistinguishably into the gray sky above drew a melancholy curtain before her windows; when it was sunny, the glare was blinding. The drawing room was immense but icy, the bedroom small and its chimney smoky. Yet though Dorothée could not help thinking regretfully of the comforts left behind at Rochecotte, when she saw her daughter again after their seven months apart, all her regrets vanished completely. Mme de Castellane was still suffering from a sore throat, but despite her poor health—which did in any case improve steadily through the winter—Pauline was by then a happy woman in the first bloom of her mature beauty and brimming over with the joys of life.

In April 1942, Dorothée traveled back to Touraine. As during the winter spent at Rochecotte the year before, the long months spent with her family (Louis and Alexandre had come to Nice for a few weeks too) had given her a feeling of contentment brought back a glow into her always anxious heart. "I have good news from the Castellanes," she announced to Bacourt on May 10, 1842. "I miss them a lot: Pauline's sweetness of temper, Henri's unfailing resources of conversation, Marie's grace —they are all such a great help to me. I can always be sure of rest with them, and without any risk of boredom; I can relax

* Driven on by political ambitions, Henri de Castellane had by this time begun building in the Cantal region, on a site devoid of trees or cultivable land, far from any road, the château where within a few years he was to ruin himself and ruin Pauline.

in their atmosphere; they've become absolutely necessary to me. I always make a place for them in all my schemes and plans for the future, and I can't imagine my old age without them. . . ."

Had Dorothée found the right climate for her existence then, for the first time since Talleyrand's death? There was reason to believe she had and that Prussia was not going to succeed in wooing her away from France. But only if one counted without the irony of fate. For fate, having once made a Frenchwoman out of the little girl whose life would normally have been lived in Prussia, was now, by a strange reversal, with less brutality than before but with the same relentlessness, with a slowly building pressure from often trivial events, driving the woman she had become back to the country of her origin, and gradually tearing her up by the roots a second time.

Early in 1842 when she was still in Nice, the Duchess had received a letter from Berlin: the Prince Hohenzollern would not have anything to do with the plans for a settlement suggested by his mother, and the Princess had just sold the entire freehold portion of the Sagan estate to her sister. This was an important transaction and one that meant another visit to Prussia for Dorothée in the course of 1843.

Despite this future prospect, the spring of 1842 was passing very gently for the Duchess in Touraine when, on June 7, a letter arrived from Pauline. Her husband was ill; the illness was the result of a fall from a horse, or else a rheumatic inflammation, no one knew, but his condition was serious: fever, delirium, nervous spasms, frightful attacks of pain, fainting fits. Pauline, lost in that desolate stretch of country, far from a doctor, was finding her isolation difficult to bear.

After heisitating for a few days, Dorothée left for Cantal. She found her son-in-law much changed: the condition of his thigh had improved, but the nervous tremors were still occasion for concern.

Dorothée found Aubijoux no less difficult to bear than her daughter did. They were living in a temporary wooden building, indeed, practically bivouacking in it. They were devoured by fleas, plagued by mice; the mountain winds whistled unopposed throughout the building, and the noise was infernal.

Until now, Castellane had refused to leave this wretched barn of a place. But one fine morning, three days after the Duchess's arival, he announced that he would like to move to Néris, the waters there having been prescribed for him by his doctor. Almost before the words had left his lips, the horses were outside the door and the baggage all strapped up. On June 25, a veritable caravan rumbled down the hill from Aubijoux. "We laid my son-in-law on a mattress then set it down on the floor of their big traveling coach, which luckily is very roomy; then all we had to do was get down out of the mountains! Apart from the Castellane coach, with them and the doctor, there was also my carriage, which contained myself and my maid with M. Vestier [an architect from Touraine who had supervised the improvements at Rochecotte] and Jacques outside, then a little tilbury with some Corsican horses pulling it and containing the cook and a local jockey; on horseback there were the business agent, a guard, and a Negro my nephew had brought back from the South of France whose name is Zéphir and who was blowing a horn.The whole thing made a very odd sight, rather like a scene from the *Roman comique*. . . . Darkness caught up with us before we had got past all the gorges, and I cannot tell you enough to what extent my cowardice shamefully betrayed me at that point: to tell the truth, I wept . . ."

Once the Castellanes were safely in Clermont, the Duchess went on ahead to Néris, reserved lodgings for them, and then, with a kind of furious haste, as though hounded by some terrible anxiety, drove on to Rochecotte.

What could it have been, this new inner distress that had produced such an obvious change in her feelings toward her son-in-law and inspired her with overwhelming uneasiness on behalf of her daughter? Both the tone of her letters during the few short days at Aubijoux and the desperate haste with which she made her escape definitely indicate that she was in some mental distress. And though it is true that she was concerned at the way Castellane's activities were jeopardizing Pauline's own fortune as well as his own, and mentioned this concern in a letter, this cause alone does not seem adequate. It seems certain that she had discovered something else, something more serious, something that threatened her daughter's whole happiness, something of which she wanted Pauline at all costs to remain ignorant.

"Have I ever told you the story of M. de Castellane's son, the one who married Mme de Talleyrand's daughter, the young lady who was probably also the daughter of M. de Talleyrand, her uncle?" Mérimée wrote on December 25, 1847, to Mme de Montijo. "He died, as you know, leaving enormous debts. His widow was inconsolable and had no thoughts whatever for the ruin of her fortunes, for it was the man alone she mourned the loss of. At the very height of her noble grief, as she was going through the private papers of the deceased, for business must always be attended to, she came upon a packet of love letters. That he had been unfaithful they made only too abundantly clear, but what she found strange was that all the adjectives used to describe this successful rival were of the masculine gender. Imagine the surprise. M. de C. had chanced upon a very handsome footman in the employ of Princess Lieven; he had persuaded the fellow to enter his own household, relieved him of his livery, and made him his steward. The steward and the rival, you see, were one and the same. . . . One day, when Mme de Talleyrand was paying a visit to M. de C.'s château, she observed the steward in question entering the room, dressed like a gentleman and preparing to sit down at table with her. 'It seems to me I've seen that gentleman somewhere before,' she said. 'Yes, behind the Princess Lieven's carriage. Have the gentleman's meal served to him in his room.' "

Mérimée had a great fondness for scabrous anecdotes. But he was often very well informed all the same. And moreover he was certainly aware that Mme de Montijo, being a very close friend of the future Maréchal de Castellane, Pauline's father-in-law, was in a position to check his story. It is therefore possible to accept the likelihood of his imputation, an imputation that Viel-Castel was to repeat several years later.

If Mérimée's story is true, then the incident between the Duchess and the steward must have taken place in 1842. After her departure for Germany in May 1843, Dorothée came back to Paris in April 1844, spent a few days at Rochecotte, then

left for Prussia once again late in June of the same year. She
was not to appear in France again until the autumn of 1847,
after Henri de Castellane's death.

It is difficult not to believe that an incident of *some* sort
occurred during that short stay at Aubijoux. On May 10, as we
have seen, the Duchess was telling Bacourt that she always
made a place for the Castellanes in all her schemes and plans
for the future and that she couldn't imagine her old age without
them; but in July, leaving her daughter to tend her sick husband first of all in Néris, then in Italy, the Duchess went to
Rochecotte and scarcely emerged from her hiding-place again
during the whole of the following summer, autumn and winter.
Only for a brief moment in the following spring, while she was
in Paris for a few weeks before traveling on to Prussia, did she
see Pauline and her husband when they arrived back from Rome.
It is certainly true that the Duchess's own private life was to
become complicated again toward the end of 1843, but the seed
of this separation had been sown earlier—in 1842.

While these personal considerations—the acquisition of the
Sagan freehold, the waning of her intimacy with the Castellanes
—were at the same time drawing Dorothée towards Prussia and
loosening still further her remaining ties with France, there
occurred a serious political event, the death of the Duke of
Orléans on July 18, 1842, that not only destroyed all the
hopes she had been nourishing for the future of her son Louis
de Valençay, but also made her lose faith in the future of the
Orléans dynasty altogether. The dead heir to the throne had
always shown genuine friendship toward Dorothée; * she could
have expected to play an influential role after his accession. In
her eyes, as in those of many other Orléanites, the Duke of
Orléans' abilities and personality had always constituted the
July monarchy's best guarantee of survival. So that this premature death was yet another contributory factor in pushing
Dorothée toward Prussia where Frederick-Wilhelm IV and the
Princess of Prussia were waiting to welcome her, where the pre-

---

* On April 13, 1840, in a codicil added to the will made on the 9th,
the Duke of Orléans had expressed a wish to leave mementos of himself to
both the Duchess of Talleyrand and the Duchess of Massa.

vailing political stability would enable her, she thought, to live in peace.

◇   ◇   ◇

When Dorothée chose to make her life with Talleyrand, she did so only after that choice had been slowly prepared for by her years at the Imperial court. Before the final decision, a decision that had meant signing away, as it were, twenty-two years of her existence, or almost all her life as a young woman, Destiny had granted Countess Edmond de Périgord one last, brief period of respite. For several months in Vienna, away from Talleyrand, she had deliberated with herself until her decision was ripe.

Now, Dorothée was once more on the brink of a decision. It was one that involved the rest of her life. As in her youth, this decision had been slowly prepared for by the years since Talleyrand's death; as in her youth too, Destiny granted the Duchess one last, brief period of respite in which to weigh her final decision.

For eight months, from July 1842 till March 1843, Dorothée lived in Touraine, in her beloved château of Rochecotte, in that house where she had always until then found security and peace of mind.

Bacourt, having returned from America in August 1842, came down to spend a portion of the winter with her there. Despite the almost daily letters they had written to each other, the two years of separation had erected a barrier between these two friends: they no longer talked exactly the same language, they no longer walked exactly in step. It is even reasonable to wonder, without any ironic intent, whether the presence of Talleyrand had not always been, at bottom, in some way necessary to the understanding between Bacourt and Dorothée. With his subordinate, the Duchess could relax from the Prince's brilliant but tiring conversation; so submissive where her uncle was concerned, it was not displeasing for her to feel that she could dominate in her turn. Once Talleyrand was no longer there, perhaps

Bacourt's manner of expressing himself seemed suddenly a little dull, the world he had to offer rather small.

While Bacourt, now in his forties, morose and prematurely aging, was struggling through his period of exile in Washington, ailing, bitter and always complaining, the Duchess, still radiantly beautiful (it was Lady Granville who used the phrase in January 1842, at Nice), was launching herself with a sort of light-hearted abandon into a new career, that of the great Prussian lady and landowner.

"I expect a visit from M. de Bacourt this month," Dorothée wrote to Barant on December 5, 1842, from Rochecotte. "I shall go through two enormous chests of papers [Talleyrand's] from England with him. . . . For the time being I shall do no more than simply go through them and make an inventory; later I will do the whole thing again better and more thoroughly. Perhaps in Rome, under your protection and with the benefit of your skilled advice.

"Yes, try to see to it that your 43-44 winter is spent at the Palais de France in Rome. If I survive that long, I promise to place myself under your protection on the Pincian Mount. You can help teach me how to live there, and perhaps how to die there too. I don't think I have very much longer to stay in this life, which, take it all in all, has proved more inimical to me than otherwise. . . ."

The Duchess, it can be seen, displayed little enthusiasm at the prospect of Bacourt's visit, and he does not seem to have displayed much eagerness himself. Yet the reunion was a happy one. In January, Dorothée told Barante: "M. Bacourt and I have been looking over an enormous bundle of papers, which we found to be in the most strange disorder. I am still delving into them. You will see for yourself what a great deal of precious material there is amongst them later on." She then added: "My health is fairly good, my life quiet and fully occupied, the weather mild, and my soul more rested."

Bacourt left in February; Dorothée stayed on for a few more days at Rochecotte on her own. How could she have guessed then, as she visited the poor and looked up at the first buds in her garden, that an epoch in her life was drawing to an end? And yet, without her knowing it, she was saying good-bye to her Touraine, to Rochecotte, as luminous and drenched with light as the Loire sky itself. When she said good-bye to this countryside where she had made her home, and felt at home, for nearly twenty years, Dorothée was in reality saying farewell to all of France. From then on, and for the rest of her life, the real background was to be Prussia, and the Duchy of Sagan's sumptuous austerity.

Part Five

DUCHESS

OF

SAGAN

(1843-1862)

HE DUCHESS of Talleyrand is here, so beautiful and young she seems quite fabulous," wrote Princess Lieven in May 1843—and she was a woman scarcely given to indulgence.

As a child, Dorothée had been skinny and sallow, rather gnome-like—unattractive despite her magnificent eyes. When she first arrived in France, the prune described by Charles de Rémusat was a disappointment to Talleyrand, and at the Imperial court Countess Edmond de Périgord went almost unnoticed.

Brought into bloom at last by her three pregnancies, her beauty as a young woman first revealed itself in Vienna, although even then in many people's eyes her dark beauty seemed· to lack the freshness and dazzle of youth. It was not until she reached her forties, her features delicately chiseled by the years, her eyes made deeper by experience, that she finally came into possesion of a beauty that was saluted by the whole world— men like Rémusat, women like Lady Granville and Princess Lieven, children like the little Gonneville girl. This ageless beauty was hers for many, very many, years.

It was a dangerous gift for a woman of fifty whose life and heart were now empty, who had already seen so many of her days wither and fall away.

A dangerous gift too for a woman who, despite her many experiences with men, must have wondered sometimes whether she had ever truly loved, ever truly tapped all the resources of her heart and mind and flesh.

And yet a precious gift nevertheless, since it was to permit her unappeased heart to experience one last love, to love and to be loved just once more.

On May 23, 1843, the Duchess of Talleyrand passed through Saarbrücken on her way to Berlin. "Here I am past the French frontier," she noted that day with a kind of melanchody. "Soon I shall have crossed the Rhine, another frontier. Every new border I cross makes me feel sadder, and when I see a black and white striped post and a strip of water they offend my eyes."

Dorothée stopped at Mannheim to see the Grand Duchess Stephanie. The Grand Duchess, anxious lest this visitor worn out by long days of traveling in a carriage should fail to take advantage of the good weather, took her for a long drive in her own calash.

From Mainz, the Duchess continued down the Rhine by boat as far as Cologne. The river was rough and the waves rose to such heights that Dorothée became rather alarmed. The banks of the Rhine she thought very fine, despite their lack of cultivated land, and she was interested in the old castles that the Prussian princes were then slowly beginning to restore. But she certainly had no love for the German inns. She found it as cold in the place where she stayed in Cologne as she had in Bergheim three years earlier; and the lack of any kind of shutters on the windows, which meant that her room was full of bright sunshine at four in the morning, merely confirmed her dislike.

At Magdeburg, Dorothée took a train to Berlin. As on the boat, she remained in her own carriage, judging this to be the most proper course in view of her lack of a male companion and the mixed nature of the other travelers. Finally, on June 2, she arrived in Berlin, "with my dress torn and only a single crown left in my pocket."

As the relationship she had resumed with the Radziwills and Alexander von Humboldt in 1840 grew steadily more intimate, so too did the attraction that the Princess of Prussia and Dorothée felt for one another gradually increase. "I dined yesterday with the Princess of Prussia," Dorothée commented several days after her arrival. "She is really a most interesting person; the persistence of the kindness she bestows on me and her ever growing confidence are making me more and more attached to her person and concerned for her future."

On June 17, the Duchess moved to Sagan, where she spent three days exploring part of her new acquisitions. Stopping in a stretch of forest, she was enchanted to find her carriage surrounded by inquisitive stags and roe deer. One of the days she spent visiting schools, kindergartens and factories, then in the evening gave a dinner for the officers of the nearby artillery park and the head of the local administration.

From Sagan, Dorothée drove over for a visit to Muskau, the estate of Prince Pückler, who was the foremost architect-landscape-gardener of the day and had promised to advise her about her park at Sagan. It was a short four hour drive, the last stretch being over a sea of barren sand. "And that makes it doubly surprising to find oneself driving immediately afterward through the freshest, greenest, most flower-filled and most perfectly kept park that you ever could imagine. It's exactly like England, with all the same care and attention and elegance lavished on everything, inside the château as well as out. . . . As I drove up, I found Prince Pückler waiting for me at the foot of the steps surrounded by grooms, footmen, Arabs, Negroes, a whole motley and strangely assorted troupe. He then showed me up to my rooms, which are decorated with the utmost elegance and attention to detail, a drawing room piled high with flowers, a bedroom all draped in white muslin, a dressing room tucked into a tower."

That evening the Duchess was shown around the rest of the château. The Princess's workroom seemed to Dorothée more like a conservatory or an aviary. "What most struck me was a portrait of the Prince fastened onto the Princess's desk with branches of bay artistically trained around it; they were not cut, but came from two bay trees in pots one on either side of the desk itself; then between the portrait and the inkstand she had placed a little vase of forget-me-nots. This is just one of the details I could tell you of this broken, mended, singular marriage that is so unlike any other, for though one often meets people in society who are separated without being divorced, it is very rare indeed to encounter people who are divorced without being separated.*

After a further month divided between Berlin, Carlsbad and Breslau, where she went to pay her respects to the Prince-Bishop Mgr von Sedlnitzky and ask his blessing, Dorothée finally arrived late in July of 1843 at Günthersdorf. There she set about pre-

---

* Having been divorced in 1826, Prince and Princess Pückler had resumed cohabitation without a second marriage having taken place.

paring the house to receive all her family, Louis de Valençay, her sisters, and her Biron nieces. But despite being taken up by these simple domestic schemes, the Duchess was uneasy in her mind, and the news of General d'Alava's death, so often her guest on the Rue Saint-Florentin and at Rochecotte and Valençay, upset her. "There is something so sobering about death," she wrote to Bacourt, "and when it begins to thin out the ranks of one's friends, as it has been doing around me for several years now, there is no way of not dwelling on it a great deal, no way of not being affected by it. It is a subject that preoccupies me increasingly, and sometimes it seems to me that I should lose no time in making my own preparations for that great and final journey."

Scarcely had these lines reached their destination than Dorothée received a first visit from one of her neighbors, Prince Felix Lichnowsky.

◇ ◇ ◇

Both in Berlin and in Vienna, the Duchess had heard a great deal of talk about this handsome adventurer who, though still not thirty (he was born on April 5, 1814), had already had a full and very checkered career.

A member of one of the illustrious Silesian families that Frederick II's conquest of that country had split between Austria and Prussia, Felix Lichnowsky, since his mother was Hungarian—a Zichy, related to Mélanie von Metternich—had been raised in Vienna. More Hungarian than Prussian, he had all the noble bearing, the charm and easy insolence of the former nationality and entirely lacked the stability of the latter. Having enlisted in a regiment of Silesian Hussars, he soon found the life dull, and saying good-bye to his tedious garrison existence he threw himself wholeheartedly—in 1837, at the age of twenty-three—into the Carlist adventure. Since he was as brave as he was rash, he quickly distinguished himself in several actions, and after being noticed by España, one of the Spanish leaders, he was put at the head of a brigade.

When España died in 1838, Lichnowsky handed in his resignation and went to the Hôtel-Dieu in Bordeaux to seek treatment for a serious leg wound. Having been put back on his feet (though he had nearly lost one of them from gangrene) by Doctor Caussade, he moved on to Paris during February 1840 and was about to set out in search of fresh adventures in Persia when the death of Frederick-Wilhelm III made him change his mind and go back to Berlin. Unstable and romantic, he was attracted by the personality of the new king—who was unstable and romantic. His stay in Berlin was brief and punctuated by several duels, one of them with the Duke of Nassau.

On January 31, 1841, the Queen of the Belgians mentioned in a letter to her mother that the evening before, at a court ball, one of the guests had been a Prince Lichnowsky who had arrived with an extraordinary son of his, "a kind of madman who is turning Berlin upside down." Two months later, the Queen returned to the subject: "The madman Lichnowsky is paying court to the Princesse de Ligne and also to one of the little Arenberg girls at the same time. He wants to marry the latter, so that both the Prince de Ligne and the Duke of Arenberg are quite furious." A daughter of the virtuous Marie-Amélie, married to her dull and tedious Leopold, whose ambitions had made him forget his gayer days at the Congress of Vienna, Louise-Marie d'Orléans had failed, quite obviously, to understand the attraction of this adventurer with the brilliant black eyes and exotic elegance of manner.

At some point, either in Paris or in Brussels, the "madman Lichnowsky" had met Liszt and become very friendly with him. He sometimes went with him on his tours and stayed with the composer at Nonnenwerth, the island on the Rhine. Liszt, in his turn, also visited Kreuzenort, the Lichnowsky family's château in Silesia.*

The Prince's wanderlust had not been stilled. His next voyage took him to Portugal, a country about which he wrote with considerable acuteness and elegance. It was on his way home from this visit, in August of 1842, that he met with an unfortunate adventure that went some way toward cooling down his hotheaded behavior. He had unwisely ventured with a Carlist

---

* Liszt always kept a portrait of Lichnowsky hanging in his room at Weimarer Altenburg.

into Spanish territory where they were both arrested and recognized. The Spaniard was hanged on the spot, and Lichnowsky was only saved from the same fate by a timely intervention on the part of the Prussian chargé d'affaires.

Being forced to witness an ignominious death at such close quarters no doubt gave the Prince cause for reflection. Possibly he realized that he had been frittering his life away that he ought to find some better use for the gifts—a swift mind, boundless energy—that he undoubtedly possessed. On returning to Silesia, he threw himself into politics—local politics first of all. He became President of the Upper Silesian Railroad, then a deputy in the provincial parliament. Within a few months his abilities had become apparent. "He was clear and precise, born to be a great politician," wrote Ernest II, Duke of Saxe-Coburg and brother of the English Prince-Consort, in his *Mémoires.* "Though if there was an obstacle to his advancement in this field despite his indisputable talents, it stemmed from the inadequacy of his education and his adventurous character."

Though by then considered one of the rising generation of political leaders, Lichnowsky did not succeed in endearing himself to Berlin society. Of different stock, a different species, he only bewildered and disturbed the solid Prussians. Still unstable, still hotheaded, he moved among the docile domesticated Berliners with the graceful yet threatening tread of a big cat.

❖   ❖   ❖

Lichnowsky and Dorothée needed only one glance to recognize and acknowledge one another. They stood out together, sharp and bright, against the grey background of Günthersdorf and its other guests.

Both had Slav blood in their veins, hers with an admixture of Baltic, his of Hungarian; both were strict Catholics in a country being overrun by Pietism; both were widely-traveled and cosmopolitan in the midst of provincials unable to see farther than their own narrow frontiers; both were intelligent and ambitious, and both, despite their Catholic faith, amoral and bound by no laws other than the ones their own pride and honesty imposed upon them; both were enemies of the conventions, of a society imprisoned by its own prejudices; both were clever intriguers and always ready to answer the call of fortune; both were politically gifted and avid for power, because both had sprung from ancient feudal families recently deprived of their birthrights by the advance of history.

True there was a twenty year difference in their ages. Felix Lichnowsky was younger than either of Dorothée's two sons, and in the eyes of this richly experienced woman he might well have appeared a little naïve and vain. But he had the beauty of a fallen archangel, a bold and adventurous air, and his laughter was the miraculous sound of youth itself.

Dorothée had not forgotten the tender memory that Talleyrand kept all his life of the Countess of Brionne, the aging woman who had given so much love to the young Abbé de Périgord. Perhaps she had sometimes thought that the Countess of Brionne had after all been the lucky one, the maternal mistress, loving, forming, protecting. And when the love was dead, the sincerest gratitude had still lived on.

If Dorothée was conquered, Lichnowsky for his part was completely dazzled. The Duchess of Talleyrand had staying with her a son more than thirty years old; yet she was still singularly beautiful, with the classical line of her neck, her white and sparkling teeth, her slim and supple waist. A great lady in her own right, very much loved by Frederick-Wilhelm IV and the Princess of Prussia, the Duchess of Talleyrand already enjoyed a very real influence in Berlin. When she took up residence at Sagan, and that event was drawing daily closer, her position would become more influential still. And lastly, to this impoverished Silesian forever fretting against the check imposed on him by the inadequacy of his fortune, there was the attraction exerted by a woman who could take wealth and luxury for granted.

Dorothée spent all of August 1843 at Günthersdorf, and Lichnowsky was her guest. The Sagan archives, even before their disappearance, had contained little indication of this relationship: Bacourt, and possibly Louis as well, did his best to erase all memory of it. However, there did still exist in the charter-room on the eve of World War II, under the heading

"German Statesmen," a file bearing the name of Felix Lichnowsky. Inside it were a few letters from the Prince to Dorothée that had lain there untouched for almost a hundred years. On November 21, 1843, Lichnowsky wrote asking for the Duchess's permission to send her a poem he had written, set to music by Liszt, at the same time thanking her once more for the hospitality she had shown him at Günthersdorf. In her reply, Dorothée expressed the hope that he would repeat his visit.

Was their relationship still on a purely social level at that time? Possibly. There is one fact however that seems to indicate their being already on rather closer terms. After spending a few weeks in Berlin during the autumn, the Duchess then changed capitals and spent the early part of winter 1843-1844 in Vienna. It is a surprising choice of residence when one remembers that her entire family was in France, and the only likely explanation for it seems to be a desire to see Lichnowsky again. The Prince had many family connections in Austria and much preferred to live there rather than in Prussia.

❖   ❖   ❖

In August 1843, Herr von Wolff had suggested a new way of settling the Sagan question. The Prince Hohenzollern was to sell Dorothée his life interest; then she was to ask for a new livery of seizin of the Duchy, fief, and freeholdings now combined, for herself, her son Louis, and her eldest grandson. The matter was expected to be settled in two weeks: it dragged on for two long months.

On October 16, 1843, the Duchess wrote to Bacourt from Berlin: "Yesterday I at last received the final version of the contract with my nephew the Prince Hohenzollern giving me full ownership of Sagan, the whole duly signed, initialed and ratified.

"I officially come into possession on April 1, but I have permission to give orders to the administrative staff immediately."

Twelve hundred square kilometers in area, the fief of Sagan

included, besides the principal town of seven thousand inhabitants, four large towns, one hundred seventy-one villages, innumerable manorial properties and a host of tenant farms. In Sagan itself there were six churches, five of them Catholic. Each house paid a manorial tax. The Duke or Duchess possessed entire jurisdiction within the estate: both the police and the ecclesiastical benefices within its boundaries depended directly upon his or her will. The fief had its own colors: blue and white. In short, the situation of the Duchess of Sagan was practically that of a sovereign, and as such was bound to be a very pleasing one for Dorothée.

After her return to Berlin late in the winter of 1844, the Duchess wrote to Bacourt informing him of her plans for the next few months: "I shall spend most of April at Sagan, then leave for Paris on about the 20th, because I want to arrive in time to be with my daughter during her confinement. I shall then go quickly down to Rochecotte, spend a few days there, and return to Germany in late June."

It is possible that Bacourt had already heard some of the rumors that were beginning to circulate on the subject of Dorothée's relationship with Lichnowsky. Even if he had not, he must have felt some astonishment at the way her visit to Germany, after so many extensions, was now apparently becoming permanent. He must have noticed too that her letters were growing somewhat less frequent, that their tone was changing. It seems likely that he made some sort of complaint.

"Having been rather busy recently, I have been forced to leave several of your letters unanswered. Great distances render such broader ways of dealing with matters permissible, although they would be more difficult with greater proximity. The late M. de Talleyrand, quite rightly, thought very highly of such methods. He used to criticize as a defect in my abilities the tendency I always had to note every point, to answer everything, to quibble, to discuss any point that was made, not to ignore small difficulties sufficiently, to be too much aware of indiscretions and demands. . . . It is now some time since I decided that the moment has very definitely come for me to treat as non-existent whatever wounds or irritates me."

Harsh and haughty words that betray the feelings of a woman anxious to defend her inner life and her independence at all costs against anyone who might think himself entitled to try to penetrate the one or set limits to the other. It was a poor augury for what was to be a difficult stay in France. It was now necessary for the Duchess to make Alexandre and Pauline accept the raising of the fief of Sagan exclusively in favor of Louis, and to make them accept, as she had also to make Bacourt and all her French friends accept, her sudden and irrevocable abandonment of the country that had been for thirty years her second home.

Antoine de Castellane, Pauline's second child, was born in Paris on May 12, 1844. On June 20, the Duchess attended the marriage service of her son-in-law's youngest sister, Pauline de Castellane, whose father was generally supposed to be Molé and a young Prussian diplomat, Count Max von Hatzfeldt. Between these two dates, Dorothée managed to drive hurriedly down to Rochecotte and strip it of all the mementoes she wished to take back with her to Sagan. She also spent some time in painful discussions with Castellane, with Alexandre de Dino, and with Bacourt.

The first two very rightly complained that they were being penalized by an arrangement that in fact constituted a vast entail in favor of Louis and his eldest son, and that was depriving them of their rightful share in the freehold bought back from the Princess Hohenzollern and incorporated into the fief. Both were at that time in difficult situations with regard to money and were consequently all the more sensitive to the financial side of the question.

As for Bacourt, though he certainly spent much of the time defending Pauline's interests, for he loved her tenderly and was concerned about her future, he must also have reproached Dorothée with her new love affair and criticized her decision, which he could not approve, to take up permanent residence in Germany.

Whatever the truth of the matter, when Dorothée left France again early in the summer of 1844 she had still not obtained her children's consent to the family agreement she desired.* With Alexandre, the break was almost total, and the Duke of Dino went to Florence to live with Edmond. With Pauline, the situation was less serious, but the disagreements between them in 1844 did widen the rift that had become apparent in 1842, and it was several years before Dorothée saw her daughter again.

Her relations with Bacourt had also suffered a change. Their correspondence, having been almost daily for the past ten years, practically stopped altogether for the next three,† and it took the shock of Henri de Castellane's death in the autumn of 1847 to bring it back to life again.

❖   ❖   ❖

Meanwhile, on April 28, 1844, the Prince Hohenzollern's proxy had duly and ceremoniously handed over all the Prince's rights in the fief of Sagan. When Dorothée returned in July therefore, it was to a Sagan that was really hers, and she immediately started work on improvements to the château and the park.

Sagan was a two-story house, built in the style of Louis XIII and entirely surrounded by a moat. Where the main drive approached the house there was a stone bridge over the moat leading to a vaulted entrance. On the park side, there were two parallel wings forming an inner court which opened into a tree-planted terrace. The château contained one hundred thirty rooms. On the ground floor there were the guest apartments. The state apartments were above, reached by a stone staircase decorated with stucco; they consisted of the royal apartment, a library, an archive room, and a suite of reception rooms. Por-

---

* It was not until September 14, 1847, that the succession to the Duchy of Sagan and the inclusion of the freehold lands in the fief was finally agreed to by the whole family. This family agreement was registered with all due ceremony on May 16, 1849. In exchange for their consent, Dorothée gave Pauline Rochecotte and Alexandre the promise of Günthersdorf.

† Though a few more letters were exchanged during the summer of 1844, the two correspondents were not in tune. Bacourt was leading a melancholy existence in Baden, Dorothée was at Sagan, doubtless with Lichnowsky.

traits everywhere: Anne of Russia, wellspring of the family's wealth; the Duke Pierre in a handsome Louis XV outfit; the Duchess of Courland and her four daughters; Proud'hon's portrait of Dorothée; Talleyrand by Gérard. In one of the drawing rooms was the heavy mahogany table on which the treaty is said to have been signed after the Congress of Vienna.*

There was also a Chinese room; then another housing the porcelain collection; also a theater, large enough for *Don Juan* to have been performed there. Beyond the armory there was a sculpture gallery. And at the very end, in one of the wings, Dorothée's private apartments.

Marie de Bunsen visited Sagan a few years after the death of the last Duke. The Duchess's apartment had been left more or less intact. Her brushes, her mirrors, her powder boxes with their filigree silver tops were still there on her dressing table. Through the glazed doors of the wardrobe closets it was still possible to glimpse a few remaining evening dresses, the necks cut very low with lace insets, and a great ball cape of purple velvet. Also, in one corner, a blue silk sunshade and a lady's riding crop, very tiny.

But it was above all in the boudoir that the memory of Dorothée was still most present. She had often sat beside the great black marble fireplace, or at the writing table laden down with the mementoes of her travels and framed daguerreotypes.

The château floors were all of parquet and shone like a mirror. There was not a single grain of dust on the precious porcelain. In the park, the flowerbeds were neat, the lawns freshly mown. The orange trees, the lemon trees, the pomegranate trees stood lined up on the terrace. But it was like the palace of the Sleeping Beauty, a spell had been cast upon it: it no longer had a master and it had lost its soul. Major von Brünneck, the administrator of the royal fief of Sagan, was a civil servant appointed by the government.

Frederick-Wilhelm IV, whose mind tottered always on the brink of madness, whose heart was perpetually wracked by anxiety, reacted violently to Dorothée's charms. And since she was a childhood companion, she understood better than other

---

* This table and most of the portraits mentioned—or at least copies of them—are now at Valençay.

people what was going on in his soul. He made a first visit to the new Duchess of Sagan as early as August of 1844, and he continued to invite himself for a stay in Silesia almost every year from then on. Queen Elisabeth did not share in her husband's feeling; she found Dorothée intellectually affected and rather disliked her. As soon as it became evident that one could not visit Sagan without meeting Lichnowsky there, the Queen stopped coming.

Yet even with her heart, her material interests and her ambitions already firmly bound to Germany again, even when the King of Prussia himself was staying in her house during that August of 1844, Dorothée had still not entirely forgotten France, or at least she said she had not. Having never been anything more, her friendship with Barante still continued, patient and detached. It had survived the difficult Restoration years without a single storm. After Talleyrand's death it had grown still deeper. The latest upheaval in Dorothée's life had brought their exchanges back to a more superficial level, but even that did not perturb the author of the *History of the Dukes of Burgundy,* "sweet Barante," as Dorothée called him. So this correspondence still continued even after the one with Bacourt had been interrupted and the one with Molé had petered out. It is only a feeble glimmer, but still it gives some light, and we have almost no other with which to pierce the darkness of those years during which the Duchess of Talleyrand, transformed into the Duchess of Sagan, would otherwise have been concealed from us entirely by the German mists.*

Before the mists came down however, Dorothée offered Barante an explanation of her recent decisions in response to a question he had asked: "I am not renouncing France, that would be neither proper nor according to the wishes of my

---

* At no point in any of her letters to Barante did Dorothée ever allude to her liaison with Lichnowsky. A great lady still, even in her failings, she intended to keep the different compartments of her life quite separate. Her friends in France were to remain ignorant, or to feign ignorance, of a matter that in Prussia was a matter of public knowledge.

Even after Lichnowsky's death, on September 18, 1848, when Dorothée was making no attempt to hide her grief from people in Germany, there was no change in the tone of her letters to Barante, except for an added note of religious exaltation.

heart! I should like to divide my life between my two countries. My affairs and my peace of mind are well taken care of in Germany; but my memories, my long past, my daughter, Rochecotte, the cellar of Valençay, there are all those things that pull me back toward France."

Well-calculated words, perhaps sincere ones; certainly they should be weighed against the harsh ones previously addressed to Bacourt. But it was seven years before they really came to have any meaning.

❖   ❖   ❖

Every new owner of the fief of Sagan was bound, within a period of one year and thirty days of his or her succession, to sue the King of Prussia for a renewal of the feudal contract, in other words for his or her investiture. Once this had been granted, on January 6, 1845, Dorothée was legally the Duchess of Sagan, and it was by this title that she was thereafter known in Germany.

The holder of the fief of Sagan, in his or her quality as a prince and lord, had the right to a seat in the provincial parliament. Being a woman, Dorothée did not sit in the house herself but appointed the governor of Breslau, Count Schaffgotsch, to represent her.

When Dorothée arrived in Berlin in 1840, she had written to Bacourt: "I am very much on my guard here as regards both politics and religion." Such reticence was doubtless suitable in a traveler still uncertain of her position and her future. But the Duchess of Sagan had too strong a taste for politics, too lively a sense of her responsibilities as a great landowner, and too deep a desire to further the career of the young man whom she now loved with all her being, whose interests were monopolizing all the resources of her mind, for her to maintain that reticence. In Lichnowsky she had found again the fierce ambition, the avid love for power that she had admired in Talleyrand—and vainly looked for in her elder son. It became her labor of love to mold this energetic but still uncultivated mind, to initiate Lichnowsky into the secrets of statesmanship that she had learned at her uncle's side. In this way she hoped to open the Prince's road to a brilliant future.

As it happened, the moment seemed favorable in Prussia for the making of swift and brilliant careers. As had been the case in France on the eve of the Revolution, the country, governed by the weak hand of Frederick-Wilhelm IV, was then prey to a strange malaise. The sovereign himself had a leaning toward liberal ideas even though he allowed himself to be swayed by the reactionary and pietistic coterie that formed his personal entourage. But since he was an authoritarian mystic, this meant on the other hand that he considered himself God's representative on earth, and as such he could not accept the possibility of discussing his will. Above all, Frederick-Wilhelm took words for deeds, and his sudden reversals of policy were a source of discontent to a body of public opinion tired of being tricked by his specious promises of political liberty.

Since there was another powerful party grouped around the Prince of Prussia, who was the childless monarch's heir, the government was soon invaded by political anarchy and the Prussian State began to totter, not beneath the blows of the opposition, which was still too timid for that, but because those who still held the positions of power were losing faith in their mission.

Given these circumstances, a bold man with a lucid enough mind and a cold enough will could certainly find a way to impose himself and work his way into the front rank. Probably this is what Dorothée hoped Lichnowsky would be able to do, but the undertaking was a difficult one for a man who was both a Slav and a Catholic; it took Bismarck, the rough Protestant junker, to succeed in it.*

The political question involved the whole of Prussia. In Silesia, alternately Polish and Austrian in its recent history, the religious question was also particularly acute. Its population was divided in this respect, the aristocracy and the peasantry being mainly Catholics, the middle classes, who were of Prus-

---

* When Ernest II of Saxe-Coburg drew his portrait of Bismarck in 1852, he remarked that in his early days Bismarck reminded him of Lichnowsky.

sian origin, being Protestants, and even in some cases Pietists.*

Firm in her faith, whatever the disorders of her private life, deeply imbued with the aristocratic ideal, Dorothée felt it her duty to head the Catholic movement in her own province, and by 1845 she had solidly established her influence from this point of view. "The coming event in Silesia is the imminent arrival of the new Bishop of Breslau [Mgr von Diepenbrock]," she announced to Barante on May 4, 1845. "I am assured that he intends to make a detour to Sagan in order to rest himself here and possibly also in order to come to an agreement with the person who, in Lower Silesia, is the leader of the Catholic population."

❖ ❖ ❖

The new Duchess of Sagan spent the whole spring and summer of 1845 in Silesia, busy making improvements to her park under the guidance of Prince Pückler-Muskau. She employed as many as one hundred fifty gardeners on this project and spent one hundred eighty thousand marks. But above all she was busy with Lichnowsky, who used to come to see her often and whom she used to go to meet, as the locals still used to recount after the first World War, at Hansdorf, the nearest railroad station to Sagan, in her handsome six-horse carriage. At the château, the Prince occupied an apartment on the ground floor; it had a secret staircase leading up to the floor above.†

Absorbed though she was by life in Prussia, and by her private life, the death of Royer-Collard awoke her from that

---

* The Pietists—also called Separatists or Spenerians, after their leader, Spener—affected extreme piety and preferred private worship to public ritual. The sect had sprung up in Leipzig in 1689 as a result of simple meetings held in Spener's house in the form of lectures and called *Collegia pietas.* Even laymen were allowed to make commentaries upon the Scriptures. The Pietists soon acquired a great following in Berlin, Augsburg, and throughout Wurtemburg.

† The Duchess of Talleyrand had converted Talleyrand's room at Rochecotte into a chapel; the Duchess of Sagan converted Lichnowsky's room at Sagan into an oratory consecrated to St. Dorothy. During her solitary old age, the Duchess often used to go there and pray for her dead.

enchantment. To her, the philosopher had been a reliable, faithful and discreet friend. As she herself confessed, he had had a great influence on the development of her ideas and the disposition of her soul "at one of those critical junctures in life that impart a positive impetus lasting throughout all the rest of one's existence . . ."

The Duchess was very much moved, very distressed by this death and recognized that she was the poorer for it. The event also made her turn her mind back toward the past, and this preoccupation with the past may have made her more sensitive to certain clashes in the present. Lichnowsky was capricious and sometimes behaved too much like a spoiled child. Dorothée was imperious, possessive and had never been able to tolerate bad manners. The relationship began to encounter trials, and the Duchess, intelligent, practiced, above all too proud to try keeping so young a lover against his will, must have decided that a separation would give the situation time to ease. But apart from this, being an independent woman used to breathing a freer air than was to be found in the restricted society of Prussia, it is possible that she was near the suffocation point after so many months spent exclusively in either Berlin or Silesia.

"I did not think, when I left Paris, already eighteen months ago, that it would be for so long a time," she wrote to Barante from Austria early in January 1846, "but you must believe me when I say that I shall not prove so great an enemy to the pleasures of my life as never to revisit France, that country, a very beautiful one after all, where so many memories are still personified for me in three or four excellent friends, and where there is a grave at which I should like to pray again, before going to meet above the man who has been the central link in my existence." At the end of this letter, the Duchess of Sagan added: "From here I shall go next week to spend a fortnight in Venice. My brother-in-law [the Duke of Mouchy, Mélanie de Périgord's husband] is going there; he has insisted that I accompany him so that I may satisfy, under reliable escort, a curiosity that I have long entertained, and the object of which I am already so close to at the moment. . . . I think that this little

Mediterranean jaunt may amuse me and refresh my mind by widening my horizon, which has become a little too restricted recently . . ."

The visit to Italy was extended. "I became full of energy the moment I set foot in Italy," Dorothée confessed to Barante on February 20. "I couldn't resist Rome, now I'm on my way to Naples, the whole thing without stopping for breath, no time for anything, but curiosity for everything. . . . The more I see of Rome the more I wish you here, it would make you so happy! You'd understand it all so quickly . . . these Roman nobles, so grave always yet never sad, go so well with the melancholy of the place, so full of light and traditions . . .

"I found Venice very curious, but I should not like to live there; it is not that the nonchalant gondola does not have its charm, but it is of the kind that Mme la Duchesse de Berry seems to enjoy particularly beside the Count of Lucchesi. I saw them idly drifting along beside one another. I don't know how I shall find Naples; I should be annoyed with it if it did anything to weaken my impressions of Rome."

It was not until April 1 that Dorothée finally arrived back in Berlin. "For the moment, I am going back like a sensible person to attend to all my business," she announced to Barante from Dresden.

❖   ❖   ❖

As Dorothée wrote these words, was she convinced in her own mind that there was no business requiring her attention elsewhere than in Germany? Lucid always, even in moments of emotional tumult, the Duchess of Sagan would surely not have denied at that moment that she had business, even pressing business, in France as well.

Henri de Castellane was continuing to ruin himself and his wife, while Pauline, blinded by love, watched him with adoration. The young wife had reason to be proud of her husband's political successes. He had been elected deputy in March 1844, before he was thirty, and therefore under the minimum age required by the law. In February 1845, he was elected again however, and was by then able to take his seat. Intelligent, well-educated, hard-working, very ambitious, it seemed certain that he would make a fine career for himself. Where the Castellanes were concerned therefore, Dorothée might well have decided that her presence in France was not necessary.

It would have been difficult for her to come to the same conclusion in regard to her sons.

In Florence, the Dinos were an unfailing source of gossip. Valentine was flaunting her liaison with Anatol Demidoff in public, and her husband was turning a blind eye to everything. Alexandre had been his mother's favorite under the Restoration. Life had come between them later, but her younger son had spent several months at Rochecotte with her since then, and in 1842 the Duchess was talking with great tenderness of her little granddaughter, Clémentine. There were three other children from the marriage—two boys born in 1843 and 1845, a girl in 1844—whom she had seen either only fleetingly or else not at all. Spendthrift and moody, Alexandre had always been quick to take offense, and quick to become offensive himself when he had done so. With a complacency that was in this case rather forced, his mother persuaded herself that she had already done a great deal for him and, in fact, that she had done enough.

There remained Louis, for whom, one must admit, Dorothée had been preparing a magnificent future in Germany. A Prussian decree had recently conferred on him the title of Prince of Sagan and made him a Serene Highness. But all these titles, these honors, these entails were going to the heir rather than to the individual, just as the Prince of Talleyrand had once obtained for Louis, his heir under the Restoration, the hand of Alix de Montmorency and the Duchy of Valençay; just as the Prince of Benevento had once obtained for Edmond, his heir under the Empire, the hand of Dorothée of Courland.

Louis, weak, good-natured Louis, so easy to live with according to his mother, had in fact been sacrificed all his life to such family ambitions. Having been recalled from Italy before his eighteenth birthday, just when he was trying to live on his own for the first time in his life, he had immediately been married off to a pretty but frivolous woman. Without a career, idle and bored, he had merely waited around for nearly ten years until he received the Talleyrand inheritance. He had scarcely moved into Valençay, however, before Dorothée took him away with her to Germany: three time-consuming journeys in 1840, 1841, and 1843 made the young man completely uncertain about what or where his future was to be and possibly also contributed to the growing rift in his marriage.

Though the Duchess had felt no scruples about hauling Louis off to Prussia with her and then keeping him there, she had not seen fit to make a journey to France herself when the Duke of Valençay was created a member of the upper chamber in April of 1845. "My son is on his way," she had written to Barante. "Let me know how he is received, I beg of you."

The almost simultaneous deaths in March and April 1846 of the Duchess and the Duke of Montmorency precipitated an open break between the Duke of Valençay and his wife, who had been virtually living apart even before that. Louis was in Germany when his wife sued for a separate property settlement; * he rushed hurriedly back to France, and it did not occur to his mother to follow him.

"The new leaves unfurling make me turn my eyes toward my fields and my woods," Dorothée wrote to Barante from Berlin in April. A few weeks later, she added: "My sister,† my nieces and nephews,‡ my brother-in-law,§ a few neighbors,# and whatever the highroads that cross here bring in the way of chance guests, all provide me with enough bustle and variety to prevent me from feeling solitary in my retirement."

❖   ❖   ❖

* The separation of property was legally pronounced in August 28, 1846. As a result of this verdict, Louis, who had given up living in the Montmorency house and moved to the Rue de Lille, became involved in a distressing series of legal complications with the purpose of obtaining an injunction against the Duchess, his wife, that would force her to surrender their sixteen year old daughter, Valentine, into the care of the Convent of Chaillot.

† The Duchess of Acerenza. The Princess Hohenzollern had died in 1845.

‡ The Biron family.

§ The Count von Schulenburg, third husband of Wilhelmine the former Duchess of Sagan.

Among them Lichnowsky.

On November 22, 1846, Vernhagen, who had known Talleyrand and Dorothée in Vienna—and not liked them—noted bitterly: "The King is quite besotted with the Duchess of Sagan, with her princely way of life, her pomp and her elegance. He has invited himself there again to hunt."

Dorothée attached a great deal of importance to this royal visit, and intended to take full advantage of it. It was to be rather longer and more formal than the preceding ones, and she had invited all the Silesian nobility to visit Sagan while it was in progress, hoping thus to establish herself at the head of the province. And she also wanted to try to insinuate Lichnowsky into Frederick-Wilhelm's good graces, for up till now the monarch had proved distrustful of her lover.

In the two years that the Duchess had been living at Sagan, she had succeeded in raising the château to a level with Valençay, or with those great English country houses she had loved so much. The carriages were magnificent, the domestic staff numerous and well turned out. When the royal hunt rode home, the road up to the château was illuminated for a league and a half with lanterns and Bengal lights.

The Duchess's plans for the King's visit were thwarted, however, by a heavy fall of snow. The railroad was blocked, and the more distant guests were forced to stay at home. "His Majesty spent the greater part of his time alone with the witty Duchess and her young and witty protégé the Prince Lichnowsky," Meyendorff, the Russian representative in Berlin, wrote on December 16, 1846, to Empress Alexandra, one of Frederick-Wilhelm's sisters. He added: "The Duchess lives in almost royal state at Sagan, she holds court, grants audiences, etc. Many people laugh about it and express astonishment at such childish pretensions in a woman of such intelligence. It is true that she needs a thick cloak if she is to conceal the extreme youth of her Catholic zeal and the longevity of her acquaintance with the ways of love. She is no less enchanting in the King's eyes than she was—she has lived so much and loved so much. The Queen views her with rather less indulgence and has not gone to Sagan."

Meyendorff was writing to the wife of Nicolas I, who was hostile to anything that might smack even slightly of French influence. The Minister was therefore aware that his acid tone would please the reader. But apart from this, it seems that he was nevertheless voicing the real opinions of a large section of Berlin society at that time.* Though so kindly disposed in 1840 and 1841, the nobility of the Prussian capital were now—late in 1846, that is—displaying a certain reserve in their attitude to Dorothée. There were many reasons for this, and most of them were the same ones that had turned Parisian society against her under the Restoration.

Her unrelenting beauty had in it something that stirred up resentment in others. It was discussed with acidity: the Duchess used to wear a three string choker of large pearls—to conceal the ravages of time, murmured unkind tongues. Dorothée learned of this rumor. One evening, as she was arriving at a court ball, perhaps wearing her great purple velvet cape, she raised a hand, and with feigned carelessness snapped the thread holding all three rows of pearls. They scattered across the floor beneath the dancing couples' feet, and the neck was at last revealed—dazzling, unlined.

The Duchess was rich and her way of life too overwhelming in its magnificence. True it would have excited no comment in Paris or London, but in Berlin, where court life was relatively austere and the aristocracy often not particularly wealthy, it was a source of irritation and annoyance, as was the persistent favor shown her by the King. Everywhere, it was she who sat next to the sovereign; she alone could chase away his black moods, gain his attention and distract him.

These two qualities earned her many enemies. Yet Dorothée did nothing to try to soften the hostility that was felt for her. On the contrary, she often allowed her contempt for people she thought inferior to show. Long accustomed to moving in the highest political and diplomatic circles, she had no use for any but the best kind of conversation, and especially not for gossip. She therefore made no attempt to conceal the fact that she enjoyed men's company, provided they were well-mannered and brilliant, and that she had very little interest in women,

---

* Meyendorff was indisputably a well-informed person. The Duchess herself said: "His is the house where the most and the best news is always to be found."

in the things that women mostly talked about, such as their houses, their children, their clothes, or even in their religious opinions. This attitude provoked the hostility of a great many women of course, and also that of all the boring men, which was to say the majority.

The only way to have avoided this hostility's being expressed was for the Duchess of Sagan to have remained absolutely beyond criticism. But in fact her name was constantly linked on every tongue with that of Lichnowsky, and not only in Silesia but also in Berlin.*

A daughter of the Duchess of Courland, whose amorous adventures had echoed all over Europe in the early years of the century, sister of the first Duchess of Sagan, whose complicated love life had been one of the entertainments at the Congress of Vienna, the companion and confidante of Talleyrand, one of the last great survivors of the aristocratic cult of pleasure, Dorothée respected virtue when it was sincere, but she did not believe in the necessity for hypocrisy. She was as innocent of shame as she was of false modesty. She was what she was: it did not occur to her to hide anything.

This attitude, a survival from the eighteenth century, when European tastes were still dominated by a cosmopolitan aristocracy, had been found shocking in France under the Restoration, for the reign of the middle classes there had already begun. In London, on the other hand, this way of looking at things, or rather of doing things, had been viewed with favor. The prevailing moral climate there had still been that of the Regency, and English high society in 1830 didn't know what prudishness was. In the Prussia of Frederick-Wilhelm IV, very provincial in all its behavior and at that time invaded by a wave of Pietism, the Duchess of Sagan's freedom of manner was as shocking as it had been in France twenty years before. The only difference was that in Berlin it also had a slightly exotic aura about it which the Berliners found puzzling at first, then definitely displeasing.

In 1840, Berlin society had been flattered to see the Duchess

* The *Neue Rheinischenzeitung* printed an insulting article under the title: *Leben und Taten des berühmten Ritters Schapphahnski* (The Life and Exploits of the notorious Knight Schapphahnski), this being, according to Bismarck, the nickname given to Lichnowsky by Heine in *Atta Troll.*

of Talleyrand coming to settle in Prussia; seven years later, it took offense at the Duchess of Sagan's attempts to play a role in Prussian politics. After all, wasn't she a foreigner?

Here, of course, we touch again upon one of the constant unhappy factors in Dorothée's life. In neither of her two countries—or at least in neither Berlin nor Paris, for her life in the country was a different matter, as we have seen—was she ever allowed to feel truly at home. The French blamed her for being German, the Prussians blamed her for being French. And possibly the principal reason for her being so happy in London was precisely the fact that in England she could accept the idea of being a foreigner and feel no need to be distressed by it.

❖   ❖   ❖

On February 3, 1847, Frederick-Wilhelm summoned the provincial parliaments to a general assembly. It was a feeble gesture toward the German liberals, who immediately began to think of the King of Prussia as a possible sovereign for the unified country they desired.

The Duchess of Sagan took up residence in Berlin at the end of February. Officially, Count Schaffgotsch was supposed to be representing her in the Diet, but it seems likely that her real representative was in fact Lichnowsky. The Duchess of Sagan's "protégé" was still not very popular in Berlin, but, intelligent and able, he played a very active role in the newly convened assembly.

Frederick-Wilhelm's opening speech to the Diet on April 11, 1847 was a disappointment: he would never allow a sheet of paper [a constitution] to come between him and his people. The crown could not and should not be dependent upon the will of the majority. The surprise was universal, the debates that followed very lively. "Berlin is no longer recognizable," Meyendorff commented three days later. "A great many people have given themselves up to the most blind and rabid opposition. The dear, dear Duchess of Sagan and Lichnowsky have also allowed themselves to be affected. . . ."

"We are living here in an absolutely new atmosphere, and

one of which there is scarcely any understanding as yet," wrote Dorothée on her side, in a letter to Barante on May 1. "The actors in this drama haven't grasped their roles too well; but a parliamentary education is much more rapidly acquired, generally speaking, than any other sort. . . ."

Prompted by the concealed influence of the Duchess, Lichnowsky was moving steadily nearer to the center of the stage. "An adventurer with no respect for either religion or the laws," wrote Meyendorff on May 14 to Nesselrode, "he has already veered towards the opposition. . . . It is a sad thing to see so much intelligence and such amazing natural ability wasted on a man of such unsound character. . . ." Doubtless Lichnowsky himself saw this detour into the extremist camp as a short-cut to power.

Meanwhile, as the career of Dorothée's protégé was taking this ill-starred turn, another ambitious young man's life was being snuffed out in France.

Henri de Castellane had never completely recovered from his riding accident at Aubijoux in 1842. In 1847, Pauline, who had recently been given Rochecotte by her mother, went to Germany on a visit. When she came home, she found her husband sad and changed, scarcely able to walk. A season at Néris only aggravated matters. The couple moved to Rochecotte, where Castellane's condition deteriorated still further. On October 16, after the Last Rites had been administered, he died.

As soon as she knew that Castellane's life was really in danger, Dorothée had rushed to her daughter's side. Bacourt was there too, his rancorous melancholy and the bitterness of his jealousy sweetened by the intervening years. He and Dorothée were reconciled, and after the Duchess's return to Sagan their correspondence recommenced.

◇　　◇　　◇

Dorothée's liaison with Lichnowsky had lasted more than four years. Each day of those years was for Dorothée yet one more reprieve, and she was well aware of it. Lichnowsky was changeable. He was also poor and burdened with heavy family responsibilities. One day he would be obliged to envisage the possibility of a rich marriage in order to repair his family's fortunes and pave the way toward his own ambitions. There was some talk of his becoming engaged to Countess Bergen, the young and pretty widow of a much older Landgrave of Hesse from whom she had inherited a considerable fortune.

Dorothée could not help but feel pain. She knew well enough that what is false today may be true tomorrow. To calm her inner torment the Duchess set out on a journey. She went to Weimar, where Liszt was conducting Flotow's opera *Martha.** She also stayed for a short while at Dresden, finally arriving in Berlin on February 24. "Alone this time," Meyendorff remarked. On that same day, in Paris, the July monarchy collapsed.

At that time the whole of southern Germany was in a state of agitation caused by a series of popular disturbances. The contagion of the violence in Paris transformed these rumblings into real eruptions. On March 13, a student riot in Vienna swept Metternich from office. Five days later, Berlin experienced similar troubles.

Frederick-Wilhelm IV's political capriciousness—he had been nicknamed "the tightrope walker"—had already brought the power of the government into contempt. The incidents in Paris and the disturbances in southern Germany had given latent discontent a tangible form. While the Rhine provinces, which were near to France, and Silesia, ravaged by famine and unemployment, were threatening to break out into revolt, public meetings were organized in Berlin during early March. The emotions behind them were only superficial, however. They could have been appeased easily enough with a few slender concessions and a little authority.

Frederick-Wilhelm orated at length and decided nothing. The feeling of rebellion grew, the demonstrations got wilder, the police began to feel they were reaching their limit, and blood was shed. Only on March 18 did the King finally order an immediate convening of the Diet and the establishment of a

---

* *Translator's note:* Since the story of Flotow's opera concerns the love of a high-born lady for a man rather lower in the social scale, and since the most famous air in the work, occurring more than once, is *The Last Rose of Summer,* it seems unlikely that attending a performance of it would have afforded Dorothée very much pleasure in the circumstances.

constitutional form of government. He also announced, as either a sop or a pledge to the believers in German unification, that he intended to take the federal reform question in hand.

These promises were well received by the middle classes. They did not, however, satisfy the workers who had been thrust into the gutter by the economic crisis, and whom the Liberal intellectuals had in cautiously stirred up to rebellion in order to force the King's hand. The applause of the former class was therefore accompanied, and very soon drowned out, by the boos and hisses of the second. Alarmed by what was happening, the troops fired, barricades went up, the insurgents broke into gun-smiths' shops, and soon there was a muddled street battle in full swing.

Circourt, the representative in Berlin of the new French Republic, followed the course of events from the Hôtel de Russie. "Near Prince Hohenlohe, who was snatching a hurried meal with his clothes in disarray and his face blackened by powder, I observed Prince Felix Lichnowsky lying on a sofa. I had known him for many years already then, that young and impoverished offspring of a great Bohemian family whose life had been devoted, partly from choice, partly because of his unfavorable circumstances, to the pursuit of adventure, and knew him to be a man who loved anything out of the ordinary, always in search of the unconventional, certain to be attracted by any kind of disorder: on this occasion he was wearing a Prussian uniform. I was revolted by the cruel frivolity of his expressions when discussing the frightful crisis that Berlin, his King, and the Prussian monarchy itself was at that moment facing; yet through this culpable folly of his there could be perceived some-thing of the martial quiver that is awakened in a man of courage by the approach of danger, by the imminence of a struggle in which he may find himself a worthy role. . . ."

Bismarck, for his part, writes in his *Memoirs:* "Lichnowsky was alternately rushing into the royal apartments with alarming news about the weakness of the troops and the shortage of ammunition and provisions, then hurrying down into the square again in order to shout encouragements, partly in German, partly in Polish, to the insurgents."

The royal troops were gaining ground, and their victory

seemed assured. But by then the consciences of kings were all uneasy; in the future, only a Republic would dare crush a riot by force of arms. Like Louis-Philippe in February, Frederick-Wilhelm in March would not give the order to fire on the people. He lost heart and insisted that his troops retire, thus allowing the city to fall into the hands of the insurgents.

The Prussian Monarchy was not in jeopardy, however, for it alone had created the present Prussian State out of the former conglomerate mass of smaller countries, all with different resources, histories and religions, and without the Monarchy, which was the soul of the state, the state itself would have crumbled. The mob therefore contented itself with humiliating the King as a punishment for his vagaries and irresolution. During the night, the rebels laid the bodies of all the dead out in front of the palace, then summoned the King onto his balcony. "Blanched and quivering," Frederick-Wilhelm stood to attention and saluted the victims.

❖   ❖   ❖

For Dorothée, good works were one of the obligations of the great landowner, and the good works had to require not only personal effort but also must result from just consideration. In France, both at Valençay and at Rochecotte, she had always supervised the local schools and almshouses. In Silesia she continued to do so. During the terrible winter of 1847-1848, when the already serious prevalence of poverty and hunger was suddenly made worse by a typhus epidemic, the Duchess of Sagan had undertaken a great number of new improvements to her estate in order to give work to as many of the unemployed as possible. It was during this winter too, in February 1848, that a meeting of all the principal Catholic landowners in the province, held at Sagan with the Cardinal von Diepenbrock also present, decided to open an orphanage for the four thousand children at that time wandering homeless throughout Silesia.

Though a target for malice among the wealthy, Dorothée was viewed differently by the poor, and when the population of Sagan besieged the town hall and barracks, the day after the riots in Berlin, the local authorities appealed to the Duchess to come to their help. She drove hurriedly into the town. Though she was given no reason to regret this gesture, her brother-in-law, Count Schulenburg, whom she had made her "major domo," was disturbed by the violent incidents that had occurred in the Grand Duchy of Posen and urged Dorothée to go back to Berlin at the end of March.

There she rejoined Lichnowsky. The young champion of the people had hoped that the new Liberal minister would offer him an important post. He was still hoping when the Diet was opened on April 2. On this occasion he was given the task of reading out the address in reply to the royal propositions. But the Prussians didn't like this foreigner with the disturbing reputation and the sharp, knowing eyes of Talleyrand's niece always lurking behind his shoulder. They distrusted him, just as the Constituent Assembly had distrusted Mirabeau.

Once the necessary subsidies and an electoral law had been voted, the Diet moved its own final dissolution on April 10. Shortly afterwards, the Duchess left Berlin and went back to Sagan. Lichnowsky had left the capital before her, on his way to undertake yet another electoral campaign. Disappointed of his hopes in Prussia, the Prince had turned his gaze towards Frankfort. For concurrent with the agitation for political freedom in the Northern States, and sometimes in opposition to it, there was also the agitation for Germany unity in Frankfort.

For a quarter of a century, Metternich had been using the German Diet not as an instrument of unification but as an instrument of reaction. It had therefore been repudiated by the Liberal exponents of unification who, taking their lead from the two German philologists Dahlmann and Gervinus, were now using the idea of the German race as a rallying point and demanding that Germany be given the right to rule itself, to emerge at last from the anarchy to which it had seemed for so many centuries to be eternally condemned.

On March 5, 1948, fifty-one representatives of the Liberal Party met in Heidelberg and instructed a commission composed of seven of those present to summon a "preparatory parliament" in Frankfort. This parliament opened on March 31 to the acclamations of an enthusiastic crowd. For some bizarre, and

peculiarly German, reason, the decisions of this body without
either a legal existence or statutory powers, and the convocation
of a Constituent Assembly elected by universal suffrage from all
the provinces that had been included in the former Confedera-
tion, was accepted by everyone, Diets and rulers included, without protest.

On May 18, the eight hundred thirty members of the new
Assembly walked in a long procession from the Roemer, where
the Emperors had once been elected, to the church of St.
Paul, where they were to sit. Lichnowsky was among their
number.

Did Dorothée feel any uneasiness, any presentiment of what
was to come, as she watched the Prince leave to begin a new
phase of his career, one that would put such a distance between
them? "It is becoming very tedious to go on living," she had
written to Barante in April. She did not go to Frankfort but
shut herself up at Sagan. She only emerged again in July in
order to travel to Töplitz and then on to Eisenach, where the
Duchess of Orléans was staying. Did she go on to Frankfort?
Did Lichnowsky visit her in Eisenach? If so, it was their last
meeting.

❖   ❖   ❖

At the first taste of power, as soon as he became involved
in national politics, the demagogue in Lichnowsky gave way
to the statesman; the aristocrat forced into the extremist party
by his ill fortune and the disdainful attitude of his peers rediscovered his authoritarian bent. In 1790 and 1791, Mirabeau
had followed the same road that Lichnowsky covered in those
short summer months of 1848. The Frenchman died before
he could be accused of treachery; but things went otherwise with
the German.

Having been sent to Frankfort by the Revolutionary party,
Lichnowsky then discovered that he had been playing the
sorcerer's apprentice, that the Liberal intellectuals besotted by
their chimerical ideals were incapable of supporting any political weight, that disorder could destroy but not create. Talley-

rand, once a friend of Mirabeau, had always loved order before all else and had inculcated this notion in the Duchess; it is therefore not unreasonable to suppose that it was Dorothée's influence that brought about this sudden change in the Prince.

Whatever the truth of the matter, Lichnowsky had before long returned to the Conservative party. If he had been a less brilliant orator, if his courage had been of a less provocative kind, probably the Democrats' fury at his defection would have been less intransigent, their hatred for him less savage, and their accusations of treachery less bitter.

When the Assembly debated the repression of the Mainz riots, Lichnowsky made matters worse. He told the house that though he disapproved of the insurgents' French sympathies he condemned them even more for the dastardly murder they had committed. At these words, the revolutionary members let out howls of rage. Arms crossed, not budging from the speaker's platform, the Prince shouted contemptuously over the din: "Is this the voice of the people? No, it is the voice of the mob." * Then he stood smiling scornfully at the appalling tumult that ensued.

Hated by the Democrats, who were accusing him of betraying them, hated also by the mob, because he had sneered at them, Lichnowsky was now in danger. Though the danger would only have been relative if, in Frankfort as in Berlin, his foreign manners, his elegance, his success with women and his duels had not made him inevitably an object of the public's curiosity as well as its obloquy.

On September 16, 1848, after a stormy session lasting twelve hours, the conservatives, with Lichnowsky at their head, fought their way to a narrow victory in favor of the armistice concluded at Malmö between the Prussians and the Danes.†

Next day, September 17, Lichnowsky wrote to thank the

* *Volk* and *Pöbel*.

† Prussian troops under General Wrangel had invaded Schleswig-Holstein, a German-speaking province to which the new King of Denmark, Frederick VII, had refused to grant a constitution. The Danes beat the Prussians at Duppel, but were nevertheless forced to evacuate the two duchies. Great Britain and France then imposed an armistice. The left-wing party in the Assembly was indignant that Prussia had not consulted that body. They saw this omission, not without reason, as a gesture of contempt for their claim to be the central power in Germany.

Duke of Saxe-Coburg for a decoration the latter had recently
sent him. He expressed satisfaction at the previous day's
triumph of reason and order over madness. "How long will it
last? Only the stars can tell us that." He added: "I am more or
less certain that I shall leave early tomorrow morning for Pots-
dam, then go on from there into Silesia."

Lichnowsky was more or less certain he was leaving Frankfort. And yet hardly was that letter sealed than he ordered his
valet to unpack all his luggage again.

What had he heard that made him change his mind?

He had heard that the extremists, inflamed by the voting of
the armistice, had decided to storm the Assembly. He had also
heard that in the meeting called to organize this riot his name
had been bandied about, that he had been declared a public
enemy, and that the revolutionaries had sworn "to scatter his
guts along the streets."

Some of the Conservatives had already left the city in panic.
Lichnowsky stayed.

Next day, the extremists marched on St. Paul's as planned.
They found it guarded by several battalions of Prussian and
Austrian troops. They were repulsed and immediately began
throwing up barricades. The troops were unable to follow up
their advantage and restore order completely because the necessary artillery was still on its way from Wurtemburg. Rash and
brave as ever, Lichnowsky rode out with General Auerswald, a
veteran of 1813, to meet the Wurtemburger troops, brief them
and give them their positions. Neither of the two men was
armed. At the Aachen gate, the two horsemen encountered a
gang of rioters. They were recognized, shot at, and the Prince
wounded. Unable to force a way through, they dismounted and
escaped into a nearby house. A woman disclosed their hiding
place. Auerswald was clubbed to death. Lichnowsky, held by
two men, was shot at point-blank range.

Body riddled with frightful wounds, arms gashed, head
covered in blood, the Prince lay where the rioters had let him
fall. The harpy who had given the two men away then came over
and struck him in fury.

Having been carried while still conscious to the home of
Bethmann, one of the right-wing leaders, Lichnowsky himself

told the story of this butchery before dying, later that night, in agony.

Dorothée had been expecting him at Sagan. How did she learn of his death? We do not know. But her grief was "complete," "uncontrollable." The Prince had made her his residuary legatee; she hurried down to Frankfort, gathered together a few relics, then returned to Silesia and went into seclusion.

Her German friends let her feel their compassion. Frederick-Wilhelm expressed his pity in delicately chosen words, and Prince Pückler-Muskau wrote to her: "I had never envied our unfortunate friend until the moment when he found in you, almost miraculously, the complement and balance of his gifts."

To her friends in France, Dorothée never spoke her grief. To Bacourt she merely said, quite simply, on October 9: "Every day brings a new horror." On October 21, she informed Barante that the struggle for Vienna would decide the fate of Germany, then added: "I am not lacking in calm or courage, nor, above all, in personal indifference—which is an amazing help in allowing one to contemplate the danger, and in deciding whether to face it or avoid it when the moment comes. . . ."

When she visited Sagan, Marie de Bunsen found a very much used prayer book in Dorothée's boudoir. It contained several pictures of dead people she had known. In her fine, flowing handwriting, the Duchess had written in German on the one of Lichnowsky: "May God keep him in His holy care, and restore him to me soon in the eternity drawing near." *

---

* Gott brachte ihn in Sicherheit, um ihn mir bald in der sich nahenden Ewigkeit zuruckzugeben.

"I NOW BEGIN to feel the great difference that exists between solitude and loneliness. For a long time I always confused these two states, which seem so similar and are yet so different: the first I can bear with ease; the second frightens me," Dorothée had written to Bacourt in June of 1840.

During the last fourteen years of her life, the Duchess of Sagan was obliged to face both states, and though she always returned to her solitude at Sagan without any feelings of terror, the loneliness she had brought upon herself by choosing to live in Prussia, and by her liaison with Lichnowsky, always weighed heavily upon her in old age. She did make several attempts to bridge the gulf dividing her from her daughter and her sons, but she never quite succeeded in doing so. "When life has been emptied of its contents, then it is as well that one's days be full, even though the soul is not. Lonely idleness is perhaps an even heavier load to bear than the burdens imposed by duties, business and inferior company," she confessed sadly to Barante in 1860, two years before her death.

Only with Bacourt was Dorothée able to revive her old friendship. And though their relationship now included new areas of reticence, it was given a touching fidelity by the memory of their past together—their memories, too, of Talleyrand, and the interest they shared in the publication of his *Mémoires*.

Dorothée spent the winter and spring months of 1849 at Sagan, entirely given over to her grief. Weary of the present, without interest in the future, she was occupied wholly by her memories, by "her heart's life-savings." On June 1, she went to Grätz, the Lichnowsky home, and prayed on the Prince's grave.

A few days after that, Meyendorff visited Sagan on his way to Warsaw: "The amiable and witty lady of the house treated me with the most charming kindness. Her grief is now turning into melancholy, perhaps into devoutness. Now that she is expiating all the errors of her past life with her present misfortunes, she disarms all malice and is simply a very superior and amiable woman. One has only to encourage her to recount her memories—not recent ones of course—in order to enjoy a conversation more interesting and more full of matter than most people's written memoirs. She still worships her uncle—and Sagan is filled with all the beautiful things he loved, paintings, chinoiseries, porcelain figures, bronzes and books. The Duchess lives in Wallenstein's château like a philosopher who has withdrawn from the world, adored by all her people, doing a great deal of good, and providing work for all the workmen in the district. She is trying to bury her unhappiness there—and since she lives alone, or almost so, I like to believe that she is at peace with her conscience. . . ."

Through and on behalf of Lichnowsky, the Duchess had taken an active, a personal, interest in Prussian politics and German politics in general. After his death, she became detached from these things, and her interest, being more distant, could take a wider view once more. With complete personal indifference, she gauged the consequences of the December elections of 1848 in France. They had brought a second Bonaparte to the front of the stage. Was he to be the link that would close this cycle of revolutions in France? In November, 1849, Dorothée went to see the Duchess of Orléans again in Eisenach. The question of a possible coalition was at that time the order of the day. The Count of Chambord, strong in the knowledge of his unquestionable rights, was in favor of it. And though Louis-Philippe didn't like the idea of giving himself the lie, his sons thought an alliance would be the best course. But the Duchess of Orléans, blinded by her ambition, was refusing to commit her sons' futures by giving her approval. Dorothée's ability to sum up situations at a glance was still as razor-keen as it had been during her years with Talleyrand: "Madame," she said to the Duchess, "you are playing the President's game for him."

In Berlin, during the few weeks she spent there in January and February of 1850, the Duchess of Sagan did not voice her criticisms, but she certainly thought that the political imbroglio in central Germany and Frederick-Wilhelm's irresolute ambitions would end up by winning the game for Austria in much the same way. In this case, too, she was not mistaken, and the autumn of 1850 saw Prussia's humiliation at Olmütz.

Before this event, during the summer of that year, Dorothée had gone to meet Bacourt again at Baden. They had begun writing to one another again after Henri de Castellane's death had brought them together in 1847, though the letters were not frequent and were very impersonal in tone. Bacourt had never been to Silesia. After his career had been broken by the fall of the July monarchy, he had gone to live in Baden. He now spent most of his time in the spa town, apart from a few weeks in the pied-à-terre he had kept in Paris and a few more with his family in Nancy.

Since Bacourt would not come to her, Dorothée made the first move. After all, doctors had been sending her to Baden all her life, so in June 1850, she went there without being sent, and stayed for two months. Bacourt, caught again in the spell of her charm, and of his own memories, forgot all his bitterness, and allowed himself to be totally reconquered. And it is also possible that the gratifying friendship he established at that time with the Princess of Prussia, a clear-sighted woman not appreciated by her unfaithful husband, also contributed to healing his wounded vanity. It is probable too, that the admiration and attraction felt by the future Queen Augusta for the Duchess of Sagan, sentiments that were never to fade, also did something, in the eyes of this diplomat who was still very much the courtier, to heighten the prestige of Talleyrand's niece. In short, the intimacy between the Duchess and Bacourt was restored; their letters to one another became as frequent and as warm in tone as they had been in the past.

❖   ❖   ❖

Baden and Bacourt represent Dorothée's first effort to shake off the spell that had held her at Sagan for so many years, to tighten the bonds with her past that she had allowed to grow weak, almost to break. Now it was time to go back to France and see her children, get back into the habit of seeing them, recover their affection, share their interests.

But the difficulty of this task was increased still further by the way in which their paths had so strangely diverged. Pauline was dividing her life between the Convent of the Sacré-Coeur in Orléans,* where she had her own private retreat, and Rochecotte, where she had established what was the equivalent of monastic rule. Louis, now completely separated from his wife, alternated between Valençay and Paris. In both places he lived the life of a bachelor, showing little interest in his children, who were now practically men, in fact, even though Louis was only forty. Alexandre, having left Florence and then grown bored with Paris, had enlisted in 1848 in the Piedmontese army. After Charles-Albert's defeat at Novara, however, the Duke of Dino had returned to his former existence, dogged by the straitened circumstances that his wife's lax behavior made even more difficult still. Their children's educations had all been left more or less to the dictates of chance, with the exception of the second son, Archambauld, whom Pauline was bringing up with her own son.

It is likely that while they were in Baden together Dorothée and Bacourt discussed the necessity of the Duchess's taking the first step in this matter too. None of her children could come to Silesia. Or would not; even if they could. The Duchess may have become entirely Prussian again, but they had remained French, and all their lives and their obligations were in France. Perhaps too, like Bacourt, they felt that it was still a little soon to go to Sagan, that certain memories should first be left to the erasing hand of time.

Bacourt, who could always be relied on for good advice, certainly tried to persuade Dorothée to revisit France. For though there was nothing much more she could do for her children, whose lives were already made—and broken—the same was not true of her grandchildren. Perhaps Bacourt reminded Dorothée then, as they began to work on Talleyrand's papers again, that the Prince had entrusted his niece, not only with the responsibility for his fame, but also with the future of his house.

Traveling by way of Hanover and Brussels, where she dined at Laeken with Queen Marie-Amélie and the Prince of Joinville,

---

* Abbé Dupanloup had become Bishop of Orléans in 1849.

Dorothée reached Paris in May of 1851. There she was reunited with her daughter and also with Mgr Dupanloup.

The Duchess's decision to live in Prussia had more or less completely interrupted her relations with the future Bishop of Orléans. They had continued to write to another still, but infrequently, and only on the subject of Pauline. Nevertheless, in 1847, during the month that Dorothée spent in Paris that year, Abbé Dupanloup had been to see her every day. Possibly he had learned from Mme de Castellane of the rift that had appeared between the Duchess and her children. Possibly Pauline had confided to him that she was worried about her mother. Possibly certain rumors had reached his ears directly, for though a priest he also had an allegiance to society. At all events, being a fisher of souls, Abbé Dupanloup could not abandon this one, twice touched by grace but now presumably in danger.

Dorothée was deeply grateful to him for all he had done in the matter of Talleyrand's retraction and for all he had done for Pauline. But at that moment she was clinging to Lichnowsky with every fiber of her being and would not yield to any influence that might have led to giving him up. She defended herself with arrogance and disdain: "I have always felt that he [Abbé Dupanloup] lacks a certain ability to make accurate appraisals of characters and situations. . . ." The Bishop of Orléans had not been discouraged. He had heard about Lichnowsky's frightful end, and no doubt thought that such a shock, and the ensuing grief, might well have revived the faith that had been thrust into the background by human passion.

On May 31, all three—Dorothée, Pauline and Mgr Dupanloup—left for Orléans, continuing from there to the little seminary of the Chapelle-Saint-Mesmin to visit Antoine de Castellane and Archambauld de Dino. Then the Duchess went on alone to Valençay. She was moved to see the things that still remained there, the things that had gone. But it was at Rochecotte that she suffered most. "This backward-looking life I have been leading for nearly a month inflicts terrible tortures on one's heart, or else one's conscience. I can only trust that it is salutary for the soul," she confessed to Bacourt on June 14. A week later, Marie de Castellane made her first communion at the convent of the Dames du Sacré-Coeur de Marmoutier. This gave the Duchess an opportunity of seeing her again, this grand-

daughter whom she scarcely knew, and for whom she now conceived a strong affection. From that moment on, she tried, with
all her strength, to assure this child of the happiness and the
social pre-eminence that she had not been able to secure for
Pauline.

◇   ◇   ◇

When the Duchess returned to Sagan at the end of August
1851, she brought back with her from those months in France
a harvest of varying impressions and melancholy expectations.
Yet there had been some good there. She had become friendly
with her children again; in the next few years Dorothée made
longer and longer visits to Nice, and even to Rochecotte and
Valençay, to be with her family. And then, the renewal of her
friendship with Bacourt had been confirmed in Baden. He
became once more the friend, the confidant, to whom Dorothée would confess not only her family worries and her political
fears, but also the stages of her spiritual progress.

Bacourt's sincere beliefs had already provided Dorothée
with an example and with support at the time when she had
first found true faith. Since those days in 1836, Dorothée's faith
had never wavered. Deeply imbued with a feeling for the French
seventeenth century, the Duchess of Sagan, like the Duchess
of Longueville or some other beautiful *frondeuse* before her,
held true to her belief no matter what the life she was leading.
Rancé had been hounded into a Trappist monastery by the
hideous memory of his mistress's corpse after her violent death.
Lichnowsky's death had been appalling. The Duchess of Sagan
must have sensed the will of God in it. She hadn't the courage
to say good-bye to life: to make her loose her hold, the Lord
had shown her the void.

Though her intelligence had long since bowed itself to her
faith, the proud and passionate heart, scarred with scepticism by
her upbringing and long intimacy with Talleyrand, still fought
back.* Yet serenity was coming to her, little by little.

* Did Dorothée console herself with another lover after Lichnowsky's
death? There were persistent rumors in Berlin to this effect. The man named
was a young architect the Duchess had invited to Sagan to design her tomb.

"I love Sagan. . . ," Dorothée wrote to Bacourt in February 1852, "I have lived through a whole soul's lifetime there, storms, struggles, alarums; and afterward, it was there too that I found calm, meditation, tranquil communion. The winding, devious ways by which I was finally led there—that is one more proof of Providence's wonderful cleverness, patience and pity. . . .

"I do not write this in bitterness; sadness, ah, that's something else! How should I not feel sadness there? Or elsewhere? Or anywhere? I had a husband but no family life; I have children who are in want; I have a few precious friends from whom I am separated; I have had guides and protectors who are no longer on this earth; my health is no longer what it was; my memories are often bitter. . . . I have known many saddening experiences, some great, some small, some through others, but mostly in myself. Does this not justify a great many sad moments? Mine are frequent, constant rather—at the bottom of my heart. They are not apparent in society, but in solitude they have room to expand, they emerge; that is why I am theirs entirely when we are at Sagan. . . ."

Bacourt must have been touched by such a letter. He decided to visit Silesia, and from that time on he and Dorothée continued to meet every year for a few weeks in Baden, in Nice, in Paris, in Prussia, or in Italy.

❖ ❖ ❖

In 1851, the Duchess had stayed only a very short while in Touraine. She had not really been aware of the way of life that had been imposed on Rochecotte by Pauline's piety, melancholy and austerity. At the end of the letter in which he told the Countess of Montijo his story about Henri de Castellane, Mérimée had added, in a moment of sensibility such as that sceptic did not often show: "Tell me, you who have studied in so many human hearts, which would bring the greater grief, to lose someone you love and esteem, or to be given the knowledge that the person you are grieving for is only worthy of your contempt?" If he had seen Pauline's life at Rochecotte he would have learned what such a torment can require of its victim.

"My daughter is proving equal to sufferings that are rare even in the sad, long chapters of human misfortunes," the Duchess herself wrote in 1848 to Barante. She did not say at the price of what renunciations Pauline, the happy and blooming young woman of 1842, had achieved this fortitude. But in 1854, when she visited Rochecotte again, Dorothée saw for herself what she had not realized in 1851, and her heart froze at the discovery. The life was that of a convent: Mass every morning, household prayers in the evening. Every meal a strictly Lenten one. Absolute exclusion of worldly topics from the conversation. A profound silence broken only when the two cousins (Antoine de Castellane and Archambauld de Dino) made some noise, or when their Abbé coughed.

Though the Duchess acknowledged with tender admiration that Pauline herself was suited to this environment she had created, she was a woman of experience and therefore felt some worry on the children's account. For what kind of a future was this cloistered existence going to prepare Marie? Perhaps it also occurred to Dorothée that too austere an upbringing is likely to produce a dangerous reaction in the opposite direction. She felt that she was too old and lived too far away to take any part in the education of her grandson, who was not yet ten, but she did suggest to Pauline that Marie might be allowed to accompany her to Rome. The Marquise de Castellane was going to winter there, the climate would be good for her, and she would be near Mgr Dupanloup, who had to be there too for the proclamation of the dogma of the Immaculate Conception. The journey would also be beneficial to the development of Marie's mind, which was lively but rather stifled by the narrow life at Marmoutier and Rochecotte. It would also add some fire to her imagination. And lastly, this journey to a foreign country might perhaps help prepare the young girl for the future on foreign soil that the Duchess had tentatively begun to think of for her.

From Rochecotte, Dorothée went on to Valençay. It would be difficult to imagine two more different ways of life. To walk into Valençay was to see again the plays being performed in the great drawing room, the returns from the hunt, all the worldly diversions that she had known there in her days with Talleyrand. Then Orléans again, where Barante came to see her.* At last, on October 5, Dorothée reached her own house on the Rue de Lille and stayed there for more than a month.

This was the first time since she had left the capital in 1843 that the Duchess of Sagan had stayed so long in Paris. She renewed her acquaintance with Paris society and was appalled at its transformation. It was now given over to an unbridled thirst for luxury, an incredible lust for pleasure of all kinds. It was also even more divided in its loyalties than it had been under Louis-Philippe: added to the Legitimists and the Orleanists, there were now the Imperialists.

Dorothée had followed the rise of the second Bonaparte, whom she referred to as "the silent man," with growing curiosity. The coup d'état and the subsequent proclamation of the Empire had not surprised her; she had merely seen it as a just punishment for the Orleanists' errors and was delighted that order had been restored in France at last, albeit a little brutally. She does not seem to have commented on the role played by Morny, Talleyrand's grandson, and the only one who seemed to have inherited any of the Prince's intelligence.

This rather academic interest in events took on a more personal note when the outbreak of the Crimean war suddenly threatened to ignite all Europe, and also when Alexandre de Dino, once more unable to bear his life in Paris, enlisted in the 1st regiment of the Foreign Legion. Appointed an acting Captain for foreign service on January 17, 1855, the Duke of Dino disembarked in the Crimea on February 5, and from then on the Duchess waited anxiously for news of this son, apparently so gifted, who had so totally ruined his life.

◇   ◇   ◇

* On October 4, Barante wrote to Guizot: "My dear friend, I am writing to you from Orléans where I am spending two days with Mme de Talleyrand. . . . She is marvelously well-preserved and does not age at all. She prefers her lordly and feudal existence at Sagan to life in France, and indeed it is understandable."

The summer of 1855, though darkened by anxiety over her son, nevertheless brought the Duchess of Sagan one cause for lively satisfaction. At the time of her most recent visit to France, in 1854, she had decided to take in hand the future of her granddaughter, Marie de Castellane, and in February of 1855, in Berlin, she began negotiations to this end with Prince Wilhelm Radziwill, her childhood friend and a son of Princess Louise of Prussia who had been such a motherly godmother to her.

The Radziwills had greeted Dorothée on her return to Prussia as a long lost relative. The relationship, close from the start, grew even closer in the course of succeeding years. The Duchess knew everything there was to know about this unusually large but united family, all controlled with a firm hand by Prince Wilhelm.* The closeness of this family group always delighted Dorothée, for she had suffered all her life from the lack of intimacy between herself and her sisters, and now she was also saddened to see how lacking her own children were in feeling for one another. In short, the desire for an alliance with the Radziwills had formed itself very quickly in her mind.

The Prince's eldest son, Antoine, was twenty-two. Very Catholic, very cultivated, very musical, good looking and sweet natured, he seemed to offer every guarantee of "a happy home life," as the Abbé Dupanloup and Mgr Quélen had expressed it once, referring to Henri de Castellane. He was also of the very highest birth; his name and kinship—his grandmother was a Princess of Prussia, his mother Countess Clary—placed him in the very first rank of European aristocracy. The brilliant match and the pre-eminent social position that Nicolas Esterhazy might have provided for Pauline were possibly to be offered now to Marie.

For Dorothée, the project had attractions other than this gratification of her ancestral pride. The great lady who had so

---

* Wilhelm Radziwill and Mathilde Clary had four children, Boguslave Radziwill and Leontine Clary—the two brothers had married two sisters—seven. The estates had not been split up and the two families lived together in the Radziwill palace. Even at family dinners there were twenty people at table. Marie de Castellane admitted later that she sometimes had difficulty coping with such a quantity of relatives, and especially with the problem of having two fathers-in-law and two mothers-in-law.

loved the world of politics was also hoping to secure her granddaughter, when the favorable moment came, an important post at court. Above all, since she was an aging, lonely woman who thirsted for affection, Dorothée no doubt felt her heart warm at the thought of having near her, in Berlin and at Antonin, in the Grand Duchy of Posen not far from Günthersdorf, that blond child with the pale eyes who had been endowed by fortune with the Talleyrands' good looks, Dorothée's own subtle intelligence, and Pauline's serene faith.

The Duchess of Sagan was rich and prepared to be generous. She had great influence at the Berlin court and was one of the pillars of Catholicism in Prussia, a fact that bore great weight with a Pole still attached to that faith in the heart of a Protestant country. Prince Radziwill was therefore most willing to accept Dorothée's overtures.

Using the Exposition Universelle in Paris as an excuse, the Prince took his son with him on a visit to France. Both then continued to Rochecotte in September 1855, and were received by Dorothée, who had arrived before them. They stayed three days. Pauline was satisfied with Antoine's religious attitude; Marie, for her part, was more affected by his "simple and noble behavior," and by his good looks. On their side, the Radziwills, father and son, observed the promise of beauty Marie gave, even though she was hardly out of the awkward stage. They also commented on her stability of character.

Father, mother, and grandmother all therefore decided to pursue the project and to attempt to bring it to a successful conclusion in Silesia the following summer, by which time Marie would be sixteen.

Dorothée went to spend her winter in Nice. Her stay there was restful even if lonely. Pauline stayed entrenched at Rochecotte, building up her courage to face the painful idea of having to go to Sagan the following summer. Alexandre was still in the Crimea, Bacourt, if he came at all, came for only a few weeks. The Congress of Paris, too pale a reflection of the Congress of Vienna, excited scarcely any flicker of interest in the Duchess.

❖ ❖ ❖

Returning to Berlin during early May 1856, Dorothée was almost immediately joined there by her daughter and granddaughter. There was then a pause of several days before moving on to Silesia, during which Antoine Radziwill came to pay his respects to the travelers and Marie de Castellane was presented to the members of her vast family-to-be.

The three women arrived at Sagan on May 15. Marie liked Sagan, even though she didn't feel it was much like being in the country. It was only a very short time however before the Radziwills announced that they were on their way. Pauline then told her daughter the reason why they were there, and was very emphatic about their desire, hers and the Duchess's, that the projected marriage should come to fruition. Though accustomed by her upbringing to an almost nunlike obedience, Marie nevertheless reacted with violent emotion. No, she could never get used to the idea of leaving France.

Despite her certainty that this marriage would make her granddaughter happy—and this time she was not mistaken— Dorothée must have felt a great pity for the young girl. She had still not forgotten the panic that she had felt herself, in 1809, when she left Germany to go to Paris. She explained to Marie that although her mother and she herself desired this marriage, they would never force her into it, since the decision to marry Antoine Radziwill implied an unconditional acceptance, by Marie herself, of a new country. Without that acceptance she would always remain someone without any country at all. And Dorothée was speaking from experience.

Antoine Radziwill stayed a week at Sagan. Marie still could not decide. To give up France was too painful for her. It was not until August, while at Töplitz, that the young girl, by then beginning to feel at home with the Radziwills, and also moved by a desire to obey her family's wishes, agreed to accept Antoine—and she never regretted it.

The marriage was celebrated at Sagan during the autumn of 1857, and Dorothée herself supervised all the preparations, determined that everything should go off with proper magnificence. Though a gratification of her pride, this marriage was also the occasion for her own farewell to society. It was, more-over, a source of profound joy. She saw it as the completion of her worldly task, her last attempt to secure for one of those dear to her the happiness that she had never known, the happiness that she had seen elude Pauline.

Her *nunc dimittis* once spoken, she began to set her life and thoughts in order. "Without wishing to complain of my family ties, I am constantly forced to recognize that though kinship of soul, of mind, cannot entirely replace that of blood, neither can the latter enable us to dispense absolutely with the former," the Duchess confessed to Barante on September 24, 1857.

"It makes no difference that I am so busy here with all the material arrangements for a wedding . . . with my big house to run, my finances to keep check on, and other people's finances to put in safety; company to receive and entertain; the King to look out for and my bags to pack for Nice; in the midst of all this varied assiduity I feel an emptiness, a thirst that cannot be slaked except in those short moments I snatch from human interests in order to retreat inside that impenetrable solitude, that quiet world into which I allow almost no one other than the Eagle of Meaux.* When I feel his wings spread hovering above me, then the weight of the day falls from my shoulders and I feel my own wings beginning to sprout. . . ."

She added: "My health still continues to subject me to a persistent series of indispositions that cannot, as yet, be said to have made me an invalid in the real sense of the word; one must be grateful, even when one is ceaselessly fighting off one pain or another."

❖ ❖ ❖

Dorothée was just beginning to improve in health when the news that Pauline was seriously ill sent her hurrying up from Nice to Paris, where she arrived early in January 1858. Pauline's convalescence proved a long one, and the Duchess stayed on in her house on the Rue de Lille. Retired now from both society

* *Translator's note:* Bossuet.

and politics, she found the French capital less unpleasant than she had in the past, and was surrounded by a small circle of faithful friends, either foreign diplomats or survivors from the July monarchy. Princess Lieven had died in 1857, and there were others, too, who had disappeared. But there was at least one addition: Guizot. He and Dorothée had always had a liking for one another and now they became friends. "Still beautiful at sixty-five. The same eyes, the same slim waist, Circe still. And the same mind, still large, free, firm, supple, sympathetic," Louis-Philippe's former Premier wrote of Dorothée to Mme de Gasparin.

From then on, Dorothée went back every year to Paris, and every year she saw Guizot again, always faithful, always admiring. It was a friendship suddenly flowering on the brink of the final separation, the memory of everything that had been their past. "After having met continually during the course of our lives, we at last stopped to talk to one another for a while," Guizot wrote in 1862. "But the interview was incomplete and very short. I still keep, and shall continue to keep, a rather hazy and yet very sweet memory of it."

Though there were no very grave symptoms, nothing precise as yet, Dorothée's health was nevertheless continuing to decline, and her liver, always troublesome, was becoming steadily more so. Talleyrand had said once: "Mme de Dino has decided to be in good health; that is already saying much, for with her the will can do a great deal." That will was now diminishing, and this being whose vitality of spirit had been forced for so long to supply her failing energy of body no longer had much desire to live. In 1860, the doctor forbade her the waters that her system could not have tolerated, and she went to "make herself snug" at Sagan, seeking rest and solitude. Even the great September hunts did not lure her from her retreat. The Duke of Valençay and his sons came to do the honors in her stead. Thus Louis was already taking up his position as heir, and assuming the role of a great Prussian landowner.

Tired and unwell, but happy to be near the young Radziwill couple, whom she referred to as her "dear children," the Duchess was in Berlin when Frederick-Wilhelm IV died on January 2, 1861. There had been three years in which to prepare for this event, yet Dorothée was nevertheless very much upset. The new King, Wilhelm, was her friend, and the new Queen was very sincerely affectionate towards her, but it was Frederick-Wilhelm who had welcomed her, helped her to establish herself in Prussia, and supported her during her difficult days. Another page had turned, and there were now not many left in her book of life. The Duchess knew it, and although her faith was deep, still there were often moments when she became disturbed at the thought. "It would be difficult to find a more efficacious piety," she wrote on March 6, 1861, à propos of Pauline. "When the present dissatisfies her or makes her sad, she walks into Eternity and rests, just as you or I might walk into our bedrooms. She sees more clearly beyond this world than she does in it. My nature is much less serious, much less strict; the future for me is at the same time certain and yet quite dark. I believe in it, but I cannot see into it."

A widower since 1858, in April 1861, Louis married Countess Hatzfeldt, whose husband had died suddenly, almost on the eve of the Italian war. The Duke of Valençay and his new Duchess came to see Dorothée in Berlin. They seemed happy together, and the Duchess of Sagan was glad to think that her son—whom she had once sacrificed to Talleyrand's ambitions— would at last know the pleasure of having a real home. For her, this marriage marked the end of another stage in her life, almost the last. On May 1 she returned to take up residence at Sagan.

❖   ❖   ❖

After hearing news of the Duchess of Orléans' sudden death, Dorothée had written to Bacourt on April 25, 1858: "I know of nothing more sad than to die like that, without having had time to prepare one's soul to face Eternity." Providence granted the Duchess her wish in this respect; she was allowed a long retreat in which to prepare herself—more than a year.

Toward the end of June 1861, Dorothée was driving back in her carriage from Günthersdorf to Sagan when she was surprised by a violent summer storm accompanied by a fall of enormous hailstones. The four horses panicked, stampeded into the ditch, and overturned the carriage. Before being carried to cover, Dorothée lay for some time exposed to the battering of hailstones. When she arrived back at Sagan an hour and a half later she was bruised all over and soaked to the skin. Dorothée, already frail and ailing, had her resistance seriously lowered by this incident, and she became ill with what the doctors diagnosed as double sciatica and abdominal neuralgia. It was probably cancer of the liver or a gall bladder condition.

Bacourt decided to spend the winter at Sagan, as though he sensed it was to be the last, and during the several weeks that Louis was in residence there, Alexandre also sent two of his children, Elisabeth and Archambauld, to see their grandmother.*

* Clémentine de Dino had married Count Orlowski in February, 1860. The Dino household had then gone through another tempestuous period, and Maurice, the elder son, had enlisted in July, 1860, in the 3rd African Light Cavalry.

Here is a brief account of Dorothée's descendants:

Apart from one daughter, who became Viscountess of Etchegoyen, Louis had also had two sons from his marriage to Alix de Montmorency. The elder, Boson, the famous Prince of Sagan of the Second Empire and early Third Republic, married Jeanne Seillère. They had two sons. The elder, Hélie, Prince of Sagan, then Duke of Talleyrand, married Anna Gould, earlier the wife of Boniface de Castellane (a grandson of Pauline), and had one son and one daughter by her. The son, Howard, died while still young in 1929. The daughter became Countess James de Pourtalès.

The second son of Boson de Talleyrand-Périgord and Jeanne Seillère, also named Boson, bore the title of Duke of Valençay until the death of his brother in 1937. At his death, in 1952, the masculine line of descent from Louis de Valençay was extinguished, since the latter's second son, Adalbert, who had been empowered by Napoleon III to revive the title of Duke of Montmorency, had only one son and the son died childless.

By his second wife, Countess Hatzfeldt, Louis de Valençay had one daughter, born two months after Dorothée's death, who was given her grandmother's name. Dorothée de Talleyrand-Périgord first became Princess Fürstenburg, then left Germany and went to live in France after her marriage to Count Jean de Castellane, another of Pauline's grandsons.

Of Alexandre de Dino's four children, only the eldest, Maurice, remained French. He had only one daughter, who married a Prince Ruspoli. Alexandre's two daughters, Clémentine and Elisabeth, both married Poles. The second son, Archambauld, became a Prussian officer. His marriage to Marie de Gontaut-Biron, the daughter of the French Ambassador to Berlin, produced four children, two daughters and two sons. The younger son, a German officer, died shortly after the 1914-1918 war. The elder is the present Duke of Talleyrand. He is without issue.

Antoine de Castellane had three daughters from his marriage to Mlle de Juigné: Boniface, who was Anna Gould's first husband; Jean, who was Dorothée de Talleyrand-Périgord's second husband; and Stanislas.

On the way back from Breslau, where they had been to receive the homage of Silesia, the King and Queen of Prussia also invited themselves to Sagan. The sovereigns must have been disturbed by the Duchess's condition, for several days later Princess Charles of Prussia—a sister of Queen Augusta who had married the younger brother of Frederick-Wilhelm IV and Wilhelm I—also a great friend of Dorothée's, arrived in her turn. The presence of her friends, her grandchildren about her, royal visits—Dorothée was touched by it all. Though less than she was by a visit from Marie Radziwill, "who radiates domestic happiness."

The weeks went by, slow and full of pain. The Duchess had scarcely any illusions about her condition, but though she was suffering a great deal, her mind remained lucid, her will firm. Every day she moved further away from the present and back into the past, "living and taking refuge in a life of thought and memories." Every day, too, she spent time meditating and preparing herself to face Eternity, as she had hoped it would be granted her to do. Gradually, without haste, she began to take leave of her friends. "Dear and very dear friend," she wrote to Barante on January 6, 1862, "you will remain till the end of my pilgrimage the being of whom I think with the sweetest pleasure and almost the only one who has never let me down in any way."

Spring came, but no improvement in the patient's health accompanied it. The doctors tried first Ems then Schlangenbad.

Marie's married life with Antoine Radziwill was a happy one. Four children were born over a period of twenty years: two sons and two daughters. A General in the artillery, aide-de-camp and personal friend to the Emperor Wilhelm I, Prince Antoine occupied a very high position in Berlin. That of his wife, confidante of the Empress Augusta, was no less conspicuous, and her salon, in which she received every evening, as her grandmother had done on the Rue Saint-Florentin, was for some time the most prominent, and almost the only one of its kind, in the Prussian capital.

At the accession of Wilhelm II, the Antoine Radziwills retired from court circles. They were nevertheless chosen by the Kaiser as his representatives at the service celebrated in Notre-Dame, in Paris, in memory of the victims of the Bazar de la Charité. Beyond the war and the hate, the German Emperor thus demonstrated his awareness that the Princess Radziwill, good German though she may always have shown herself, had remained French at heart. And Marie de Castellane was so still when she died in 1915, at Kleinitz, the Silesian château she had inherited from Dorothée.

It was from the latter place that the Duchess wrote to Barante for the last time, on July 13. The letter was a farewell: "Ems did me a great deal of harm. I don't expect Schlangenbad to work wonders either. I see no way out; but there is an end, and perhaps not far off now: I still have two more weeks here, then I shall return to my home in worse health than when I left it. There is nothing left for me to do now but hide myself away, suffer, remember, wait, and prepare myself as best I can in the meantime. I try very hard. Is that enough?"

Dorothée returned to Sagan on August 3. She knew that she was doomed and began calmly preparing for her death. Always a solitary person, she did not wish for the presence of her children, not even that of her daughter. Pauline was at Roche-cotte, worried, but kept in ignorance of the truth by the doctors. The Duchess did not send for her.

She scarcely wrote any more. On August 13, she asked Fräulein von Bodelschwing, the faithful lady-in-waiting who had come to her from Courland in 1850 and been with her ever since, to tell Barante that the memory of him would be with her until her last breath, and on the 26th she sent Guizot a little note written in pencil.*

Alone, Dorothée was not afraid of dying. When she heard that her family had discovered the gravity of her condition from the newspapers, and that they were about to descend on Sagan en masse, she was much disturbed and sent for Bacourt. She had counted on his devotion to her, and she was not disappointed. He hurried to Sagan. Together, they set all Dorothée's affairs in order. Bacourt had already been appointed her executor, and on September 9 she also handed over all Talleyrand's papers into his care and keeping.† Lastly, it was Bacourt she charged with the task of conveying to Marie Radziwill her last hopes and wishes for the young girl's future.

---

* On October 1, Guizot wrote to Mme de Gasparin: "The Duchess of Dino's death was a real grief to me. . . . Her mind was superior, her heart generous and loving no matter what the errors of her life, and her presence enchanting."

† Talleyrand had imposed a delay of thirty years between his death and publication of his memoirs. Bacourt died before this period had elapsed, in April 1865. Talleyrand's *Mémoires* were eventually published by the Duke of Broglie in 1891.

Bacourt had been with Talleyrand on May 17, 1838; he was also with Dorothée at the moment when, no longer in pain, at peace with men and at peace with her God, she died quietly on September 19, 1862.

Both the judgments and the sentiments inspired by the Duchess of Dino are extremely varied. Talleyrand and Bacourt both loved her, long and faithfully. Her mother, her sisters, even her sons, displayed what was almost indifference toward her.* Society, whether in Prussia or France, judged her with severity, but the population of Sagan sincerely wept her death.

Can the heart, the character, the intelligence, the behavior, the environment, and lastly the rôle of the Duchess of Dino provide us with an explanation of these disparities?

Because of her loveless childhood, Dorothée's own heart was never easily won or very generous; it was deep and it was demanding. She had a need to dominate in her relationships, and her devotion, which was very real even though it lacked tenderness, was almost an annexation. "I need to take care of people, to devote myself to them, to surround them, to be useful to them," she wrote once to Barante. Moreover, she could never truly love unless her mind was involved as well as her heart; whenever the former began to lose interest, then the latter grew cool.

She had little human warmth; no sentimentality whatever; a sensibility entirely controlled by her intelligence. "I lost M. de Talleyrand fifteen years too late or too early, at the age when it is most difficult to muster the necessary resources for embarking on a new life." And when she one day came upon a note her uncle had written her expressing his affection, she was surprised by her own emotions: "You would not believe how much that little scrap of paper disturbed my heart."

Mistrustful of herself and others, Dorothée was nevertheless a sincere and actively helpful friend. On the other hand, always thin-skinned, she was too ready to take offense, and swift to break off a relationship at the least sign of neglect, or of what

---

* Prince Hohenlohe, King Wilhelm's representative at the Duchess of Sagan's funeral, has underlined this fact with a ruthless pen.

she took to be such; in short, difficult to love: her friendships frequently ended in bitterness and hostility.

Her heart did not play a great part in her love affairs; they were all, in varying admixtures, the products of sensual need, intellectual involvement, and ambition. No romantic frenzies, simply physical or intellectual inclinations to which she abandoned herself with an eighteenth-century woman's unfettered morality and lack of prudery, and which involved no promise of fidelity, even less of duration.

Though she thus seems to have been a little unfeeling, even egocentric, in her relations with those close to her—her relatives, her friends or lovers—one of the first of the many contrasts apparent in this woman is provided by her kindness and gentleness to the poor. With them, she shed all her constraint of manner, as though she were sloughing off some painful garment woven of all her anxiety, her suspicions, her rancor, and emerging as herself, as the self she might have been if her own unhappy life had not crushed her into a different mold. But perhaps too "because the individuals do not enter into the interest they inspire. . . ." The cry of a solitary and disenchanted heart that is terrified by human contacts and must repel them.

It took the complete love that she felt for Lichnowsky, then the rending horror of his death, to break the shell around that pride-clad heart, to let Dorothée discover the sweetness in a truly trusting affection. It was then that she wrote to Bacourt, "that in the midst of this utter bankruptcy that is our life . . . the affection that we feel ourselves, even more than that we may inspire, is our true wealth, our treasure. . . ."

❖   ❖   ❖

From Batowski, Dorothée had inherited that unstable, melancholy Pole's own unquiet nature, together with attacks of wildness, black moods, and above all a perpetual feeling of insecurity. "I am a very strange little animal; the doctor tells me daily that it is a nervous state, imaginary, my own caprice; what is quite certain is that I am energetic, gay, despondent all in sudden fits; that I don't have enough self-control, or rather that I allow my nerves to control me." Or again, these lines to Barante: "You are not like me, you don't have a black, bilious humor that wells up and makes everything look dark, that freezes the heart, saddens the mind, brings a terror of the future, strips the present of all pleasure, and tarnishes the past."

As a defense against this distress of mind, Dorothée locked herself away behind the pride that certainly seems to have been the dominant factor in her character, with all the nobility and sense of duty as well as the narrowness and arrogance that accompanied it. No stiffness however. Dorothée was a Slav and possessed all the sinuosity of that race. She spoke only with measured frankness and never said more than she wished to say. She also measured out her loyalty. With the exception of Talleyrand, to whom she attached herself truly, and who remained for her till the very end "a wizard, complex, never the same," she lent herself but never gave herself.

What is true of her relations with people is also true of her political allegiances. Cosmopolitan, as they called it then, stateless, as we should say today, those allegiances changed at the dictate of her interests or her emotions, and this fundamental lack of sentiment in such matters, this total aloofness of the heart, always lent a hint of duplicity, a shadow of equivocation to her expression. It should also be added that she had retained from her German upbringing a strange mixture of arrogance and obligingness that bewildered those of pure French blood.

But beyond the caution and the reticence, the skillful silences, the reserved confessions, the Duchess always kept a lofty soul, driven steadily toward her God by a series of violent impulses. Above all, her conscience always remained true to itself. She might deceive others, but her pride would never allow her to deceive herself, and the judgments she passed upon herself were without indulgence. "That is what saved my soul," she wrote in October 1834, "because it has always prevented me from confusing good and bad; I have never allowed one to usurp the place of the other in my mind, or in my conscience; and though I may have burdened the latter with sins, I have at least kept it free from errors. It is a big difference, and one that always leaves the possibility of retracing one's

steps. Truth of mind, truth of heart, those are what it is important to preserve; for they, in their turn, are what preserve the
worth of a character, and enable us to reach our end, though
not without faults, still without cowardly evasions."

❖   ❖   ❖

The one thing we can admire unreservedly in Dorothée is
her mind. Supple and strong, firm and lucid, robust and swift,
that mind was furnished by experience, and also by vast reading, whose subject matter had been dictated by an eclectic taste
and an instinctive feeling for greatness. We have already noted
how much Dorothée admired Bossuet; she also loved Fénélon:
"It is impossible in reading him not to be inspired with a love
for what is good and beautiful, and with the desire to live better
so that one may die better." Though she retained all her life
a preference for seventeenth-century writers, and though she
showed little interest in the Romantics, either the novelists or
the poets, she always kept herself extremely up to date in all
matters to do with history and politics, and she thought highly
of *Port-Royal* and *Les Moines de l'Occident*. Even after her
return to Prussia she did not abandon her interest in French
literature, but she also began to read enormous quantities of
German works. In short, a vast and well-assimilated cultural
background, which her daily contact with the most brilliant
minds of the century enabled her to develop and use. "During
the four years she spent in England," Talleyrand wrote of his
niece, "she had completed all that growth of which her superior
mind was capable, and which placed her in the first rank of
the most distinguished persons of the age."

This intelligence, never led astray by a heart almost always
firmly under the control of her will, was what provided Dorothée with her swift and accurate power of judgment, which
never became entangled in the irrelevant details of any problem but pierced straight to the core. Since her emotions never
swayed her head or confused her thoughts, she was able to evaluate any situation she was faced with and appraise men of
her own world without risk of errors. She sometimes made mis-

takes when the future was a factor in the problem, for she lacked intuition, and she was also liable to error when judging certain people not of her class, whether it was Napoleon, whom she only began to understand somewhat after the July revolution, or whether it was someone like Balzac, whom she found "heavy and commonplace," lacking in spirit, and whom she also lashed out at for attempting to portray duchesses.

Dorothée was brought up in the rarefied atmosphere of a small German court. Above all, she was brought up in an obsolete world, a world that was a whole generation and one revolution behind everyone else. Her long intimacy with Talleyrand had then aggravated the tendencies implanted in her by that upbringing. A daughter of the eighteenth century, she assumed that her birth gave her the right to do anything she pleased, and therefore displayed an aristocratic disdain for public opinion. This attitude, at a time when the middle classes were beginning to impose their very different concepts of society and morality all over Europe, explains the severity of certain judgments passed upon her.

She was not only a stranger to her own times however, but also to the countries in which she lived, and because of this she always had two worlds, two environments, both of them without frontiers: the European courts, and the countryside. A great lady without a country of her own, she was always at home with kings and diplomats, in the artificial atmosphere of royal courts, in the world of international high society. She had the artificial manner, the studied poise of that environment. But the other Dorothée, the intelligent, practical woman who never lost sight of reality, was different; she loved the land, she enjoyed the simple, real life of the country, ruled by the ineluctable cycle of the seasons. For the peasant, his field is his universe, his true, almost his only homeland. The same was true of the Duchess at Rochecotte, and even more so at Sagan.

◇   ◇   ◇

Again and again we meet the words "intrigues" and "ambition" when reading what her contemporaries had to say about

the Duchess of Dino. But are these terms justified by the rôle
she played and by the way in which she used her influence?

It is difficult for us to evaluate the influence that Dorothée
achieved during the years she spent in Prussia, though we can
enumerate its facets: Catholic influence in a Protestant country;
French influence in a German court where nevertheless French
was the language usually spoken; political influence through and
for Lichnowsky during the troubled years of 1847 and 1848.

On the other hand, the rôle that the Duchess played during
her years with Talleyrand is much more fully documented. Up
till the moment of the July Revolution, Dorothée's influence,
though one may sense that it was already very real, is scarcely
apparent on the surface. She certainly did not dictate the
Prince's decisions, even though she may have suggested certain
courses or strengthened certain of his opinions by creating a
particular atmosphere around him, by expressing her own feelings, by making introductions. Then followed the period in
England. By that time, fifteen years of life together had bound
the minds of Talleyrand and the Duchess of Dino in so close
an intimacy that they were almost one. At the same time, the
advanced age of the one and the growing maturity of the other
had established a balance between the two that was expressed in
a perfect communion of ideas, a perfect "team spirit"; so that
the term "influence" becomes inadequate to describe what was
an understanding too deep for either of them consciously to
manipulate the other. After 1834, everything changed, and
from then on it was Dorothée who was the active partner,
whether when persuading Talleyrand to take the decisions that
she considered necessary, or when using the still considerable
prestige of the Prince, as well as her own influence, to achieve
the outcome she desired in a moment of governmental crisis.

Would it be correct, then to use the terms "intrigues" and
"ambition" when talking of this period?

Intrigues? Politics is essentially nothing but a play of
intrigues, and the Duchess was simply one of the last political
grandes dames, a survivor of that race of women who used once
to make and unmake political leaders, or change the diplomatic
policy of a State from an armchair in their salon, yet were
never for all that accused of "intrigues." What are called her

"intrigues" are therefore perfectly explained by Dorothée's intellectual bent and by her avowed love of politics.

Ambition? The Duchess cannot be said to have been greedy. In 1816, she linked her fortunes to those of Talleyrand when he was in complete political disfavor. In 1834, she first persuaded the Prince to leave his post in London, then urged him to refuse another in Vienna. There was then a possibility that Talleyrand might serve an honorific term as Premier, with Thiers as his principal minister. In 1834, Dorothée dismissed the idea; in 1836, she yielded without reluctance to Royer-Collard's insistence that she prevent Talleyrand from accepting.

The Duchess had ambition certainly, but it was almost always of the loftiest and most disinterested kind. She played a large part in the services that Talleyrand rendered France, and indeed all Europe, during his last years; it was to Dorothée also, to her well placed ambition, that the Prince owed the order and the dignity that did such honor to the closing moments of his life.

❖   ❖   ❖

No portrait of Dorothée would be complete without a few words on her gifts as a writer.* To begin with, in 1822, during a period of melancholy, she wrote her *Souvenirs,* in which the lucid thought, the lively style and the vigorous expressions are all indicative of the writer's character. The portraits are excellent: the seven year old girl, "small, very sallow, excessively thin"; the Comtesse de Provence, "her grey hair cut to look like a hedgehog." And there are striking descriptive phrases: Prussia laid waste by war where "the little crosses in the graveyards seemed to be more tightly packed." The account of the betrothal to Edmond de Périgord is moving; the discretion of the words employed does not conceal the cruelty inherent in the

---

* The Duchess did not disdain the additional prestige that these gifts might earn her in the eyes of posterity. It seems probable that she showed the manuscript of her *Souvenirs* to Molé at the time of their reconciliation, after her return from London, and it was on her orders that Bacourt compiled the *Chroniques* and handed the resulting text to Marie Radziwill.

situation, and this deliberate dissonance is handled with rare ability.

The letters to Vitrolles are direct and full of life, those to Barante more superficial, at least in the period of the Restoration, yet even in them the spontaneity is still there. It seems clear that there was at that time a discrepancy between the Duchess's attitude in society and what she wrote; the phrases dictated by her situation on the one hand, the true expression of her nature on the other.

The July Monarchy brought a change in her correspondence, as well as in her correspondents. The letters to Madame Adélaïde are flattering and devious, those to Thiers entirely political. The more than a hundred and fifty letters to Barante, however, are more interesting. And finally, there are the four volumes of the *Chroniques*, for the most part compiled from letters to Bacourt.

Dorothée always wrote well, and when lamenting her loneliness or her sufferings, confiding her anxieties over Talleyrand's soul, or her tender feelings for her daughter, she produced some deeply felt and truthful phrases. Nevertheless, her letters are often weighed down by their political contents, and though the powers of judgment displayed in them have grown deeper with age, experience, and the habit of responsibilities, the spontaneity has gone. There are letters to Bacourt and letters to Barante that sometimes repeat one another, as though, having given one form to her thought, Dorothée was not interested in attempting to vary her methods of expression for each recipient.

One must admire the observer who kept Bacourt up to date for thirty years with the behind-the-scenes activities of European politics and amused him with the latest court and salon gossip; one must also admire the reader who could make such telling comments on the books she read, and the traveler who painted such pretty pictures of Rome and Venice for Barante. The documentary value of such a correspondence is considerable. But the letters and the *Souvenirs* written under the Restoration are more engaging. Beside the official portrait, they are the sketch from nature.

For us, however, all these writings, the *Souvenirs*, the

Chroniques and the letters, have one essential quality in common. Together, they form the mirror in which, through half a century of history, throughout the course of a life abundantly endowed with exceptional gifts, with intelligence, with beauty, with power, yet always lacking that "respectable, ordinary kind of happiness it is only given to certain women to know," we see reflected a noble, difficult and tormented soul. It is in them that we can see and sense, living and suffering, loving and praying, Dorothée of Courland, Duchess of Dino, that "rare and great woman" * who was Talleyrand's last love.

---

* Guizot to Barante.

BIBLIOGRAPHY

MANUSCRIPT SOURCES IN FRANCE

Archives nationales.
Archives du ministère de la Guerre.
Archives du ministère de la Marine.
Archives de la Seine.
Bibliothèque Thiers: Fonds Masson.

PRINTED SOURCES

MEMOIRS OR LETTERS OF THE DUCHESS OF DINO

Souvenirs, Paris, 1908.
Chroniques de 1831 à 1862, Paris, 1909, 4 volumes.
Lettres à Madame Adélaïde, in *Nouvelle Revue rétrospective,* Paris, 1901 and 1902.
Lettres à Barante, in Barante: *Souvenirs,* Paris, 1901, 8 volumes.
Lettres au comte Molé, 1830-1851, in *Revue d'Histoire diplomatique,* Paris, July-December 1947.
Lettres à Adolphe Thiers, in *Revue de Paris,* July-August 1923.
Lettre à Talleyrand in *l'Amateur d'auiographes,* new series, Paris, 1909.
Lettres à Vitrolles, in Royer (Louis): *La Duchesse de Dino et le Baron de Vitrolles,* unedited letters, 1817-1829, Grenoble, 1937.

MEMOIRS OR LETTERS OF TALLEYRAND

Mémoires, Paris, 1891-1892, 5 volumes.
Lettres à Madame Adélaïde, in *Nouvelle Revue rétrospective,* Paris, 1901 and 1902.
Correspondance de Talleyrand et de Bacourt, in *Le Correspondant,* March-July 1893.
Lettres à Caulaincourt, in *Revue des Deux Mondes,* October-November 1935.
Talleyrand intime d'après sa correspondance avec la duchesse de Courlande en 1814, Paris, 1891.

PRINCIPAL MEMOIRS OR CORRESPONDENCE CONSULTED

Abrantès, Duchess of, *Mémoires*, Paris, 1831-1838, 18 volumes.
Apponyi, *Journal du comte Rodolphe Apponyi*, Paris, 1913-1926, 4 volumes.
Bacourt, A. Fourier de, *Souvenirs d'un Diplomate*, Paris, 1882.
Barante, Prosper de, *Souvenirs*, Paris, 1901, 8 volumes.
Bernstorff, E. von, *Ein Bild aus der Zeit*, Berlin, 1899, 2 volumes.
Berry, *The Berry Papers*, 1763-1852, edited by Louis Melville, London, 1916.
Beugnot, Count, *Mémoires*, Paris, 1866, 2 volumes.
Bismarck, *Mémoires*, Paris, 1889, 3 volumes.
Blennerhassett, Lady, *Talleyrand, eine Studie*, Berlin, 1894.
Blessington, Lady, *The Idler in France*, Paris, 1841.
Bocher, Charles, *Mémoires, 1816-1907*, Paris, 1906-1907, 2 volumes.
Boigne, *Mémoires de la comtesse de Boigne*, Paris, 1908, 4 volumes.
Broglie, Duke of, *Souvenirs, 1781-1870*, Paris, 1886, 4 volumes.
———, *Mémoires*, I, 1825-1870, Paris 1938.
Broglie, Duchess of, *Lettres, 1814-1838*, Paris, 1896.
Broughton, Lord, *Recollections of a Long Life*, London, 1909, 4 volumes.
Castellane, *Journal du maréchal de Castellane, 1804-1862*, Paris, 1895-1897, 5 volumes.
Castellane, Boni de, *Mémoires*, Paris, 1924-1925.
Caulaincourt, *Mémoires du général de Caulaincourt*, Paris, 1933, 3 volumes.
Chateaubriand, *Mémoires d'outre-tombe*, Paris, 1948, 4 volumes.
Circourt, Count of, *Souvenirs d'une Mission à Berlin en 1848*, Paris, 1908.
Clary et Aldringen, Prince, *Trois mois à Paris lors du mariage de Napoléon*, Paris, 1914.
Coigny, Aimée de, *Mémoires*, Paris, 1902.
Combe, Colonel, *Mémoires*, Paris, 1853.
Coulmann, J.-J., *Réminiscences*, Paris, 1862-1869, 3 volumes.
Creevey, Thomas, *The Creevey Papers*, London, 1902, 2 volumes.
Cussy, Chevalier de, *Souvenirs*, Paris, 1912, 2 volumes.
Czartoryski, Prince Adam, *Mémoires*, Paris, 1887, 2 volumes.
Lettres inédites de Dalberg à Talleyrand, in *Revue d'Histoire diplomatique*, April-June 1937.
Dosne, *Mémoires de Mme Dosne*, Paris, 1928, 2 volumes.
Ernst II, *Aus meinem Leben und aus meinem Zeit*, Berlin, 1887-1889, 3 volumes.
Falloux, Count of, *Mémoires d'un Royaliste*, Paris, 1925, 3 volumes.
Gagern, Baron de, *Mein Antheil an der Politik*, Stuttgart und Tubingen, 1823, 1845, 3 volumes.
Gayot, André, *Une Ancienne Muscadine, Fortunée Hamelin*. Unedited letters, 1839-1851, Paris, 1911.

————, *Guizot et Madame Laure de Gasparin*, Paris, 1934.

Gentz, *Tagebücher von Friedrich von Gentz*, Leipzig, 1873-1874, 4 volumes.

Gorsas, Jean, *Mémoires, Lettres inédites et Papiers secrets*, Paris, 1891.

Gorsse, Pierre de, *Aimables inconstants*, Paris, 1961.

Granville, Lady Harriett, *Letters of . . . 1810-1845*, London, 1894, 2 volumes.

Greville, Charles, *The Greville Memoirs*, London, 1855-1887, 8 volumes.

Griois, General, *Mémoires 1792-1822*, Paris, 1909, 2 volumes.

Gronow, *The Reminiscences and Recollections of Captain Gronow*, London, 1862.

Guizot, *Lettres de M. Guizot à sa Famille et à ses Amis*, Paris, 1884.

Gyp, *Souvenirs d'une petite Fille*, Paris, 1927.

Hanoteau, Jean, *Lettres du prince de Metternich à la princesse de Lieven*, Paris, 1909.

Hohenlohe-Ingelfingen, Kraft von, *Aus meinem Leben*, Berlin, 1897-1907, 4 volumes.

Holland, Lady Elizabeth, *Lady Holland to Her Son, 1821-1845*, London, 1946.

Houssaye, Arsène, *Les Confessions. Souvenirs d'un demi-siècle*, Paris, 1885-1891, 6 volumes.

Hubner, Count of, *Neuf ans de souvenirs d'un ambassadeur d'Autriche à Paris*, Paris, 1908, 2 volumes.

Kielmannsegge, Countess of, *Mémoires sur Napoléon*, Paris, 1928, 2 volumes.

La Rochefoucauld-Doudeauville, Duke of, *Mémoires*, Paris, 1861-1864, 15 volumes.

La Tour du Pin, Marquise de, *Journal d'une Femme de cinquante ans*, Paris, 1913, 2 volumes.

Lejeune, General, *Mémoires*, Paris, 1895, 2 volumes.

Lichnowsky, Prince Félix, *Souvenirs*, Paris, 1844.

Lieven, Princess of, *Correspondence of Princess Lieven and Lord Grey, 1824-1841*, London, 1890, 3 volumes.

————, *Letters*, London, 1902.

————, *Lettres de la princesse de Lieven à M. de Bacourt*, in *Le Correspondant*, August, 1893.

Marbot, General Baron, *Mémoires*, Paris, 1891, 3 volumes.

Marigny, Mme de, and T. R. Underwood, *Paris en 1814*, Paris, 1907.

Masuyer, Valérie, *Mémoires*, Paris, 1837.

Mérimée, Prosper, *Sept Lettres de Mérimée à Stendhal*, Paris, 1898.

————, *Lettres de Prosper Mérimée à la comtesse de Montijo*, Paris, 1930, 2 volumes.

Metternich, *Mémoires, Documents et Ecrits laissé par le prince de Metternich*, Paris, 1884, 8 volumes.

Meyendorff, Baron Peter von, *Ein russischer Diplomat an der Höfen von Berlin und Wien*, Berlin, 1923, 3 volumes.

Michelet, *Sur les chemins de l'Europe*, Paris 1893.

Montcalm Marquise de, *Mon Journal (1815-1819) pendant le premier ministère de mon frère*, Paris, 1935.

Montet, Baronne Joseph du, *Souvenirs*, Paris, 1904.

Nesselrode, Count of, *Lettres et Papiers*, Paris, 1908-1912, 11 volumes.

Neumann, *Diary of Philipp von* . . . , London, 1928, 2 volumes.

Noailles, Marquis de, *Le Comte Molé*, Paris, 1922-1930, 6 volumes.

Orléans, Duke of, *Lettres 1825-1842*, Paris, 1889.

Orléans, Louise-Marie d', *Lettres intimes*, Paris, 1933.

Orléans, *Journal de Marie-Amélie, duchesse d'Orléans*, Paris, 1938, 3 volumes.

Pasquier, Chancellor, *Histoire de mon temps*, Paris, 1893-1895, 6 volumes.

Pichot, Amedée, *Souvenirs intimes sur M. de Talleyrand*, Paris, 1870.

Potocka, Countess, *Mémoires*, Paris, 1897.

Prussia, Princess Louise of . . . , Princess Antoine Radziwill, *Quarante-cinq ans de ma vie*, Paris, 1911.

Radziwill, Princess Antoine, *Souvenirs*, Paris, 1931.

Raikes, Thomas, *A Portion of the Journal Kept by . . . from 1831 to 1847*, London, 1857, 4 volumes.

Reiset, Viscount of, *Souvenirs*, Paris, 1899-1902, 3 volumes.

Rémusat, Charles de, *Correspondance de M. de Rémusat*, Paris, 1884-1886, 6 volumes.

————, *Mémoires de ma vie*, Paris, 1958-1962, 4 volumes.

Stendhal, *Journal*, Paris, 1937, 5 volumes.

————, *Correspondance*, tome VI, Paris, 1933-1934.

Varnhagen von Ense, *Tagebücher*, Berlin, 1905, 15 volumes.

Viel-Castel, Count Horace de, *Mémoires sur le Règne de Napoléon III*, Paris, 1883, 6 volumes.

Villemain, *Souvenirs contemporains*, Paris, 1864, 2 volumes.

Villemarest, C.-M. de, *Monsieur de Talleyrand*, Paris, 1834-1835, 4 volumes.

Viennet, Jean-Pons, *Journal de* . . . , Paris, 1955.

Vitrolles, *Mémoires*, Paris, 1952, 2 volumes.

Weil, Commandant M.-H., *Les Dessous du Congrès de Vienne*, Paris, 1917, 2 volumes.

PRINCIPAL BIOGRAPHIES OR STUDIES OF THE DUCHESS OF DINO, BACOURT, AND TALLEYRAND

Arrigon, L.-J., *La Duchesse de Dino et la fin de Talleyrand*, in *Revue des Deux Mondes*, March-April 1955.
Bunsen, Maria von, *Talleyrands Nichte*, Stuttgart, s.d. (1935).
Feckes, Elizabeth, *Die Herzogin von Sagan*, Bonn, 1917.
Lamy, Etienne, *L'Enfance d'une Grande Dame*, Rouen, 1908.
Lacour-Gayet, G., *La Duchesse de Dino*, in Revue de Paris, December, 1922.

Dumaine, Alfred, *Notice sur M. de Bacourt*, in *Revue d'Histoire diplomatique*, 1928.
Monod, G., *Monsieur de Bacourt et la Duchesse de Dino*, in *Mémoires de la Société des Sciences morales, des Lettres et des Arts de Seine-et-Oise*, tome XVIII, 1894.

Bertaut, Jules, *Talleyrand*, Lyon, 1945.
Brinton, Crane, *The Lives of Talleyrand*, London, 1937.
Duff Cooper, *Talleyrand*, Paris, 1937.
Lacombe, Bernard de, *La vie privée de Talleyrand*, Paris, 1910.
Lacour-Gayet, G., *Talleyrand*, Paris, 1928-1934, 4 volumes. *Talleyrand et Royer-Collard*, in *Revue Mondiale*, January, 1928.
MacCabe, Joseph, *Talleyrand*, London, 1906.
Madelin, Louis, *Talleyrand*, Paris, 1944.
Michaud, L.-G., *Histoire politique et privée de Charles-Maurice de Talleyrand*, Paris, 1853.
Missoffe, Michel, *Le coeur secret de Talleyrand*, Paris, 1956.
Paléologue, Maurice, *Talleyrand, Metternich et Chateaubriand*, Paris, 1924.
Sainte-Beuve, C. A., *Monsieur de Talleyrand*, Introduction and Notes by Léon Noël, Monaco, 1958.
Vivent, Jacques, *La vie privée de Talleyrand*, Paris, 1940.

MISCELLANEOUS

Angot, E., *Louis de Talleyrand-Périgord*, Paris, 1911.
Arrigon, L.-J., *Une amie de Talleyrand*, Paris, 1946.
Crozet, R., *Le Château de Valençay*, Paris, 1930.
Dard, Emile, *Napoléon et Talleyrand*, Paris, 1935.
———, *Dans l'Entourage de l'Empereur*, Paris, 1940.
Daudet, Ernest, *La Princesse de Lieven*, Paris, 1903.
Dino, Duchess of, *Notice sur Valençay*, 1848.
Dyssord, Jacques, *Les Belles Amies de M. de Talleyrand*, Paris, 1942.
Grunwald, Constantin de, *Metternich*, Paris, 1938.

Hildebrand, K., *La Société de Berlin de 1789 à 1815*, in *Revue des Deux Mondes*, March, 1870.

Lafue, Pierre, *Histoire de l'Allemagne*, Paris, 1950.

La Garde-Chambonas, Count of, *Fêtes et Souvenirs du Congrès de Vienne, Tableau des salons, scènes anecdotiques et portraits*, Paris, 1901.

Malo, Henri, *Le Beau Montrond*, Paris, 1926.

Masson, Frédéric, *L'Impératrice Marie-Louise*, Paris, 1902.

Mirabeau, Countess of, *Le Prince de Talleyrand et la Maison d'Orléans*, Paris, 1890.

Rosenthal, David-August, *Konvertitenbilder aus 19°*, Schaffhausen, 1865-1870, 3 volumes.